'ZiNE

OTHER BOOKS BY PAGAN KENNEDY

Platforms: A Microwaved Cultural Chronicle of the 1970s

Stripping and Other Stories

Spinsters

PAGAN KENNEDY

'ZiNE

How I Spent Six Years of My Life in the Underground and Finally . . . Found Myself . . . I Think

ST. MARTIN'S GRIFFIN NEW YORK

Design by Pei Loi Koay

Library of Congress Cataloging-in-Publication Data:

Kennedy, Pagan.
Zine : how I spent six years of my life in the underground and finally . . . found myself . . . I think / Pagan Kennedy.
p. cm.
ISBN 0-312-13628-5
1. Kennedy, Pagan, 1962- —Biography. 2. Periodicals, Publishing of—United States—History—20th century. 3. Literature publishing—United States—History—20th century. 4. Underground press—United States—History—20th century. 5. Women authors, American—20th century—Biography. 6. Women publishers—United States—Biography. I. Title.
PS3561.E4269Z467 1995
818'.5403—dc20
[B] 95-21097
CIP

First St. Martin's Griffin Edition: September 1995
10 9 8 7 6 5 4 3 2 1

CONTENTS

PROLOGUE

FOR SIX YEARS, I published a magazine all about myself. In it, I documented everything from my dreadlock hair-care tips to the antics of my roommate's pet pig to my travails as a struggling fiction writer. *Pagan's Head* (as the magazine came to be known) was just a little Xeroxed, stapled-together thing that I handed out to friends and acquaintances—but it changed my life. I began publishing it in an effort to procrastinate, to trick people into liking me, to get dates, to turn myself into a star, and to transform my boring life into an epic story. And the scary thing was, it worked.

I did get fans, friends, and dates—people responded to the *Head* with far more enthusiasm than I had ever anticipated. More to the point, the magazine imparted a surreal, cartoony quality to my life; during the years when I published *Pagan's Head,* I existed on two levels. On the one hand, I was just another out-of-whack, directionless woman trying to muddle through her late twenties; on the other hand, I was the star of my own story, a story illustrated by cheesy clip art and half-assed cartoons and photos chosen because they made me look like I had high cheekbones. On the one hand, I was a frustrated writer, receiving rejection letters from *The New Yorker* for my short stories; on the other hand, I was a publishing dominatrix who demanded my readers send me money, toys, and fan letters—and I got them.

My *Pagan's Head* phase lasted from the time I was twenty-five until I was thirty-one. Now I'm thirty-two and I think I've come out the other side. I seem to have lost the urge to live on two levels; nowadays, just dealing with ordinary life seems complicated enough. I look back on the

Head years with bemusement and some shame. What the hell was I thinking? A whole friggin' magazine all about myself? Geez.

I suppose I did it because I was shy, frustrated, and fucked up. But, really, I remember those years as mostly happy, suffused with the candy-colored glow of a Saturday morning cartoon. A time when all that mattered was adventure. A time when art could still save my life.

BACK TO PAGAN

ONE DAY in September 1987 my friend Billy, a bassist from the band Hell Toupée, loaded my stuff into his decaying car and drove me down to Baltimore so I could become a student at Johns Hopkins University.

I'd found out I was accepted into the graduate writing program several months before. I remember standing in the graffiti-splattered living room of the "E Ranch," a punk flophouse where I lived, and tearing open an envelope with the Johns Hopkins insignia on it. The letter inside congratulated me for being awarded a teaching fellowship—a full scholarship plus a stipend. As soon as I saw that, I started screeching the way people do when they choose the right door on "Let's Make a Deal."

At the time, I was working as a copy editor—I held a full-time job and, on top of that, wrote fiction for several hours every morning. I was slaving away at it because I had a mission: I wanted to write the Great American Underground novel. This was in 1987, before the media had noticed that there was a youth underclass living in group houses and subsisting on temp jobs—later we would be given labels like "Generation X" and "slackers." But in the eighties, we were stereotyped as young Republicans climbing the corporate ladder. For instance, after Bret Easton Ellis's *Less Than Zero* came out, I felt like puking. He tried to describe people my age, but it was such a stupid, shock-value version of us. We were supposed to be spoiled brats, rapists who drove Jaguars and snorted coke. It sounded like the story of our generation as dreamed up by some forty-five-year-old ad man (or maybe Aaron Spelling).

Of course, there was another reason I'd prayed I would get into Hopkins. Being a disaffected slacker type, I hated to work full time. I saw grad school as my escape from office drudgery, a beautiful year of getting free money while I hung out, wrote, thrift-shopped, made jewelry, and dozed in the sun.

I intended to live for nine months on the $5,700 stipend. Right from the beginning, that affected many of the lifestyle choices I made in Baltimore. No graduate housing for me—way too pricey. Besides, I didn't want to live too near Hopkins, that uptight campus with its ties to the Department of Defense.

Actually, I ended up loving Hopkins, or the writing program, anyway. I loved being in a place where fiction mattered more than anything else, where all I had to worry about was teaching and writing. True, none of the other writers came from the punk underground; most of them planned to become professors or return to their corporate jobs or become mothers. But they were warm, talented people who cared about writing, about living honestly. And though they seemed conventional on the surface, many of them shared the mental quirks and the morbid tendency toward self-scrutiny that had always set me apart.

My (nonwriting) friends teased me about being a hypochondriac, but at Hopkins I was suddenly surrounded by a horde of hypochondriacs, other people with such overdeveloped imaginations that they, too, couldn't keep dreadful thoughts under control. One of my fellow grad students went to the health clinic after he discovered a red dot on his hand; the nurse took a quick look and referred him to a shrink. We writers noticed every spot and speckle on our bodies, anything that could bloom into death. In the same way, we scrutinized our stories for any tiny flaw that would doom the polished piece to literary oblivion. We could spend half an hour arguing over one word. We sought no less than perfection in our stories, to enter the pantheon of Nabokov and Joyce and Beckett and Woolf.

As a writer, I belonged at Hopkins. But the part of me that was Pagan didn't. I was getting by on $500 a month, hanging out with Hungarian performance artists and hippie musicians, and living in a neighborhood where many students refused to go at night. No matter what city I moved to—Baltimore, Boston, New York—I always seemed to end up in the same place: Underground USA, a low-rent sideshow of people who didn't just *make* art—they *were* art. I had one friend who used a diving shirt as her jacket. I went around bedecked in chicken bones and beads, carrying a Muppets lunchbox.

Which brings me back to my mission: writing the Great American Underground Novel. In some ways, I succeeded with this at Hopkins. That year, I wrote the first story I ever had published in *The Village Voice*, an epic about two garage-band rockers who travel to Graceland. But in the long run, I lost track of my mission. By the end of my stay in grad school, I had stopped writing about the hipster demimonde and begun trying to produce "normal" fiction.

Why? Well, before I went to Hopkins, it never would have occurred to me that I could get a job teaching college-level English. But one day, I glanced around the cafeteria table where we grad students hung out and realized that many of my peers *assumed* that they would go on in academia. They were desperate to publish stories in *The New Yorker* or *Grand Street* or the *Atlantic Monthly,* not just to be validated as writers but also to plump up their résumés. To get a fat academic job, you need to publish and publish well, in tony magazines or with a respectable house like Ticknor & Fields. (*The Village Voice* definitely does not count.) That pressure, the need to publish respectably, affected their work—and my work too. Because in some part of my brain (maybe the reptilian subcortex that gives us our will to survive) I was thinking, Why not teach? After all, what else will I be fit for once I have my degree?

Maybe those of us who went to grad school in the mid-1980s had a particularly strong need to conform. Unlike writers who came of age in the swinging years, we were faced with a conservative fiction market. Realism, "yuppie fiction," and minimalism were hot. *The New Yorker* seemed to publish story after story about people getting divorced in Westchester. Pieces about punk-rockers wouldn't get you very far. You were supposed to invent "ordinary" characters conducting "ordinary" lives: Updike lives, *New Yorker* lives.

We graduate students were well equipped to make a living—if one could be made—by producing 1980s fiction. We knew how to invent imaginary people, how to give them jobs and lovers and worries, how to craft our work, make it realistic and powerful. But did we know how to invent ourselves? Did we know how to transform our own lives? Could we go through the looking glass and enter our own fictional worlds? I thought less and less about such questions as the months passed. Even as I learned to be a better writer, I forgot why I'd begun writing in the first place. By the time I graduated from Hopkins, all I cared about was flexing my literary muscles and building up my résumé.

And then I moved back up to Boston. Oh God, that stifling summer of 1988. I sat on a sweltering little porch and dutifully started a novel—the kind of novel that I thought I *should* write, one that had nothing to do with me at all. The kind of novel that might get me a job. It was a story about two spinsters who cross the country in 1968, the language full of frills and metaphors. I labored on it all summer, imagining what *The New*

York Times would say when my book came out ("Kennedy's historical novel is nothing short of a tour de force"). Sometimes I stood gazing at myself in the bathroom mirror, posing for the author photo that would appear on the back of my novel. Other times I agonized at how slow my progress was—I couldn't wait to finish the novel so I could land a teaching job and escape from copyediting forever.

That fall, I moved to a group house, a rambling Victorian mansion with fireplaces and stained-glass windows and eight weird residents. In the heyday of that house on Farrington Avenue, only one or two of us held real jobs. We sat around working on projects, gossiping, making cookies, practicing guitar, designing clothes, refinishing furniture. I subsisted, as usual, on part-time copyediting.

That year it seemed as if everyone I knew had suddenly decided to produce a homemade Xerox magazine (or "'zine"). My roommate Donna collected the ravings of insane people and turned them into pamphlets; Seth published a cartoon 'zine; Jason color-copied his psychedelic collages; Tony made comic books; Rob was working on a surrealist literary thing; and on and on. At the highest pitch of the scene, the 'zine publishers formed the Small Press Alliance. (The group fell apart after Shiva, the god of destruction, whispered into the ear of an anarchist pamphleteer that he must destroy the alliance and sue its members for "harassing" him.)

My friends couldn't understand why I didn't have my own publication. I often contributed cartoons and essays to other people's 'zines, so why didn't I just buckle down and start my own? I kept trying to explain that I couldn't do a 'zine because—no offense—I was a real writer. *The Village Voice* had started publishing my reviews and short stories. And I was still working on that novel in progress, which I had begun calling my "nov in prog" because I felt the need to make fun of it in front of my slacker peers.

And then, I don't know, one day something in me snapped. Boredom, really, that's what I should attribute it to. I had to do something with myself, because God knows my fiction wasn't going too well; some days I found I couldn't write at all. So I started a 'zine, telling myself it would be just a little Xeroxed thing to send to friends far away, a kind of letter. Maybe, too, I'd hand out a few copies to acquaintances in Boston. But that was all. Just for fun.

Deciding to publish the 'zine was like giving myself permission to loosen up after years of trying to attain perfection and aping "respectable" fiction. For so long I had hidden behind a narrator, but now I would finally let myself speak. Instead of using metaphors and codes to make my point, I would talk plainly. That must have been exactly what I needed, because suddenly I began churning out essays and drawings and cartoons.

Almost instinctively I broke every rule of respectable fiction. I published my own work (for serious literary types, self-publishing is considered a sign of rank amateurism). I drew pictures. I wrote unpolished sentences and hardly went back to revise. I even scribbled in last-minute notes. And most important, I talked endlessly about myself.

Rule number one of fiction is this: Try not to write an autobiographical story, but if you do, then make sure you "write against yourself," that is, show yourself as a loser, a jerk or whatever. This has the paradoxical effect of making you, the writer, look like a great person because you understand and admit to all your flaws.

Well, life is too short. So in my fanzine, I dispensed with all the wise head-shaking at my own folly. Intead, I let my ego out of the box. I indulged in an orgy of self-adulation. I wallowed in the mud of narcissism. What a relief after so many years of self-effacement!

I did everything they'd told me not to do and I loved it. My fanzine was a fuck-you to *The New Yorker* and the University of Iowa and the Bread Loaf writers' colony and Ticknor & Fields and Raymond Carver and agents named Bitsy and John Updike and the twenty-two-year-old novelists that *Newsweek* told me hung out in the hottest clubs and English Comp jobs. The whole respectable writing crowd could gather in their country club, sip tea on the long green lawns, and discuss elegant style without me. Once I discovered my 'zine, I no longer wanted to belong.

Besides, in some backward way, I had finally learned how to write the Great American Underground Novel—though it ended up being a 'zine instead. And why should it be a novel? What literary masterpiece could have captured my life as well as a Xeroxed pamphlet full of scrawled cartoons?

Once I started doing the 'zine, I knew I was on to something. I was happy here in my room—drawing a cartoon about summer camp, writing about my trip to Knoxville, choosing cheesy illustrations from clipart collections. It reminded me of when I was a little kid, eight or nine, and I used to make my own books. I had rediscovered the sheer delight of creating something. How had I forgotten that this—this absorbed, tongue-between-the-teeth, little-girl feeling—was the essence of art? Oh calloo-callay I had found it again, hidden tide pool of my own thoughts, secret garden, kiddie pool.

Godhead is light. Nescience is darkness. Where there is Pagan there is good gossip
BACK TO PAGAN
Issue #1
usually $2, but for you... $1
I'm such a mirerable reject. No, I'm not, I just need something—but what could it be? I know, I'll dye my hair. No, that's not it, I have to learn German so I can go to Berlin. Naw, I hate to even leave the house. Ice cream? Combat boots? Therapy? No, no, no. I KNOW, I'll do a MAGAZINE. Everyone else I know does one. And it'll be all about me!
S STOP
In this issue you WON'T Find
• An interview with John Wayne Gacy
• Endless references to "Bob" and Slack
• Poetry
• Drawings of rotting corpses
• Anarchist rants

ARE YOU LIKE SUSAN? and Pagan?

Do you want to see what you have in common with gorgeous Susan Dey? Take our match-up quiz below and see if you and Susan share the same dislikes and likes! Just mark an X in the box labeled *YOU* whenever you answer the question *YES*. Susan's already taken the quiz—now it's your turn!

	SUSAN	YOU	PAGAN
Will you one day cut your hair and don corporate clothes to play a TV lawyer?	☒	☐	No way
Do you care for your hair with good habits to keep it clean and shiny? + L.A. Law blond	☒	☐	☒
When you feel hungry between meals, do you reach for a juicy crisp apple?	☒	☐	and a couple of Oreos
For a well-balanced meal you always include protein and vegetables?	☒	☐	forget the protein
Always keep your clothes in good condition by sewing on buttons and mending tears?	☒	☐	are you kidding
Do you love carnival rides?	☒	☐	Meat is murder
Do you enjoy going to amusement parks to eat hot dogs, candied apples, and fluffy cotton candy?	☒	☐	man
Love sipping hot tea with honey on rainy days?	☒	☐	Any day!
Have naturally long eyelashes?	☒	☐	None
Do you pout when you can't have things your own way?	☐	☐	You bet
Make a special effort to return phone calls?	☒	☐	You bet!
Like to eat out rather than cook?	☐	☐	Sure
Like wild, funky outfits that are daring?	☐	☐	+ tacky
Are you anorexic?	☒	☐	No way!

Thanks to Steve for loaning me his Partridge collection

Remember--

The address of this magazine is 14 Farrington Ave. in Allston, MA. This is *not* my house--big mean guys with no sense of irony live there and will beat you up if you mess with them.

Pagan Pipes Up

Dear Friends:

I read those other self-published magazines--the angry-collage, gross-out punk 'zines with names like *Eating Jesus' Snot*. Who are these publishers anyway--didn't they used to be high school rejects like everyone else? Don't they visit their grandparents or give their moms a call just to say hi? Don't they ever feel left out at parties or sometimes leave a club because the music's too loud? Are they really that cool, that angry?

This magazine will try to be different. Even if it is for unrecognized messiahs, arm-chair revolutionaries, motorcycle mamas and angelic hop-headed hipsters, I want it to be *nice*. It won't make you feel like you aren't cool enough to even be touching it. The print won't be so small that you have to strain your eyes, because that's just not thoughtful. And you won't feel left out. I'll introduce you to my friends, my phobias, my jobs, my deep thoughts about life and my sinus problems. And if I don't have anything nice to say, I'll try not to say anything at all.

A SPECIAL FIRST-ISSUE FEATURE: WELCOME TO THE WORLD OF PAGAN

You're probably wondering if my being named "Pagan" means I have anything to do with the Wiccans, or the Neo-Pagans. It does not. Although I can see the

point in running naked through the woods as a method of worship, frankly, I would worry about being bitten by ticks (they can give you deadly Old Lyme disease). Also, I have no desire for men named Graywolf to try to help me open up my lower chakra.

Not to brag or anything, But I was given the name "Pagan" way before Paganism was cool. In high school I had a groovy, alway-in-trouble Pakastani friend who liked to go around asking people, "Can I call you Broomstick?" or "Can I call you Aluminum Siding from now on?" So one day after I attempted to stage a protest because we had to say prayer in our school assemblies, she asked if she could call me Pagan. It was the only time one of her names actually stuck.

I've resisted putting out my own magazine for some time, since I thought it would divert my energies from my career as a promising writer. That career began when I was just out of college and a big Pooh-Bah in the New York writing scene "discovered" me and decided he would make me famous. But he never did get around to making me into ~~the~~ a 22-year-old literary genius. (What did I do wrong? Was I supposed to have slept with him?) Nonetheless I must not have lost my lustre as a promising young writer, because a few years later I won a grant to study writing at Johns Hopkins University. For a year, I taught writing, hung out with writers, felt guilty whenever I wasn't working on a new story. At Hopkins, writing seemed serious, the focus of your life and the cause of your early death.

But you know what I realized in Baltimore? I'm shallow. I don't want to write deathless prose. I just want to create stuff like I did when I was eight years old--like when I tried to make a one-armed bandit out of a dog-food box or when me and my sister built shopping malls for our pet turtles. And that's what self-publishing is, in a way. You don't have to compare yourself to Beckett or Nabokov. You don't agonize over every word. Instead of making something for strangers, you make it for friends--who'll forgive if your cartoons are wobbly or your prose wanders.

One final note: You may think I'm self-obsessed, since so much of the magazine is about my life. Well, okay, I am. But I like to read gossip about other people's lives too--confessional I'll-give-you-the-embarrassing-details stuff like Aline Kominsky-Crumb's cartoons--so darn it all, I'm not going to feel guilty.

Travel Talk

My friend Donna is a millionairess and I myself have a vague knowledge of computers that allows me to command hundreds of dollars per hour as a free-lancer. So we decided to squander some of our wealth by taking a trip through the South.

At first we planned to drive down in a '62 Dodge Dart--not that either of us had one. We'd sing "Me and My Bobby McGee" as we drove. We'd wash our clothes in the bathrooms of highway gas stations. We'd sleep on piles of Spanish moss in Lousiana swamps, clutching sticks with which to fight off zombies. We'd stop at every trashy tourist trap we'd read about in *Roadside America* (the world's largest peanut, the Tupperware museum, Condederama).

But we never did find that elusive Dodge Dart, so we settled for a less authentic solution: We booked plane tickets going to Knoxville, Tennessee, and leaving from New Orleans two weeks later. We thought we'd drive to New Orleans in a rented car--a pale approximation of the originaly Bobby McGee, zombie, gas station plan.

Our friend Trevor picked us up at the Knoxville airport and escorted us to his bachelor pad. This turned out to be a sort of concrete bunker with a "technology pit," a living room full of electronic instruments.

And then it was off for a tour of Knoxville's sights--which we exhausted in about twenty minutes. For scenic thrills, there was the 1970s (?) World's Fair abortion. That is, Knoxville built a bunch of weird, stupid-looking monuments in preperation for the World's Fair, which ended up being held elsewhere. A gigantic, Cyclopean "Tower of the Sun" dominates the Knoxville skyline, like a disco ball on a pedestal. Underneath it flows the Tidy Bowl blue waters of a man-made lake, complete with fake waterfalls.

The Tower of the Sun looms over Knoxville.

We lunched at the Vatican, Knoxville's equivalent of CBGB's. True to Southern style, this hang-out centers around food--a pizza joint decorated Pope paraphrenalia where they blast Sex Pistols from coffin-like speakers. The guy who owned the place was about eighteen with spiked hair, a country boy gone wrong--but not too wrong because Southern punks are sweethearts.

We had to go back to Trevor's bachelor bunker, as he had to do some "work." The poor guy did piece work--constructing hideous globular "fashion" belts for a few bucks each. As he wove blue lycra through plastic blobs, he told us about his recent arrest. He'd been to an Anarchists' conference in Toronto; the Anarchists had demonstrated by running wild in the streets; a policeman was about to beat a woman and Trevor grabbed his arm to stop him; Trevor was arrested for assualting an officer. Trevor seemed more world-weary than I remembered him, and I suppose it was his brief stay in prison (*prison,* not jail) that changed him.

It should be noted that most of the time I was in the South, I was crippled with a sinus infection. You may laugh, but it is truly awful to have your ear feel like it's full of lead shot. The only way I could get relief was to drop a constant stream of Sudafeds, those little red pills that are over-the-counter's answer to amphetimines. My heart was always hammering and I couldn't stop gnawing on my tongue. In this state of mind, trying to comprehend the South was like trying to watch a tape of "Hee Haw" on fast-forward.

That night, we went to the Posse House--the home of a band of earnest young Anarchists who like to throw firecrackers in the kitchen and listen to Public Enemy. They were very nice boys, but when I requested a pillow and a blanket, the deranged Dixies seemed not to understand. They wanted to give me drugs, not blankets, and so I sunk into a sick puddle on the carpet while they toked up and talked about a world without law.

Next day, it was off to Gatlinburg--a place where in-bred Southerners go to honeymoon, and also where Jim and Tammy Bakkar hid out after all the hoopla. On the way, we hit Pigeon Forge, a highway strip of souvineer warehouses, Elvis-impersonator lounges and a town where the natives always think it's Christmas. We stopped in at Hillbilly Village, a flea-bitten bunch of exhibits celebrating hillbilly humor. The best was a crooked old outhouse: Open the door and a hillbilly dummy on the can says "Shut that thaing," or "Hand me a corn cob." Corn cobs, Trevor had to explain, are what hillbillies use for toilet paper. In fact, he had to explain most of Hillbilly Village to us.

Gatlinburg was a tourist trap's tourist trap: dinosaurs roam freely in its many mini golf courses and scary fat people with no minds parade around gnawing on hunks of fried dough. Every inch of sidewalk is crammed with something to grab your attention: get a T-shirt with your head on Elvis's body, play skeeball, have a wooden plaque made to hang in front of your mobile home.

In the center of it all looms the Space Needle. You pay a few bucks to ride the slowest elevator in the world up to a round, covered platform. Up there it's like being in a spaceship hovering several hundred feet in the air, except instead of walls there's a flimsy, waist-high fence. You can only see Gatlinburg if you look straight down; all around you are the Smokey Mountains, huge and flat against the sky, unscarred by ski trails, the most beautiful mountains I've ever seen. It was silent up in the

The author enjoying a ride at Gatlinburg and looking way too much like Paul Williams.

Space Needle. It would have made a good church. They should have holy men chanting up there, each facing a different direction, all garbed in matching T-shirts that said, "My parents went to the Smokey Mountains and this lousy shirt is all they bought me."

A faux gravestone for a moonshiner at Hillbilly Village.

Down on the ground, I went into religious ecstacies of another sort at the Guinness Book of World Records Museum, where we saw the longest mustache, the tiniest woman and a filmstrip about a man who cut a tree into bite-sized splinters and ate the whole thing. But these were nothing compared to the last exhibit. There on a pedestal was the object about which I'd had so many fevered childhood fantasies: the real, actual Batmobile. It looked like a cartoon come to life, with orange neon bats on the hubcaps and two-foot-high tail fins. Everywhere signs warned us not to touch the Batmobile. This spurred Trevor into an anarchistic frenzy. What kind of goddamned government is it anyway that doesn't let you touch the things that it brainwashes you to love on TV? Shouldn't the Batmobile belong to everyone?

"I have to touch it," Trevor said.

I panicked. The Batmobile was surrounded by sirens and closed-circuit cameras. Not only that, but this was *the Batmobile*. Wouldn't bat radar sense his touch? Wouldn't it emit bat anarchist-killing vapors? I begged Trevor not to, but he leaned over the ropes, his hand hovering inexorably closer and closer to the bat door. The tips of his fingers met the shiny, black surface and ... nothing happened.

We were elated. He had touched the Batmobile and gone unpunished; he had gone up against the system and come out unscathed, man. It was time to leave the Guinness Museum. Outside on the sidewalk, still high from Trevor's brush with the Batmobile, we squinted in the sudden sunlight. I was flooded with happiness, and actually feeling proud of America, my country tis of thee, where they put you in a museum for eating a tree.

A lot more happened when we were down South, but I don't have any more energy left to tell you about it, so too bad.

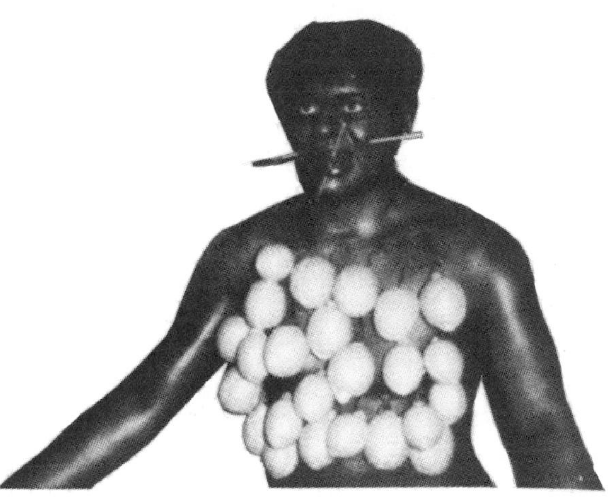

A guy at the Ripley's Believe It or Not Museum takes the lemon pledge.

MY GREEN SNEAKERS

by pagan

ugly, practically unreadable Letraset bought at yard sale

STAR-KEDS

In exchange for agreeing to go to Camp On-the-Rocks,* my mom let me buy my dream shoes... a pair of neon green high tops.

KEDS

But I was really supposed to wear stupid-looking orthopedic shoes

veil of tears

In order not to undo all the "good" of my orthopedic shoes, I was only allowed to wear my sneakers for an hour a day...

Come over quick before I have to take off my sneakers

Those happy hours were all too brief...

CAMP SUCKED. Let's just say it wasn't the place for a budding intellectual.

allergy tree

mean dogs

COMPETITIVE GAMES

When I got home, my father snuck in my room one day and threw out the sneakers. My mom said it wasn't his fault. The toxic green color of the sneakers had driven him temporarily insane.

THE END

Shoe circled by crown o' thorns

* name changed to avoid ugly libel suit.

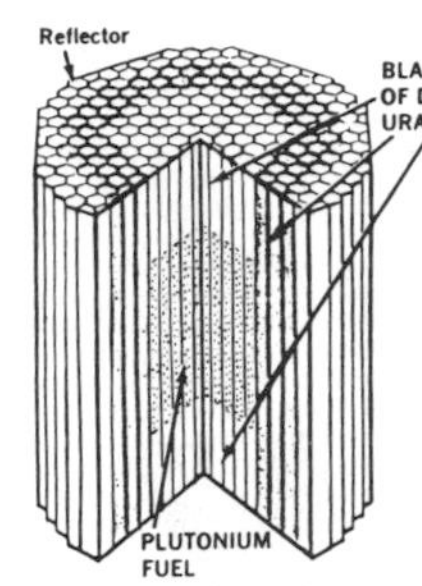

Personality from my Past

Andy was the guy in my freshman dorm who never left his room--always in there grinding away at physics. He looked normal enough: button-down shirts, Wallabees, short hair. But every word out of his mouth hinted at some rich and twisted inner world. Now, of course, I can't remember any of the things Andy said that so amazed me. But I do remember one time, junior year, when some friends and I had gone over to his apartment and found him in a strange mood. Suddenly he disappeared into his room and came out wearing a white suit jacket and a piece of cotton taped to his lip. When we asked him what he was up to, he said he was Mark Twain.

After he graduated, he received a huge sum of money to study in an Ivy League PhD program. I haven't heard from him for a few years now.

Andy is our featured Pagan Personality for this issue. In the following selections from his letters to me (written mostly during school vacations), you can see how ingenious he was. Andy turned his grudges against minor characters in his life into baroque systems of belief and secret mythologies. Hail Andy!

12/30/84
... I thought your analysis of my misanthropy was amusing but, on the whole, totally wrong. You said that I hate people who broach my exterior formality. I think what you meant was "breach" (I may be wrong on this), but worse than that, I think your misguided. ... I love informality. The people I hate are the ones who (a) aren't nice to me or (b) remind of people who, at one time, were not nice to me.

In fact, I believe these are sounder than the frivolous criteria you seem to use. You hated Dennis simply because he was a wimpy, humorless little scientist who slept with your friend, and that's not being fair to him. On the other hand, I hated him because he was competitive and offensive and peed on the bathroom floor. These are good reasons. You hated Rhonda immediately and for no good reason at all (though I have to admit you were right on that one) while I remember taking pains to compile several good complaints against Scott and still managed to hate him before that became fashionable...

10/17/84

...I am glad to hear you are a fact-checker at the Voice. My brother was a fact-checker for Rolling Stone once and whenever they didn't get enough mail for their letters column they would make up some and sign his name to them. It was pretty degrading, but they eventually repaid him by offering special acknowledgment to him in the preface of the rock & roll histories. I tell you this so you know what lies ahead...

8/10/83

...This week, my boss is away so I have to deal with all the severe loonies who work in the office. One woman, whose name I dare not mention, wants me to be her son, and made me so angry today that I cracked her head open with a garden shovel. She complains about her mother--who is relentlessly and selfishly dying a protracted death--and then eats tuna salad sandwiches that render the air unbreathable...

7/13/82

...On Tuesday I went running for the first time since high school. I did, of course, inhale a large insect that flew across my path. I also enjoyed the way my underwear rides up until I feel like I'm wearing a piano-wire bikini.

Please enjoy these healthiest and happiest years of your life. Your aren't getting any younger.

Mint, regular or new gel,
Andy

I hope you have enjoyed the featured Personality for this issue. Wherever you are, Andy, I hope you are enjoying these healthiest and happiest years of your life too.

EARTH MOTHER PAGE

(hand-written to look like The Moosewood Cookbook)

All my life, I've been terrible at anything practical. I made a rotten feminist, because I couldn't pour herb tea without spilling it all over myself. But Jung says if you're weak in any of the four areas (thinking, feeling, intuition, perception), you should try to build it up. So, I've been attempting to do all the Earth Mother things — cooking, gardening, nurturing. Here's a bunch of my fave down-to-earth things to do.

Let's Make Some "Never-Get-Cancer Miso Soup"

1. fry up some onions + garlic
2. meanwhile, chop up broc, carrots, tofu, zuccini, etc.
3. Start that water a-boilin
4. dump in veggies, onions + garlic
5. clean up, let soup simmer
6. pour some not-boiling water into a bowl and mush in some miso until you have a hideous mess. Don't look at it, just dump it in the saucepan.

WARNING: Never boil miso, or else all the anti-cancerettes will die.

Cleanse a Crystal

What if your new crystal has some heavy vibes left in it by its previous owner — then it would actually be sapping your energy instead of healing you. So make sure you soak it in a bowl of salt water.

Let's Grow Wacky Grass!

Dump grass seed in piles around your yard. When it comes up, you have thick grass "pillows" all over. Fun to stand on barefoot!

Clean the Bathroom

Drink 3 cups of coffee and then scrub one tile until it's perfect.

Make "Feminist" Popcorn

The secret is in the topping! Melt some margerine and mix it with nutritional yeast — flakey yellow stuff you find in bins at the health food store. This yeast is high in vitamins and magnesium — which means it's an excellent anti-depressant. Many times a few teaspoons of yeast have made my life seem to have meaning again.

I WAS A
HIPPY VAMPIRE
PEAVEY
I was an ADDICT
and BLOOD
was my fix!
THE
VAMPS

2

PAGAN'S DISCOVERED TO BE SEVENTH PARTRIDGE

IN FALL OF '88, when my first full-page article appeared in *The Village Voice,* I hoped for a little taste of fame. At the very least, I thought, my friends in New York would call me to say they'd seen the piece. Well, though the *Voice* had something like 50,000 readers, nobody ever mentioned the article to me. It was as if my work had disappeared into a black hole.

A few weeks later, the first issue of *Back to Pagan* came out. It had a circulation of fifty—I handed them out to pals and housemates, and also mailed copies off to friends in other cities. Soon after I distributed the 'zine, people began calling me to tell me they'd read it in one sitting, and then had lent it to their friends; acquaintances would ask me how they could get copies. Through some kind of weird publishing karma, *Back to Pagan* proved to be far more influential than the *Voice*—at least in my little circle. *Back to Pagan* traveled through the world with a magical ease, flying from hand to hand and ending up in every group house in Allston.

One day a guy came up to me at a party and said, "I know you. You're Pagan. My roommate left your magazine in our bathroom. It's so great. I want to subscribe."

"Wow, thanks," I said. Though I'd been continually surprised by the way *Back to Pagan* got around, I had never expected this to happen—I never expected *people I didn't know* to read the 'zine and become *fans.* I think that night at the party was the moment when I began to grasp the awesome potential of *Back to Pagan.* It wasn't just a 'zine, it was a social tool. Strangers would read it and think I was a self-assured scenester. Better yet, guys would dig me.

At the same time, the whole project could be dangerous—not dangerous like bungee-jumping, but dangerous like a junior-high dare. ("I dare you to go up to that guy and tell him he's cute." "I dare you to wear that T-shirt that says I'M WITH THE ASSHOLE.") Back then, back when I was twenty-six, that was exactly the kind of danger I was drawn to. I wanted to create a fabulous persona for myself, to turn my life into a Douglas Sirk movie set in urban hipsterland. More than to write novels, I longed to become a fictional character myself.

Nothing happened with the guy at the party—I probably minced away from him in embarrassment. But something in my brain clicked. Suddenly I realized that I didn't have to wait for the literary establishment to anoint me. If I wanted to, I could do it all myself, turn myself into a star by publishing the 'zine. It would be like cutting out the middleman: Instead of waiting for some publisher to promote me, I'd just promote myself.

Better yet, I could turn myself into whatever I wanted to be. For instance, during my preteen years, I'd always dreamed of running away to join the Partridge Family, living with them in their bus, jamming in their garage. So in the second issue of my 'zine, I finally made good on this childhood fantasy. On the cover, I announced that I was the seventh member of the Partridge Family, and I inserted myself into a group photo of the band. There was something oddly satisfying about remembering what I'd wanted so badly at age nine or ten and then being able to give it to myself.

Actually, my obsession with the Partridge Family was probably the cultural low point of my childhood. Mostly, I read. I adored all the childhood classics about fantasy lands: the Narnia series, *Alice in Wonderland, The Phantom Tollbooth, A Wrinkle in Time.* I'd lie on my stomach, following the words frantically; sometimes, instead of getting up to pee, I'd cross my legs and hold it in because I couldn't bear to break the spell for even a minute.

But I was always frustrated because I didn't want just to read books, I wanted to be a character inside one of them. I loved *Alice in Wonderland,* loved the book so much it almost hurt. I was desperate to follow Alice through the looking glass into that nonsense world where I knew I belonged. At eight years old, I'd stand in front of the mirror, concentrating, searching for some doorway, some hint in the reflection that another world lay behind the glass. But no, the world in those mirrors was just a backwards version of mine; and the girl there, misting the glass with her breath, was only a backwards me stuck in the year 1970 and the state of Maryland, a sweaty little girl wearing Huckapoo shorts and blue-green, oval-shaped glasses.

My 'zine was a way into Wonderland, a secret doorway into that backwards world of the mirror. From now on, I would be in character in a story of my own invention.

BACK TO PAGAN'S HEAD
(formerly Back to PAGAN magazine)
Cartoon by Tony Fitzgerald
STICKERS!
Big, Kissable Photos of David Cassidy
I was HOT FOR NIETZSCHE
MY HAIR
now stars in kung-fu movies
merely a replacement for the other, REAL Chris
PAGAN!
too young
anorexic
always seeming to have lumps on top of his head
My friends
too old
PAGAN DISCOVERED TO BE SEVENTH PARTRIDGE

HAVE A SAFE AND PSYCHEDELIC SUMMER

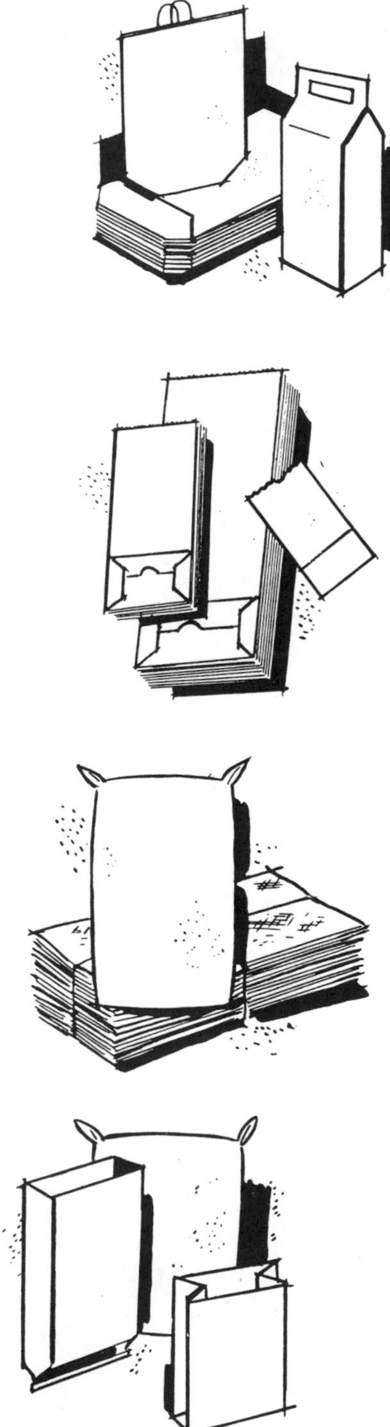

Dear Friends:

How thrilled I am to be bringing out another issue of *Back to Pagan's Head* (formerly *Back to Pagan)*. I hope you like our new look. But remember, even though we've gone high tech (using those layout boards with non-repro blue lines on them), we still feel as close to each and every one of you as when we were just a small-time operation run out of Pagan's room. In line with a snazzier layout, we've changed the magazine so no one will confuse it with one of those embarrassing New Age crystal newsletters.

I think you'll find a lot to luv in this issue of BTPH. A FAMOUS Boston underground cartoonist was sweet enough to help me bring my Jeapardy fantasy to life. You'll also find out about my secret love for Frederick Nietzsche and David Cassidy. And best of all, the back cover is a sheet of stickers. Wear BTPH stickers on you shirt, bike, hat or leather jacket and make a political statement as well as a fashion statement.

Spring finds Pagan in good spirits: I've quit my job and am gearing up for a Summer of Luv. (During a "Summer of Love" you have to drop acid and give people backrubs; but during a "Summer of Luv" you watch reruns of "The Mod Squad" and eat Fudgicles.)

Actually, my new career is writing book reviews. Sometimes all my pieces are due on the same day and it's just like being in school again, except harder because the papers I write actually have to be *good*. Watch for my reviews at your local newsstand in *The Village Voice,* the *Boston Phoenix* and the *Boston Review*.

Just one last thing: Please, for your own good, do not leave the city this summer! There are huge, microscopic, crazed ticks out there, and they're determined to make us all arthritic zombies. Stay on the pavement; do not touch leaves. Oh, and don't go to the beach because of the deadly rays being spewed out through the rotting ozone layer. And don't touch other people. Your best bet this summer is to stay in front the TV.

Safety first! Luv,

Pagan ♡

MY JEOPARDY FANTASY
by PAGAN UND FITZ
I WEAR A LEATHER BIKER JACKET AND SKULL JEWELRY, WHICH MAKES THE OTHER CONTESTANTS AFRAID OF ME...
PAGAN
BILL
COMPUTER PROGAMMER
FINANCIAL CONSULTANT
$ 0
$ 0
$ 0
I LIE TO ALEC TRIBEC...
MAY I ASK HOW YOU GOT THE NAME "PAGAN"?
MY PARENTS WERE HIPPIES!
I WAS CONCEIVED DURING A RITUALISTIC ORGY!
$ NADA
I LUCK OUT ON THE CATAGORIES...
UFOs
Copy Editing
Sinus Problems
German Philosophers
Allston Diners
Death Of The Planet
The Partridge Family
...AND GET ALL THE ANSWERS RIGHT!
WHAT IS A "RHINOPLASTY?"
BING
WHO WROTE "BEYOND GOOD AND EVIL"?
BING
WHAT IS THE OZONE LAYER?
BING
WHAT IS DANNY BONADUCE?
BONG
AS THE CREDITS ROLL, ALEC DECLARES HIS LOVE FOR ME...
MARRY ME... I BEG OF YOU...
COULD YOU PHRASE THAT AS A QUESTION, PLEASE?
YAWN
GRIP
JOEY TISSUE
ALEC TRIBEC'S SUITS BY MR. GUY
GAFFER
BILL DING
BUT THE BEST PART OF THE FANTASY IS WHEN I MEET MR. GUY!
SORRY, BABE...
I DON'T DO AUTOGRAPHS...
©1989 PAGAN-FITZ

PAGAN personality

We met simply eons ago during freshman orientation at Wesleyan University, at a get-to-know-your-dormmates beer bash. Max was named Matthew at the time, and he wore geek glasses and shapeless hand-me-downs. Gregarious Pagan (I had already been nicknamed Pagan) had to draw out shy Matthew, but eventually we began talking--about what we were supposed to be doing to fulfill our roles as stereotypical college students (i.e., ordering out for pizza and screaming "paaarrrty"). Pagan recognized in Matthew a soulmate, someone equally obsessed with self-parody. At the same time, he seemed pliable--apathetic and agreeable--so I knew I could force him to go along with all my kooky schemes. In fact, Matthew became the charter member of the pogo-sticking team I started (hey, I was 18).

Max and I play in Planet Love. He hasn't refined his image yet.

But all the while, he was subtly shaping me from hick to hipster. When I started college I had decided to be a drugged-out hippie. My method of becoming one (in hindsight) was typically Pagan. Rather than just acting spaced-out and leaving it at that, I announced to everyone that I wanted to be a hippie and agonized over every detail of my groovy wardrobe and aggressively retro vocabulary. (This was in the dawn of the eighties, before the sixties became passe.) Matthew's parents were REAL (suburban) hippies, so I looked to him for advice. He kept telling me, like a Zen master uttering a koan, "As long as keep thinking about being a hippie and talking about it, you'll never be one." But though he discouraged my obsession, it was he who taught me about the Fugs, Mary Quant, Iron Butterfly, paper dresses and freaking freely.

I think he changed his name to Max senior year--at any rate, the new name was the capstone of the gradual image change he'd engineered during his college years. Matthew was a shy, awkward loner; Max was the flashy lead singer of Planet Love (the psychedelic band he and I formed with three other pals). Matthew wore frayed button-down shirts; Max sported plastic jewelry, red-and-white Coke pants and golf shoes. Matthew majored in physics; Max majored in art. Matthew stood in the corner watching; Max circulated at parties.

Matthew/Max wrote me the following letters during college summers and right after graduation (I lived in NYC, he in Boston). Many of my readers may know Max in his present settled-down-with-Marcus, gadabout-Allston, recession-proof, red-wine-in-chipped-glass incarnation. To you I say, There was once another Max. Look ye, and learn.

1982: I'm enclosing a photograph of a pinecone sitting on a lawn chair. It was taken with a Polaroid "Big Swinger" camera c. 1968, which I found lying around the house. To take a picture, you look into the viewfinder and turn the knob until the red and black checkerboard says YES, press the button, pull on the tab, pull out the picture, count to 15, remove the cover from the picture (while avoiding the deadly oog) and coat it with that special coating, also deadly. And this is what you get [vague, fuzzy picture]. I think it's the amazing the lengths that some people will go for the novelty of instant pictures.

1983 (?): Hitchhiking today I got a very interesting ride from an old lady in a white Rabbit (no pun intended) convertible with the top down. When I got in she had the radio turned to top volume playing WPRO, the loud obnoxious rock station from Providence. She had to turn it down successively lower after I got in to get it to a reasonable volume. Then she told me about how her local residential association would not allow 1) marked driveways 2) laundry hung out to dry 3) cows in the fields.

1983: My first day at work [at the restaurant] was a wedding between a Jewish woman and a Puerto Rican man. Dan, the chef, kept complaining about the spics and their faults as a race and let fall such aphorisms as "You can take a spic out of Puerto Rico, but you can't take Puerto Rico out of a spic" (which I still haven't quite figured out). I'm afraid I might call him Archie by accident or let on in some way that I think of him as being from New Jersey. For the wedding, he made a punch out of Kool-Aid, gingerale and a bit of fresh citrus. "They'll never know," he said, but it tasted like Kool-Aid to me and I told him so. He says at the end of the summer I will cook as well as him, and it was difficult to restrain an inappropriate smile.

What can I read? Please send suggestions in your next letter. It's so *embarrassing* taking great authors out of the library but that was all I saw that I wanted. I was mortified on my second trip to the library and *couldn't* take out *Ulysses* and ended up taking out the shortest book by Thomas Mann that I could find, and the librarian told me it was very funny and I was "in for an exeperience."

1984: I didn't say, or at least I shouldn't have said, that I didn't think I wrote well, because it's beside the point. I just can't be bothered to spend any time on it. Anyway, enough things have been written already and I'm quite satisfied to read them, which is not to discourage you. In fact, the more I think about it, the only thing I really want to do is be a rock star--it is a predicament. If nothing else, I'm at least too old [22]. I like my job, but when there starts to be more creativity and responsibility involved, it will give me headaches.

I've been trying to say "I 'spect," and otherwise eliminate unnecessary syllibles.

Elton John just amazes me.

1985 and Max is trying to start a new rock band: You can console yourself, selfish as you are, that things are difficult for a band in the real world. There are NINE people at last count--of course some will drop out--but you see I was searching for something to offset our extensive rhythm section, and then suddenly there were all these people and conflicting view points. I just want people to dance and be happy! And I know certain factions are behind me. We'll probably all hate each other just like a real band, except we won't be famous.

This picture, taken only a few weeks later, captures that crucial moment when Max's look came together.

I'm in heaven when I listen to my "Peanuts" soundtrack album.

My boss, the art director, is going to be on a local Donahue-type show as a member of an INTERFAITH MARRIAGE. It strikes me that this kind of thing wouldn't happen in NYC.

...You know talking about ideas can become tiresome for me. But your interpersonal problems--indeed anyone's interpersonal problems, if they are truly problems and not just bitchy complaints--are fascinating. If I do not respond it is only because I have nothing to say.

Forever my love, Max

PAGAN'S HAIR: A HISTORY

Age 0: first aware of hair.

Age 7: I wanted long, hippy hair, but my mom said I had to get it cut short because I always got gum stuck in it. I didn't see what was wrong with having globs of gum in my hair (and still don't). Above is pictured my primal hair trauma scene.

AGE 11: I was a budding skate punk. My mother had given up on my hair. If she tried to take me to Mr. Bernard (her hairdresser) I ran upstairs screaming "I HATE YOU" and slammed my door.

AGE 16: My best friend was the perfect hippy. I was pale and dumpy and hated nature, but at least my hair was long.

When we grow up, we'll live in Montana and embroider our jeans and eat sprouts and marry cute boho hiker boys! Don't act so worried, Pagan.

* She succeeded in all this and more.

FRESHPERSON YEAR, COLLEGE: I discovered feminism + drugs. Strange objects lodged in my hair + stayed there for months.

Nicht ist wahr

Alles ist erlaubt

AGE 20: (shown with young Fred Nietzsche lighting my cig.) I discovered German philosophy. Cut my hair, dyed it black. I tried to muster amor fati in the face of a meaningless universe. Times had never been better for my hair.

SENIOR YEAR

← This is a picture from the yearbook! Here Donovan helps me tune my guitar. (enhanced)

As guitarist for a band called "Planet Love" I plunged headlong into MOD. My hair? Well, my dream was to have a '60s stewardess-style bubble cut, but it never worked out. I realized to get hair like that, you'd have to live like a '60s stewardess. But I did change my hair from Being-and-Nothingness black to Cissy (Family Affair) red. It was a time of experimentation—one last fling before the Real World of sensible hair.

Since NYC, I've been living in Allston, mostly, a town where cool hair is a major concern. I've got short hair in front, long in back. I've been braiding jewels and bubblegum toys into the back part—though I'd prefer to have dreadlocks. That doesn't seem possible. I have been told you can get dreadlocks by soaking your hair in 1000-Island dressing + toasting it in a toaster, but I'm not willing to go that far.

get it? Like Van Halen's "Hot for Teacher"

HOT FOR NIETZSCHE

I was touched by Walter Kaufmann's account of Nietzsche writing Thus Spake Zarathustra in the final days of his life. "He is shy, a little stooped, almost blind, reserved." He speaks to others "as a man who has been unused to talking." Yet, when he goes up to his room in the boarding house, he writes "until his eyes burn," pouring out frantic, brilliant passages. Kaufmann says "The key to Zarathustra is that it is the work of a profoundly lonely man."

My fave. passage from Zarathustra

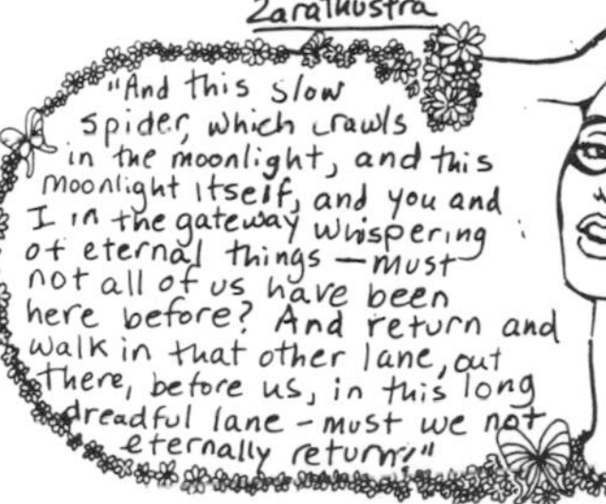

But after college, I forgot about everything but being a famous writer. I lost my copy of The Portable Nietzsche.

About George Sand: "This fertile writing-cow who had in her something German in the bad sense and who was only possible during the decline of French taste... rant, rant, rave..."

More than you even wanted to know about the

partridge family

If I was already a social reject at eight, blame Bobby Sherman. He was the teeny-bopper idol with a round, dimpled face, a suede jacket with super-long fringes, and--my third-grade shame--a TV show that was after my bedtime. So I had to hang out with the prissy girls with "Campus Queen" lunchboxes while the really cool girls, who had Bobby Sherman lunchboxes, sat in a circle rehashing the last episode of "Here Comes the Brides."

At recess, the leader of the cool girls, Sandra, would say, "Only people who love Bobby are allowed on the jungle gym," and I would be left standing on the wood chips because, by "love Bobby" I knew she meant owning his lunchbox and all other official Bobby Sherman-trademark products.

But what was her love for Bobby in the face of an uncaring universe? Where is Sandra nowadays--is she a stockbroker, banker, anchorwoman? Does she still think about Bobby? I doubt it very much. I, on the other hand, think about him all the time. Wherever she is, I'm sure Sandra is climbing the jungle gym of respectibility while I stand here on the wood chips of righteousness, clutching my Bobby Sherman albums.

Bobby was the first of his kind (if you don't count The Monkees, that is). He was never a real rock star; he was just a piece of bubblegum cooked up for us pre-pube girls by a corporation. Some guy on Madison Avenue noticed that it was the teeny boppers who spent the most cash on Beatles paraphrenalia, so why not create a puppy-eyed idol aimed right at the crotches of girls still into stuffed animals? Bobby was the avatar of a long line of made-for-TV "rock stars" such as David Cassidy and brother Shaun, Leif Garret and Rex Smith.

I never got to hear Bobby's music back then, except once on TV special. He wore his trademark jacket and leaned over ladies in the audience, singing "Julie, Julie, Julie" to them individually (Elvis-style).

And I may have never seen his show, "Here Comes the Brides," but thanks to a hippy baby sitter, I got to stay up and watch the first episode of "The Partridge Family." That's the one where Danny brings the Family's demo tape to Reuben Kinkaid. Danny finds Reuben asleep in a motel room, with a mask over his eyes to block out the afternoon sun. (This intrigued me--perhaps it was the moment I saw Reuben thus that I made a crucial lifestyle choice.) When the Family gets their first gig, they're so nervous that Mom tells them to close their eyes and just pretend they're practicing in the garage. The "closed eye" theme figures prominently in that first episode, setting the tone for a show that would close its eyes to most of the realities of the early seventies.

That episode was my first introduction to the crazy, raucous world of rock 'n' roll and it blew my mind. I had already learned about life from the Brady Bunch, but the Partridge Family taught me about COOL. Ostensibly, the message was that the family that rocks together talks together, but the show only made me realize how square my parents were. Why didn't they buy us a school bus? Why couldn't we turn our garage into a rock 'n' roll practice room? All of a sudden I saw how they were screwing up my life with their classical music, sensible meals, station wagons and bedtimes. In fact, watching "The Partridge Family" was almost agonizing because I wanted so badly to run away and join the Partridges, except I couldn't since they weren't real.

My parents showed they weren't entirely square by bumping my bedtime up by a half-hour on Fridays so I could watch the Family. My little sister and I went Partridge crazy. We knew all the words to "I Think I Love You" (or "Wathink I lav ya," as David pronounced it), "I Woke Up In Love" and "I Can Hear Your Heartbeat." My sister, still somewhat confused about her identity, had her hair cut just like David Cassidy's.

My best friend had already claimed David, so I took Danny as my 4ever 2gether tru luv. Actually, I liked Danny better anyway: He was a precocious nerd, always making wisecracks that marked him as a budding cynic. Recently, I was shocked to read in *The Enquirer* about what had happened to actor Danny Bonaduce, who so sensitively portrayed Danny Partridge. For a while, he was acting in sleazy kung fu movies, but when he couldn't even get those jobs anymore, he worked

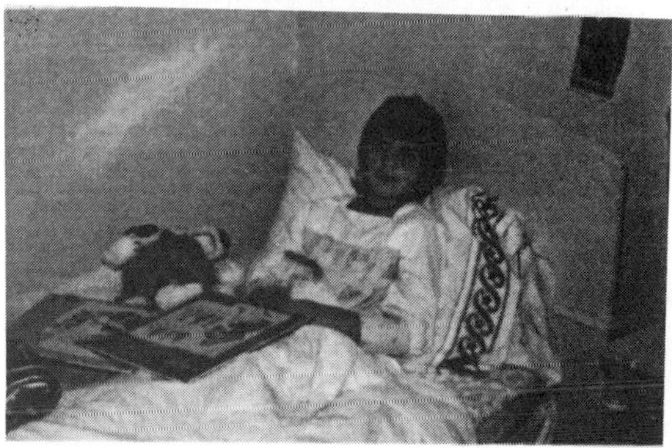

My sister with David Cassidy haircut.

in a bar where the boss yelled at him, "Faster, Partridge, faster, you're not a TV star now."

My best friend, Anne, and I lived on the hazy edge between reality and our Partridge-based fantasies. She had one of those giant posters of David Cassidy's face in her room that the ads in teen magazines describe as "kissable." It wasn't actually kissable at all becuase his lips were as big as our heads. You had to choose between kissing the vast expanse of his upper lip or of his lower lip--it wasn't good practice for kissing real guys unless you were planning on giong out with a hydrocephalac. Instead, we started doing striptease acts in front of David's huge face, tossing our shorts, shirts and underwear all over Anne's room.

My sister had a teepee, which inspired a Partridge-Indian game that summer. Anne and I were squaws, waiting for our braves (David and Danny) to come home from the wars. Our "Partridge Family" trading cards became Indian bark-paintings of our beloved husbands. We worked ourselves up into a frenzy of frustration imagining that David and Danny were about to walk into the teepee any minute and say "How."

A year or two later, it was Anne who convinced me that "The Partridge Family" was stupid and that they weren't real rock stars (she had older, hippie sisters). Hiding my tears, I gave away my PF records to a younger kid. I tried to like The Beatles, even though their TV show was just a stupid cartoon. And eventually I reconciled myself to a life without Partridges.

MY THEORIES

In college, I became an American Studies major, which gave me an excuse to obsess about "The Partridge Family" and all the rest of the junk culture I've always been in love with. From my new perspective, I could admire how brilliantly that show had co-opeted the ideas and styles of its time.

First of all, the PF's bus is a sanatized version of the school bus used by the Merry Pranksters (the band of psychedelic pioneers of the early sixties). The Pranksters' bus, covered with acid-inspired swirls of color, allowed them to haul loads of tripping people around to freak out unsuspecting small-town America. Via a system of loudspeakers and musical instruments on the roof, the Pranksters could braodcast their own atmospheric "music" to unwary gas station attendents, policemen, etc. Thus, the bus, which carried a platoon of protohippies ready to take over and freak out whole towns represented a threat to normals--isn't being "freaked out" hippie slang for being threatened?

The PF's school bus was entirely different. The Family didn't live in it, or braodcast insane music and ranting from it --they *used* it to get to their gigs. And though the bus was many colored, the colors were contained within Mondrian-like black lines, as if to reassure viewers that nothing was going to get out of hand. While the Pranksters' bus said, "Caution: Weird Load," the PF's bus warning read "Caution: Nervous Mother Driving."

Whether or not the creators of the show were aware of the Merry Pranksters, they were certainly attuned to a myth of the time: Hippies traveled around in painted buses. The brilliance of the PF was that it twisted that myth around so the bus was no longer threatening to normals. The Pranksters had a saying: "You're either on the bus or off the bus." The appeal of the PF was that it allowed Middle American viewers to feel they were "on the bus" that was ordinarily so frightening.

And then there is the incredible way the show glossed over a much-discussed issue of the early seventies: the generation gap. If anything, rock was the force that alienated teens from parents, and yet, in the world of the PF, it is what brings families together. It's hard to believe that Mom and

teens Laurie and Keith can all agree on what music to play.

In fact, "The Partridge Family" *was* modeled on a real bubblegum-rock family, The Cowsills (who sang "Indian Lake"). But, if memory serves, none of the Cowsill kids had hit their late teens--and certainly none them were pop idols the way David Cassidy is portrayed to be. The PF makes the male rock star--ordinarily a symbol of sexuality and rebellion--palatable to TV viewers by placing him in the

drugless, sexless world of the Cowsills.

It would be much harder to imagine a rock star son living with his family if Mr. Partridge was alive. But it is precisely because there is no male authority figure that the family has to turn to rock 'n' roll for its livelihood. Presumably, if there was a Mr. Partridge to bring home the bacon, this family would be as respectible as the Cleavers. But the male leader (Kennedy?) is dead and the family (the U.S.?) has to make do with a feminine leader with little earning power. (Perhaps Shirley Partridge was a symbol for President Johnson, who espoused feminine values of caring in his Great Society programs. Or, more darkly, perhaps she symboloizes Nixon, who was "a woman" because he was losing the battle with Vietnam and a "bad housewife" because he could not stop stagflation.) Until it finds a new "Mr. Partridge" to keep the kids in line, the "family" will have to reconcile itself with the anarchic forces of rock 'n' roll.

MR. PARTRIDGE R.I.P.

MY DREAM LIFE ILLUSTRATED

He fell in love with a dwarf. And he asked the dwarf, "How come everything makes sense, but at the same time doesn't make sense at all?"

There were four questions, but this was the first and most important.

My friends and I are traveling across the Midwest when we find a Shriners' Lodge and decide to go in. As we file in the door, a man hands us the little magnets with Shriners symbols on them that you sometimes see stuck on cars. On the back of the magnets is a drug that immediately begins to work on us.

Inside, the building looks like a church, except a swimming pool takes up the entire floor. Instead of being white, pasty and fat, the shriners are dark men who wear nothing but swimsuits and fezes. One of the men is standing in the pool, dispensing more of the drug from a floating tray. Suddenly, I am frozen as I stand on the cold tile, for I know the secret of the Shriners, which is also the secret of the Midwest.

Mina said, "I had a dream about you."

I said, "Don't tell me," because I knew it meant something horrible, but she told me anyway.

She said, "I dreamed about your house. No one was there. The wind was whipping through it. All the doors were banging like drums."

I realized that everyone has one Tru Luv® and that you know immediately when you see him or her.

I was looking out the window at people passing on the boardwalk. A man stopped and looked through the window at me. Except for his clothes and haircut--which were from some other era, perhaps the 1940s--he looked ordinary. We stared at each other, knowing we were each others' Tru Luv.® Then he walked on because there was nothing to say.

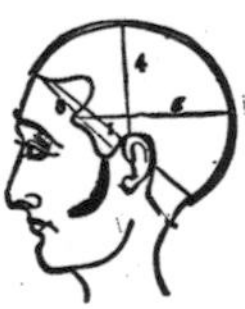

Elvis was tied up in a chair when a bottle exploded. His wife's face was covered with glass shards. It wasn't his wife, it was a man. We were all reduced to the level of animals.

Elvis's daughter was possessed with insane fits. This is what convinced him there was a spirit world.

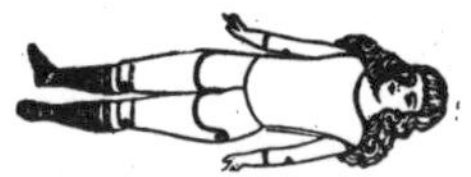

A demon child is running around the room. She has all the answers.

"Wait, wait, wait," I say, "I have an important question." The demon child stands at attention.

"How come there has to be evil?"

The demon child wrinkles her gray face and waves her hand at the sky, "Ever think that maybe <u>He</u> is?"

Gee Pagan, WHY ARE THERE STICKERS IN THIS ISSUE? well I'll tell you

One time, Max and I went to visit Maggie at her college. I had just graduated from *my* college and was thinking about what I really wanted from life. What I really wanted was to be standing on a balcony over a crowd of millions all yelling with one voice the name of their savior, "Pagan, Pagan, Pagan." I wanted to be Gandhi without having to spin my own cotton; Florence Nightingale without getting blood on my hands; Florence Henderson without having to do the Wesson commercials. But if that was my career goal, how would I build my resume?

Maggie lived in a hippie house where everyone painted their fingernails different colors and cooked brownies all the time. Unfortunately, she had to finish a paper, so Max and I ended up tripping with two of her housemates, Jenny and Tod.

I don't remember much about the beginning except that we shopped at the Salvation Army, but soon we had to leave because of the horrible vibes. Then we ran around in an underground railroad tunnel for a while. After that, we walked back up to the school, and Todd left us, lured away by a bunch of boys playing electric guitars in the student center.

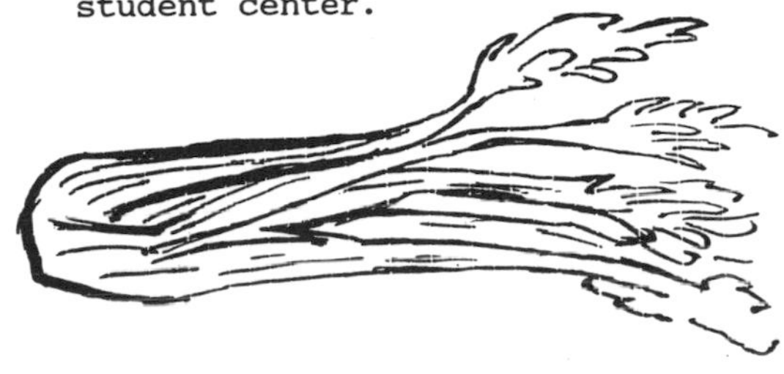

So Max, Jenny and I ended up lying in the hall of some dorm near a water fountain.

I started talking about my career goal--to be worshipped. Max has been a guy in search of a god, so all of a sudden we realized that we had symbiotic needs: I needed to be worshipped; he needed to worship.

Max started to grovel in front of me. He wanted to carry my jacket, to punish himself for me. I got mad: I was not going to be a Christian god, demanding sacrifice and guilt.

"Well then, how do I worship you?" Max said. He was getting up to drink from the water fountain.

I said, "You have to worship me in everything. I am the water you drink. I am the carpet. I am you. But most of

Me when I was "God": absolutely hideous

all, you must think of nothing but me."

Jenny, who's the type to go along with anything, took up the new religion too. She prayed for a backrub and I gave her one.

Then I had a revelation. I felt like God bossing around Noah. I said to Max, "You have a button maker. When you get home, you have to make thousands of buttons that say, `More happiness for Planet Earth.' If everyone wears the buttons, it'll usher in a new age."

Next we went to Store 24 to get celery. Jenny and Max walked two steps behind me--but otherwise we tried to act normal so no one would know I was God.

That night, Max had to take the train back, since he had a job. The next day, I felt terribly contrite and called him long-distance. I said, "Look, you've got to stop worshipping me right now." He was all too happy to agree.

A while later, Maggie showed me a photo she took of me when I was God. I look awful--all marshmallow puffy and pale. I'm lying on a bed staring at the ceiling and frowning, as if aware of my terrible responsibility.

Well, Max never did make the buttons. He was going to, but his machine could only make big ugly buttons, and neither of us thought that would be right. So, though it is about four years later, I'm finally fulfilling my prophesy: On the next page you'll find a sheet of "More happiness" *stickers*. Please, for the sake of the planet, wear them on you, your bike, your refrigerator--and trade 'em and collect 'em all!

STICKER SAMPLE

INSTRUCTIONS:
Couldn't afford the real kind with sticky backs so, cut as close as you can to the art and use glue on the back. Good luck

3

GOSSIP!

BACK TO PAGAN wasn't really written by me, only by one part of me—a voice, a persona. This was Pagan, the cartoon character (from now on I'll refer to her as Pagan[1] to distinguish her from myself). Pagan[1] was revealed to me in the first issue as a bratty, self-obsessed, neurotic, and sarcastic woman. At the same time, she was redeemed by her genuine desire to be a good person, by her self-mockery, her humor, and her friendliness. She was a camped-up version of myself, a full-blown fiction. And yet, she was also the one who authored the 'zine: It was she who turned her career history into a cartoon, she who reprinted a particularly stupid letter from one of her readers and then ridiculed it. She did everything in a childlike frenzy, working by instinct; whereas I, the serious writer, labored away methodically on my fiction.

In the first issue, Pagan[1] was still a tentative presence. It was in the second and third issues that I began to understand her. Pagan[1] had none of my own vulnerabilities: She didn't worry about offending people, or making bad art, or deferring to others. I recognized her as the id girl, too churlish for the real world.

I had a lot more readers now because I'd listed the fanzine in *Factsheet Five* (a Who's Who of 'zines). I began to receive piles of mail from subscribers, correspondents, art-types who wanted to involve me in their projects. I wrote back to people in my Pagan[1] voice, flippantly demanding they send me money or toys.

One of the most scary and wonderful of the letters I received was from a guy in Kentucky, an anarchist friend-of-a-friend. He said he wanted to run a Pagan fan club. He had me fill out a long questionnaire, information he would use for his fan newsletter. The questions perfectly echoed the dopey kind of interview you'd read in an issue of *Tiger Beat* from the early seventies: What's your favorite color? What do you eat for breakfast? What are your turnons and turnoffs? It seemed like he might spin off a 'zine from mine, sending dispatches to hipsters all over the nation about my doings. (What really happened was that he lost interest after a while.) Pagan[1] loved this overblown adoration, but it made another part of me—the sensible part—squirm. Did I really want to be an idol, except in my own imagination? Did I really want to turn into a cartoon character? When yet *another* guy wrote me that he, too, wanted to start a fan club, I said no. I didn't want this thing to spin out of control.

Still, Pagan[1] began to invade more and more of my personality. The way I dressed, for instance: I'd always worn thrift-shop assemblages, but now my look grew more costumelike. I began wearing this 1940s housedress with pockets that resembled oven mitts, paired with a belt emblazoned with tin cows.

And Pagan[1] began talking through me—mainly when I was at parties or in other situations where I could put on a kissy-kissy, debutante-from-hell personality without scaring everyone too much. In my six-inch-high platform shoes (found in the basement of my group house), I'd totter around, hugging people and having long conversations with strangers about candy cigarettes and "Welcome Back, Kotter."

A few blocks from my house, there was a grotty performance space where people would show industrial films or do readings. For a few years, it seemed like I knew everyone who gathered for these performances—and I buzzed around, gabbing and showing off, very aware that I was an Allston celebrity. (This wasn't too much of an achievement, considering that Allston is several blocks in diameter.)

Being Pagan[1] was like taking a vacation from my normal personality, the cautious workaholic. I turned into her when I met new people. She became a coping mechanism. I learned to be bold, though what I showed off was an invention, a fictional character; in some ways I was more cut off from others (except my close friends) than I had ever been. She was taking over.

BACK TO PAGAN

formerly "back to pagan's head" magazine

SPECIAL REPORT
A Partridge family Scandal

as seen on TV

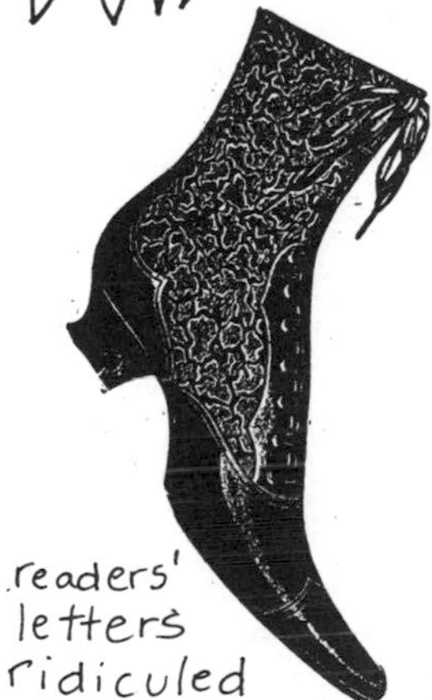

readers' letters ridiculed

the magazine by and about a self-obsessed woman

Secrets from my family's history

trauma s of one of my childhood friendships.

confidential letters from my friend Maggie that she doesn't know I'm publishing

on-location reporting from my dream life

Learn how to join a Pagan fan club that wasn't even started by me!

The 12 Stations of ~~the Cross~~ *my career*

1

I realize that I'll JUST DIE if I don't become a writer.

2

I take my first writing class.

3

I join the editorial board of my college's feminist newspaper.

4

I graduate, do an internship at the Columbia Journalism Review.

5

Get free-lance jobs at the Village Voice.

6

Study with Gordon Lish and get published in The Quarterly.

7

Earn an MA in Fiction Writing.

8

Move to Boston; learn to copy edit for computer magazines.

9

Become a regular writer for the Voice's Literary Supp.

10

Get an agent.

11

Several editors express interest in my book.

12

But they all reject it.

The Gossip Page

It Really Came Together When Mom Sang Along?

by Ingrid

Oh Shirley, if only loving were still as simple as singing a song. If only **David** and **Shaun** had stayed home with you; if only you hadn't married that "Hollywood Squares" glad-hander **Marty Ingalls.** Shirley, we hardly knew ye. Yes, that's **Shirley Jones** as in Partridge.

The story you are about to hear has just made the jump from the West Coast to the East. Show-biz agents with nothing better to offer their clients are dishing them this sorded tale of leather and whips--that is, I heard it from my friend, who heard it from his agent. Unfortunately, you can't verify the facts with Shirley. She's left the country.

Shirley and Marty have a nice house in Bel Air. The house has special room just for fun, with lots of leather suits and whips and cuffs, all Shirley-sized and ready to clip on or zip up.

And one day Shirley and Marty--oh, let's just call them S&M--were doing their thing, Shirley completely encased in leather and hanging upside-down from the mirrored ceiling with manacles around her motherly wrists and ankles, when Mary started having a heart attack.

~~Meet~~ Beat Shirley Jones

He's blue on the floor; Shirley is screaming louder than usual; the neighbors come running but they can't get in. They call the Bel Air police, who break in and shove Marty into an ambulance--but they can't cut Shirley down! (Notice the trail of reliable witnesses.) Finally, they call a locksmith. Shirley rubs her wrists and, we assume, tips them all nicely.

Mary has recovered, but S&M seem to sad or worried, or perhaps embarrassed, to return to Bel Air. Last anyone heard, they were in Greece, where I suppose that kind of thing is OK. It makes you wonder what little **Tracy** and **Chris** are up to.

THE WORLD'S FIRST GOSSIP

LETTERS

I love *Back to Pagan.* I am in the process of finding special places for the stickers. The whole package from front to back is all wholly pure hoot, no negative projections.

The only qualification I can not is the little reference/ allusion in the first issue to Pagan being a writing fellow at Johns Hopkins University. It makes one suspect the whole Pagan creation is only an illusion.

Mr.Psuedonym
Iowa

"Pagan" responds:

You're the only one who's figured it out. Pagan Kennedy is merely a character created by a style council. We realize there's a big demand out there for a star who's cool but also frumpy and shy; intellectual but fascinated with pop culture; self-promoting but also anxiety-ridden.

That's why we're launched this little magazine. We're testing the "underground" consumer market's response to the Pagan Kennedy character. If she's popular enough, we'll get a team of writers to come up with a novel "written" by Pagan. If that turns a profit, why then, we'll hire an actress, give her the trademarked "Pagan" glasses (another product tie-in), dress her in black tights and a ripped dress and send her out on tour.

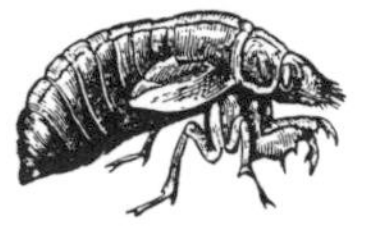

From the Southern fan club:

Things are as usual here in Kentucky, which means everything seems like a cross between *Children of the Corn* and *The* Ninth *Configuration,* with random cuts into *Rumble Fish* and "Hee Haw," scripted by Kafka and directed by Luis Bunuel on Quaaludes and Listerine.

What are you going to be for Halloween? I'm still deciding between an evil perverted clown, a zombie Elvis, Twiggy or an amorphous enigma. On the other hand, should I stay home and distribute subversive literature to the kids?

Regarding the fan club funds, we've already received a few thousand dollars this month, plus several strands of David Cassidy's hair--should be enough to let you quit your job.

Pagan responds:

See the back cover for details on joining the fan club. Remember, every dollar you slave at your job to send to the fan club keeps Pagan unemployed.

I plan to be Liberace for Halloween, but I'll probably have an anxiety attack at the last minute and stay home.

From my long-lost college pal Jim, who was also the drummer in Planet Love (Pagan played guitar in that unforgettable band):

I love your magazine. You do chicken right. I laughed, I cried, I called my lawyer.

I am enjoying NYC strangely and truly. I'll probably get hit by a truck or deadly virus to make up for my recent good fortune: I've signed on with this gallery, which has just moved to big-fucking-deal Soho. And Mr. Director hinted he would give me a solo show sometime. Where's that truck? Smell that virus?

From *Spew and Review:*

A friend of mine gave me a copy of *Pagan's Head* and I was knocked over by the coolness of the contents. I'm talking Bobby

... letters ...

Sherman and Partridge Family here, two of my long-time rock heroes. I'm 25, so I grew up grooving to them, plus the Archies, Osmonds, DeFranco Family, Cowsills. Now that's real rock. Ever notice how the older boys in the Cowsills all look like Chip and Robbie from "My Three Sons"?

In addition to all those childhood favorites, as I got older I discovered reruns of "The Patty Duke Show," which in turn led me to Patty's great LPs, all of which I now proudly own. Forget her acting cuz Patty was a righteous rocker! And her hairdos were always the coolest. I know that if I were a girl, I'd wear my hair in either a flip or a beehave.

Bob(by) K.

Dear ▬ Pagan's agent

Thanks so much for sending me Pagan Kennedy's collection of short stories, ELVIS'S BATHROOM, which I read with pleasure. I feel I almost should say I reread these stories with pleasure; I've been an admirer of Kennedy's for some time and have always kept an eye out for her work. "Elvis's Bathroom" was in the same VLS issue as an excerpt from ▬ ▬ which I published this spring. I remember ▬ in another incarnation when it appeared as a "Pagan Kennedy to Q" piece in THE QUARTERLY. Kennedy is an extremely inventive writer with a great ear for dialogue. I especially like her quirky sense of humor as evinced in stories like ▬ She manages to be hip, knowing, and savvy without being dismissable and flip. That said, I'm afraid I will not be able to make an offer on this collection, as fine as it is. The reason has less to do with the fiction than with the situation at ▬. I'm afraid the climate here is not too hospitable to short story collections unless they can fall under the guise of the related collection cum novel like ▬ I'm sorry to have to pass for such a relatively bureaucratic reason, but given I know that Kennedy's interests -- at least as far as this collection goes -- would be better served elsewhere.

Please congratulate your author on a thoroughly entertaining and diverse collection. I'm confident she'll be published and published well. I'm only sorry it couldn't be at ▬

Sincerely,

Editor at a major NYC publishing house

DIAGRAM OF PAGAN'S HEAD
(from above letter)

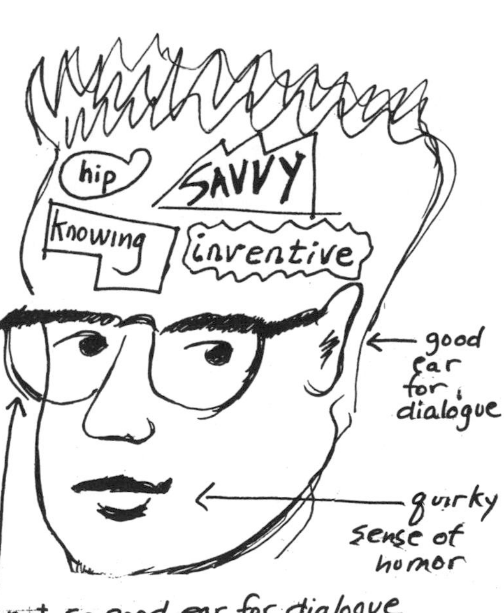

My Best Friend Anne

BY PAGAN

At least they have a roof over their heads, but it probably needs reshingling.

Anne's sisters shown here as boys.

Good-for-nothing physicist.

Even though my parents were dubious about her, she and I were always together.

The treehouse in my backyard was our fort.

← Anne and I shown here as middle-aged men.

Anne lived next door. Her parents were divorced, and her dad almost never came around. My parents didn't like Anne's mom because she didn't keep her lawn mowed, slept on the floor, and was into Zen.

all my love to Chartpak for these easy-to-use tape lines

Young Pagan demonstrates

We had a secret whistle.

TOP SECRET DO NOT TELL RUSSIANS.

How to Perform Our Whistle:

1) Put tip of yr. tongue on roof of yr. mouth and make r-r-r-r-r-r sound.

2) at the same time, screetch.

3) While you do above, put 2 fingers in yr. mouth, as if y're performing one of those really difficult, macho-boy whistles.

(Last step optional.)

Many thanks to the Dover Clip Art series for providing drawings for scenes too emotionally charged for me to attempt

When she left, my life was worth less than a used Bandaide®

But → we still wrote though. But one day, I got a very weird letter from her.

Dear Pagan,
I am finally so happy. I joined a youth group and we all love JESUS the only-begotten son of our Lord.
I want you to love JESUS too. He has changed my life.
God Bless you.
I love you, Anne.

← word of evil power

FUCK You, JESUS. You took away my best friend.

This only confirmed my feelings about religeon.

Years spun by. Once and a while I got a letter from Anne – she was always in some new religeon or else home for messed-up kids. It turned out she was schizophrenic.

When I was 25, I had moved to a certain city to get my MA. One day, I got a call...

Pagan, this is Anne. Your Mom gave me your number. I live here too, only I'm in Sunny Acres. Things have been hard. No one's com- ing to see me. Re- member Sherry? She wouldn't. I still luv Jesus. I luv you so much please take care. Come visit me, okay. God bless you.

The Art of Fiction John Gardner

↖ don't let cool veneer fool you. It's the same old nerdy Pagan.

Pagan Personality

Other friends may come and go, but Maggie is my all-time, official Best Friend. Our friendship, fittingly, began on the phone. She was doing an article for the school paper on people who'd applied to college early decision, and so she called me up to interview me. I can't remember what either of us said, but we quickly realized we were soulmates, that is, we both despised our high school and thought its authority figures were ridiculous, Pere Ubu-style dictators. If this seems like a pretty pedestrian cynicism, it wasn't in our all-girls' prep school , where everyone was blonde and cheery and poised for a future of hosting Junior League teas.

Maggie was always in trouble. She chalked up endless afternoons in detention by coming to school late every day (this was a private school and it was very easy to be bad). Another way to stir things up was to break the ultimate girls' school taboo: Mags and another friend walked through the halls hand in hand so everyone would think they were dykes. Once they even chased after the heiress to the Marriot foods fortune screaming, "We want your body."

Maggie was so bad that there was a teachers' meeting JUST ABOUT HER!

She had great parents, too. Both were lawyers and transplanted New Yorkers. They were my dream parents--they tried to "rap" with us, and even claimed they wouldn't be upset if we smoked pot. (Of course they were lying about the pot, but it was a start.)

But all middle-class parents have certain phobias in common: Both Maggie's mom and my mom got really upset if you drank milk straight out of a milk carton and then put the carton back in the fridge. When asked why this was inappropriate behavior both moms (independently of one another) had the same answer: "That's what people do in the slums." So we developed a code. If, say, she was at my house and wanted to drink out of the carton, she'd say, "Are we in the slums?" If I said, "No," that meant my mom was home and Maggie had better use a glass.

Maggie went to Brown and majored in India. She learned to speak Hindi and spent several months in Banaras. She wrote her thesis on how Gandhi wasn't such a great guy after all. She now lives in New York and works at an Asian film archive, cataloging Indian movies (there's some great, cheesy musicals) and thinks she'll probably go to grad school in Hindi.

In some ways, I feel she's living one of the lives I could have chosen. I've always been interested in (my imaginary) India, where everyone grooves to the sitar and wears gaudy psychedelic clothes. But instead I became an American studies major, so I rely on Mags to teach me Indian show tunes and cook me chapati.

HER LETTERS

From DC:

So far I've spent my time looking for a job, pretending to apply for stuff in the fall and having sex. One thing that's a pain is that Scott has this incredible concentration span. Although I've given up TV for now, I guess growing up on it has made me want to do everything briefly. Scott likes to fool around for four hours. That's why he gets such good grades ...

DC, later:

Josh wrote me a nice letter, despite the fact that he can't gossip. Sure, I misjudged him as a softie at first, because unfortunately, he has the most lovely languid bulging eyes I have ever seen. I mean, I love the way he could always just barely muster the energy to lift his briefcase...

I just got fired from my job canvassing for SANE. I came back from five hours on "conservative turf" and the one mean director screamed at me for only raising five dollars.

He said, "Frankly, you don't show any promise at all." I knew he said this to all the other new canvassers. Exhaustion got the better of me and I said, "I don't like to be threatened; it doesn't make me work better."

I probably wouldn't have said this had I not been the product of a society that doesn't always place much weight on whether you have a career if you're a woman; I couldn't believe being fired would mean losing anything...

From Karachi, Pakistan, and environs:

I got to go into the farmers' village with Saira [another of our high school buddies] speaking to the people in Urdu. The women took us by the hand and showed us everything. They are absolutely gorgeous and decked out in spectacular stuff they've made but don't sell because, "Who's going to take it to Karachi?"

The social classes are so deeply embedded, there's no way to step outside of them, even as a visitor, and the weirdest part is that no one at all would like you to.... Every vehicle is covered with colored and carved metal ornaments. Will bring nice presents.

From Banaras, India:

...To move from shopping to other things, of which these days it often seems there are few, when are you going to visit me? You would love shopping here! I mean it, you would just freak out in appreciation of the sixties flashback effect.

I am only just beginning to appreciate how difficult it is to really experience India in a way that goes beyond fascination with the material. Not just the shopping, but getting used to what Americans would consider an incredible mess: no hot water, no running water, never being in the house alone, cows, water buffalo and elephants in the street, wild cats, mice, ants, a rat in my hair at night. After two months I can say I'm getting pretty used to that.

Now I must come to terms with my Indian family's never questioning anything, never analyzing anteing, downright never discussing anything at all other than when I will return in the afternoon--and the fact that in a way I respect that sort of life, even prefer it to the American way of perpetual criticism.

These days I'm looking into ashrams. I'm hoping to find one to live in for the next month or two. I looked at one after a few days of attempts at finding it (no street signs, and people usually give you the wrong directions with smiling faces rather than say they don't know). It's the women's' section of the Ramakrishna ashram. There's only three monks though, and one's a man, the social outcast type who can't have a conversation. The other two are a sexy thirty-year-old Australian freak and a fat old jolly Indian.

Oh where are the thriving familial communities, or a phone

book to find them with? I could hang out with a bunch of Brahman virgins doing puja all day but I want to do something more relevant to justifiable jollydom and complacency.

Now I'm thinking I want to be a rabbi when I come home. It would be a culture I could understand for once. I could sit around and gossip all day, too.

Anyway, I hope when I get back we can spend some time together. My travels have taught me that the girl next door really is a very special friend.

END~

HENRY ADAMS: hot, single and dead

OK, everyone except for the American history majors out there are probably wondering who Henry Adams is. Well, you know that guy John Quincy Adams, the sixth president of our country? Henry's his grandson. Henry was also the son of Charles Adams, our ambassador to England during the Civil War. Henry himself was mainly a gadabout who wrote trenchant political analyses and never missed a good party. I'm now reading his book, *The Education of Henry Adams,* in which he tells the story of his life in the third person, never missing a chance to gossip about political celebs of his day or put himself down with a sarcastic quip. In short, *The Education of Henry Adams*--though in book form and written at the end of Henry's life--was the *Back to Pagan* of its day.

Pretend this is
Henry Adams during the fortunate years

I've only gotten halfway through the book, but already I'm suffering from a wild, incestuous lust for Henry. Why incestuous? Well, my grandmother has always said we're related to the Adamses, so Henry's my cousin! Will a mere century and the fact that one of us is dead and that we're related keep Henry and me apart? No way.

What's so amazing about Henry is that he sees Civil War America with the eyes of our own time--he is well aware of the shifting of power from the aristocrats to the bureaucrats. Moreover, he spends his twenties casting about for what he wants to do, hanging out with his pals, and trying this or that occupation without much hope of settling down to do anything. He's just like me and my friends!

There are other shocking similarities between Henry and Pagan. Henry, born in Boston, moved to Washington, DC; Pagan made the opposite migration. Henry and Pagan both write for The Nation, and both are free-lancer writers. Both are self-obsessed, and sarcastic. And they both write about themselves in the third person.

So, without further ado, I'd like you to meet my dream guy, Henry, through his writings.

Here's an account of 6-year-old Henry's run-in with his grandfather the ex-president: "[Henry] distinctly remembered standing at the house door one summer morning in a passionate outburst of rebellion against going to school." Henry's mother had almost given up trying to get the boy to leave the house, when suddenly the door to his grandfather's study swung open and the ex-President appeared. Slowly, and without saying a word, he walked the boy to school, winning Henry's admiration. "The [ex-]President, though a tool of tyranny, had done his disreputable work with a certain intelligence. He had shown no temper, no irritation, no feeling."

Alfred, Lord Tennyson

detested strangers but loved pets?

Here's Henry on why the literary parties of London were so dull: "Sydney Smith, who had amused, was dead; Thackeray died at Christmas, 1863; Dickens never felt at home, and seldom appeared, in society; Bulwer Lytton was not sprightly; Tennyson detested strangers; Carlyle was mostly detested by them; Darwin never came to town." Whew, can this man gossip!

Henry on why he decides to be a journalist: "The press was still the last resource of the educated poor who could not be artists and would not be tutors. Any man who was fit for nothing else could write an editorial or criticism. The enormous mass of misinformation asccumulated in [Henry's] ten years of nomad life could always be worked off on a helpless public."

Henry, starting out as a political writer, is taken by a friend to meet the President, because that's considered the first step in any aspiring journalist's career. Back then, getting an appointment with the Prez was no big deal (no harder, say, than it would be nowadays to line up an interview with one of the cast members of the original *Star Trek)*. Henry relates that the meeting was "brief and consisted

ULYSSES S. GRANT

in the stock remark common to monarchs and valets that the young man looked even younger than he was." Afterwards, Henry decided he wasn't impressed with Andrew Johnson. He "was not the sort of man whom a young reformer of 30 ... was likely to see with enthusiasm." Boy, things were different for writers then, huh?

Henry, like many other young men of his time, supported the election of Grant, only to realize when it was too late that Grant was a scoundrel. Henry lamented this turn of events not for the sake of his country, but because of what it would do to his career. "As for Adams, all his hopes of success in life turned on his finding an administration to support. He knew well enough the rules of self-interest. He was for sale. He wanted to be bought. His price was excessively cheap, for he did not even ask for an office, and had his eye not on the government but on New York [ie, publishing].."

So check out The Education of Henry Adams and you'll find that our forefathers weren't all boring guys who wore wigs and knee-high socks. Henry and his famous pals could get pretty nutty sometimes, and if they were alive today, they'd probably be hanging out in Allston, eating at Greek diners and trying to form a band.

the PAGAN KENNEDY
fan club
southern chapter
HEY KIDS !!!
As you sit in your room with the door locked, listening to Ed's Redeeming Qualities, munching generic lemon sandwich cookies and root beer, reading your copies of BACK TO PAGAN'S HEAD over and over and ovo again, don't you feel a tad isolated from your idol, never knowing when the fickle winds of fate may blow a scrap of news about P.K. your way? Don't you wish there existed a way to better CONNECT with the awesome personage that is Pagan Kennedy?
WELL, WHIMPER NO MORE!!!
We here at Artwerx Laboratories are proud to bring to you The Pagan Kennedy Fan Club. Now you can be a part of that ever-growing circle of truly cool individuals who are perpetually "in-the-know" about the latest P.K. gossip, often before P.K. has heard about it herself! Impress your friends when you tell them you're a member of this ultra-prestigious club!
HOW DO I JOIN??
Membership in this exclusive organization costs a mere dollar. Most of the proceeds will go to financing Pagan's activities, and keeping her mighty head afloat till that big book contract comes in. We'll keep you posted on the ups and downs of her meteoric rise to literary stardom, and bring to you, whenever possible, schedules and tour dates! Be the first on the block to know if/when Pagan's coming to YOUR town. As a member, you'll receive periodic updates and newsletters alerting you to the latest scoop on the She-Pope's doings, and a membership card suitable for carrying in your wallet, framing, affixing to your forehead, etc. The card will also get you VIP treatment at hotels, casinos, restaurants and gas stations in Dobbstown. So send that dollar today to PAGAN KENNEDY FAN CLUB,

4

PAGAN'S ANCESTORS SPEAK OUT

AS I GEARED UP to produce Issue Four, I was in a funk. It was spring 1990 and I was still working freelance at *PC Week*. This was a spiritual and moral defeat for me because I'd been trying desperately to get out of my rut. In the fall, I had applied to two nearby graduate schools: Brown and Harvard. I wanted something like the sweet deal I'd gotten from Hopkins—a scholarship and hefty stipend—but I wasn't willing to move out of Boston.

Actually I didn't really want to go to grad school, I just wanted to find some way, any way, to escape from my copyediting limbo. I wanted to be whisked out of the computer-publishing dungeon by the Fairy Godmother of academia, who would wave her magic wand and grant me a stipend. Not surprisingly, both schools turned me down. Academia is not a Fairy Godmother, it is a Cruel Mistress who punishes you if you are overqualified (as I was for the Brown writing program) or underqualified (Harvard, Religion).

By spring, I'd come up with Plan B. Instead of being a *student,* I'd be a *teacher.* Admittedly this was not nearly as attractive as Plan A, but it seemed inevitable. After all, I did have "terminal degree" in writing.

The thing was, unless I wanted to teach at a community college in South Armpit, I would have to have a book. And I don't mean "have a book" as in owning a book, I mean "have a book" as in "have a baby." Which meant I needed to finish my novel and start sending it out to publishers. Which meant that I was developing a screwed-up relationship with my creative work. Instead of working on my novel because it was *fun* or *important* or *meaningful,* I was trying to finish it so I could get a better job. The logic went something like this: published novel = working in academia = never having to copyedit again = getting out of my rut = being happy.

I dubbed the summer of '90 the "summer of self-improvement." Not only did I plan to finish my novel, I would also exercise every day, learn to cook better, explore my spirituality, wear nicer clothes, and read all the Great Books. In short, I intended to make myself into a perfect human being within three months. I assumed that when I attained perfection, I would finally get out of my rut.

But, of course, the deepest rut you can climb into is the pursuit of self-improvement. With so much to accomplish, my schedule became absolutely rigid: write in the morning; go to work; go running; cook a nutritionally sound dinner; read difficult books; sleep.

In the other issues of *Back to Pagan* I'd managed to make my life sound exciting, even when it was pretty boring. But now my life had become *so boring* that no amount of hyperbole could make it interesting. That's why in Issue Four, I didn't talk too much about what I was doing. Instead, I focused on the "background material" of my life: family history, ideas, anecdotes from my childhood.

This distracted me from the pathetic little problems that had been obsessing me. How can I make the ending of the novel work? Do you have to read Milton to be considered educated? Why do I feel so *blah* about everything? Is having a relationship worth going through the hell of dating? To paraphrase Sartre, my problems had become so metaphysical as to be embarrassing—and my problems weren't even *that* metaphysical.

Working on *Back to Pagan* was a relief because it helped me to ask different questions about my life. What does it mean to be descended from southern slave owners? What was it like to grow up under the Nixon presidency? In this issue, we meet another side of myself: Pagan, thoughtful citizen of the United States, a gal who's merely a fly caught in the great web of history.

As I explored some of the deeper motifs of my family and my life, I felt a weird sense of wonder—every time I looked at what had happened to me, I found more memories and stories to tell. If that sounds snotty, let me hasten to add that I'm not just talking about myself. I realized that *everyone* is endlessly complicated. And *anyone* could write hundreds of thousands of pages about their own history and ideas—and it would *still* be interesting, if it was written well enough and had enough pictures. We are all endlessly unfolding fanzines.

BACK TO PAGAN

Issue #4; Summer 1990, "The summer of self-improvement"

$1 free to Pagan's special friends

I wish I didn't have to marry the beard boy, but it's the only way to create Pagan

Only about a century until Pagan's born!

Virginia Tucker née Brooke c.1850

Daughter of Judge Henry St. George Tucker and Anne Evelina Hunter of Winchester, Va.

Henry Laurens Brooke, c.1850 Esquire, from Stafford County, Va.

ALSO INSIDE:

- My memories of Nixon
- Rejection letters
- The Pagan–Elvis link
- Danny Bonaduce
- Gossip, gossip, gossip
- Religion, religion, religion
- And of course, the latest on my hair and career

IN THIS ISSUE:

Pagan's ancestors SPEAK OUT!

Update on my Life

HAIR

My friend **Jan**, an official in the **Visual Department** at Filene's, dyes her hair white-blonde. Last time she did a touch-up, she used the leftover dye on me. Now I'm blonder than I've ever been in my entire life--blonder even than back when I was a normal, wholesome, blue-eyed child named Pam.

photos: 2-minute photo booth

Blonde Pagan

Readers of issue #2 may remember that I was trying to grow dreadlocks--not so much because I really wanted them as because it was the ultimate hairdo challenge for someone with nary a curl. I did in fact achieve dreadlocks, and without having to use messy 1,000-island dressing or toasters. I simply braided my hair and never took out the braids.

However, most of my dreadlocks were more like long rat's nests. Actually, they were really like just plain rats, a pack of rats hanging off my head. (They say in Boston there are two rats for every person. I was just more honest about it than most people. I cut off all of them except one perfectly

page # → ①

ADVERTISEMENT

THIS IS JOHN TRAVOLTA *speaking for....*

WATER

Did you know that like our planet, our bodies are mostly water? Well, back when I was a "Sweat Hog" I thought I could sweat all I wanted without danger to my body. And in "Saturday Night Fever," I danced and drank the night away, without thinking that I might be depleting important bodily fluids. But the hedonistic '70s are over. I survived because I learned to replace fluids. How about you?

Actor John Travolta

Whether straight from the tap, from the bottle or from a purifier, enjoy CLEAR, NATURAL WATER. Remember, Doctor says at least eight glasses a day.

BROUGHT TO YOU BY THE NATIONAL WATER PRODUCERS' UNION and instant lettering

Update (con't.)

formed dread. My remaining dread acts as a conversation piece, of sorts. At parties, people fondle it and say, "Ewww, what is this?"

GAVE UP POPEDOM

Loyal Paganologists probably already know that for years I have been the Pope of All New England for the Church of the Subgenius. Even when I was living in Baltimore, I held the position. Well, the arduous duties of ministering to thousands of souls hungry for spiritual knowledge and guidance got to me. Actually, I just became embarrassed to be associated with the church--which these days has been flooded with sci-fi nerd-boys. And I'm bored of "Bob."

This is not a mistake, it's a literary device

Anyway, in a ceremony held at the Coffee Clamp, I handed over my Popedom to Mark Morey, a young, idealistic art student and impresario. I gave him the sacred Pope hat, as well as a sceptor made out of one of the aforementioned cut-off dreadlocks.

CAREER

It's humiliating, but I'm employed. I've had to start free-lancing at a place where I used to hold a job--copy editing at PC Week magazine. Back in the PC Week's Golden Age (1986), we put out the magazine in rare lapses between making personal calls, quizzing one another with a pack of Canadian Trivial Pursuit cards and revealing secret crushes via the computer message system. Now, the computer market is in trouble and it's all seriousness at PC Week.

From 9:00 to 12:30, I'm a famous writer, pounding out deathless fiction and trenchant cultural criticism. From 1:00 to 6:00, I'm a cog in the corporate world, honing sentences about weapons-system applications development.

As for my real career, I had an article leading the arts section in The Nation about comic books, for which I received two (2) hate mail letters. I also have a feature story about environmental magazines coming out in the Voice this summer. My agent is sending out my new short story: So far we've only heard from The New Yorker. (See "Featured Rejection Letter of the Issue," below.)

In search of a life without copy editing, I applied to grad schools (see "My Religion," Page 9), and was roundly rejected, perhaps because the schools could tell my only focus in the academic world was on the stipends.

NEWS FLASH

This just in! Pagan won an arts grant from the fine state of Massachusetts for her fiction. The triumphant Kennedy said she'll use the money to buy a big-screen TV and a VCR.

*

Back To Pagan was mentioned several times in a Boston Herald article about the local small press. The article included a picture of Pagan, who was sucking in her cheeks in an effort to simulate high cheek bones.

FEATURED REJECTION LETTER OF THE ISSUE →

↑ crappy Letraset I bought used at the now-defunct Handyman Fix It Shop

(2 page)

Jan 16th

Dear Pagan's agent

I think this is beautifully written, and the last passage is just wonderful, but it's a little too circumscribed to work out here. It's convincing and dear and the friendship with Nira is described perfectly, but it's a little bit confined: the story of a season in college and a young woman's emergence from an idea of intensity that confounds and discombobulates her. But it's a good story all the same and I hope you'll find a good home for it.

the frat next door
A TRUE STORY
script and drawing by Pagan
Lookat those chairs in the frat boys' yard. Hic.
They'd look great in our Kitchen. Hic.
Meet my housemates Kathy + Lesley, a coupla architects from Texas. They're not always drunk like in this story, though...
In a few minutes...
Hurry, Lesley
Shhh... Hic.
C'mon. This way
Wow!
Hey, girls, over here. Down in the basement. C'mon.
Shower cap
This is what they see:
An endless array of frat boys in showercaps and underwear.
3

Hey, what is this?
We're pledges. We've been down here 2 days, living on peanutbutter + pickles.
Girls, guess what? That guy has a black dick!
You do? Let's see.
OK!
Hey, that's not black!
censored!
4
EPILOGUE: The chairs are in our kitchen now. They look very nice.

MY MEMOIRS OF THE NIXON ERA

reprinted from Zontar magazine with the permission of the author

by Pagan

In 1972 I was ten years old and a Nixon supporter. That's how it was: you liked whichever candidate your parents told you to like.

I grew up in D.C. and went to a school full of Democrats. All the other kids were behind McGovern and it became my own personal crusade to defend Nixon.

Back then, political arguments went like this:

Some kid would say, "Nixon sucks."

"Nuh-uh, McGovern sucks," I'd say.

My mother had told me the cold, hard political truth: McGovern had promised to give everyone in America two-thousand bucks, and where did he expect to find the money to do that?

Then there was the Eagleton thing. I didn't know exactly who Eagleton was, but he had something to do with McGovern. My friend explained it to me: Eagleton was crazy so they'd hooked him up to a Frankenstein machine and electric sparks came out of his ears and eyes. I was never even sure whether Eagleton was a human being: I pictured him as the eagle from the American presidential seal, only instead of lightning bolts in his talons, he held sparks.

My dad, trying to explain the meaning of the word "nix" to me, said that people who didn't like Nixon chanted "Nix on Nixon." I knew those people were wrong, but I liked the sound of that chant anyway and would--with some sense of shame--repeat "nix on Nixon, nix on Nixon" under my breath when I pretended to be a soldier and marched down the street.

The Nixon years passed quietly in the Pagan household. I only knew about Vietnam because some kids' parents let them have aluminum bracelets engraved with the name of a prisoner of war or a soldier missing in action. As with other kiddie consumer items-- Wacky Paks, Zots, Pop Rocks and Clickety-Clacks--if you owned one of those bracelets you were cool. If you didn't, you were a social reject.

My mom wouldn't let me have one of those bracelets because a) she wasn't sure if it was an anti-American statement and b) the bracelets had sharp edges and my mom was afraid that if I fell down, I would inadvertently slash my wrist and bleed to death.

The Watergate hearings were a special time for me. For once, my parents joined me in my favorie activity--watching TV. Unfortunately, the show they wanted to watch was the most boring one I'd ever seen: hours and hours of men talking into microphones.

Most importantly, the Watergate hearings were a time of togetherness. It was like a snowstorm--our parents were forced to stay home in front of the TV. Our neighbors became friendlier and dropped by to talk politics the way, in a snowstorm, they would drip by to borrow our shovel. Everyone got along because, finally, here was a political event that everyone could agree on. Nixon was a crook--no two ways about it.

That's why, as far as I'm concerned, the Age of Aquarius didn't dawn during Woodstock or the Summer of Love. It dawned during Watergate.

Elvis and Pagan: 10 amazing similarities

By Jimmy Guterman
Watch for Jimmy's book about the Sex Pistols, 12 Days on the Road, coming out in Sept. from Wm. Morrow & Co. (really!).

lived in Graceland . . . . visited Graceland
dyed blonde hair black . . . . dyed black hair blonde
united black and white music . . watched "Eyes on the Prize"
often tailed by fans . . . . often tailed by hair
two vowels in first and last names . . . . ditto
took psychedelic drugs . . . . . . wears psychedelic clothes
made comeback TV special . . . . . . returned to PC Week
died in his bathroom . . . . dyed hair in her bathroom
produced by Sam Phillips . . . . owns a Phillips screwdriver

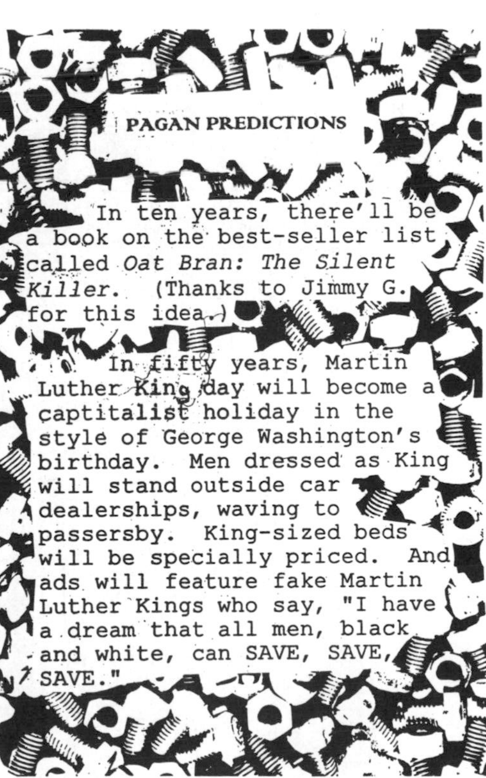

PAGAN PREDICTIONS

In ten years, there'll be a book on the best-seller list called *Oat Bran: The Silent Killer*. (Thanks to Jimmy G. for this idea.)

In fifty years, Martin Luther King day will become a captitalist holiday in the style of George Washington's birthday. Men dressed as King will stand outside car dealerships, waving to passersby. King-sized beds will be specially priced. And ads will feature fake Martin Luther Kings who say, "I have a dream that all men, black and white, can SAVE, SAVE, SAVE."

Personalities from my Past

What follows is a series of cartoons and drawings (actually only three because all the artists who promised to give me work ended up spacing it) based on letters written by Pagan's Southern ancestors between the years 1831 and 1869. How on earth do I have these letters in my possession?

Well, there's a noble tradition of spinsterhood in my family. If you don't marry and produce scions and scionesses, then you're expected to concern yourself with writing the history of our family (or a whitewashed version of it). For instance, one such spinster's life work is a biography of several of our ancestors. She's ninety and only half way through. Last time I saw her, she threatened to leave the task to me when she died.

Anyway, about ten years ago, some other spinsters (actually I have no idea whether they were really spinsters) went through the family papers to compile the letters of our ancestors Henry Brooke and Virginia Tucker Brooke. Cousin Henry served as the "Receiver of Alien Property" for the Confederate government--but we think "treasurer" sounds better, so that's what we say he was. Cousin Virginia was the granddaughter of Saint George Tucker, who wasn't really an actual saint, but rather an important man-about-town in Williamsburg. They were cousins of Robert E. Lee and pals with Jefferson Davis.

Anyway, my parents got this book full of our ancestors' letters at one of our family reunions/conventions. (Every few

years, our relatives organize a "Tucker" reunion. Hundreds of descendents of Saint George Tucker--our first ancestor in America--gather to meet one another and discuss geneology.) I "borrowed" the book full of letters from my parents, who seemed to have forgotten about it anyway.

At first I imagined that I'd be able to read through the letters, acquaint myself with the my ancestors and partake of their juicy gossip. However, the letters are nearly impossible to follow. For one thing, everyone has the same name. If they're not Hunter Tucker Randolph, then they're Randolph Hunter Tucker, or perhaps Saint George Tucker Hunter.

VIRGINIA TUCKER BROOKE
c. 1850
attributed to
William James Hubard

The first in Pagan's family to wear dreadlocks.

Also, people back then never gossiped. All they did was declare how much they loved and missed each other, apologize for not writing or tally up the sick in their family--so-and-so has the augue, while whositz has the bilious fever. I guess gossip is a luxury of the healthy.

I have a complicated relationship to my ancestors, those patricians who lived on plantations. Back in college, when I was an aspiring revolutionary, I kept my past a secret from my friends. Oh how I wished for backgrounds like theirs; how I longed to tell stories about Jewish intellectuals hanging out at coffee shops near Washington Square, discussing the ideas of Izzy Stone; how I wished that I, too, was descended from wild-eyed wobblies and 1930s Communists who fought for justice, who believed in a better world. If you were descended from people like that, how could you doubt your own goodness?

Over the years, it was my wonderful grandparents who taught me to appreciate my own, real past. Our ancestors did not fight for social justice, they fought to protect Southern traditions and Southern land --and to keep alive a way of life that was vanishing. For instance, one turn-of-the-century lady in our family was ordered by the state of Virginia to cut down all of the cedar trees on her property. Some fancy agriculturists from the city believed that the cedar trees were responsible for an apple blight. Well, our cousin Violet refused to cut down her cedar trees, but the state workmen came anyway. So she threw their tools in a river. Then, while they were still fishing their saws out of the water, she hired a little boy to climb the cedar trees and tie an American flag to the top of each one. She hoped that the workmen wouldn't risk causing the flags to land in the dirt. When the workmen nonetheless began chopping, she drove to the state capital and staged a one-woman protest. This is the kind of eccentric heroism that runs in my family.

Mostly it is my grandmother who remembers stories like that. She was raised by her cousins on a plantation called Rion Hall. I saw that place when I was a little girl; it had an impressive entrance, but narrow steps and mean rooms upstairs. My grandmother remembers an old spinster living in one of the stifling third-floor rooms. The kitchen was a free-standing, whitewashed building a few yards away; the slaves (and, later, servants) lived in the second story above the swelter of the ovens.

Both my grandparents always loved to tell stories about the South in its flower, before "the War." (There's only one war that matters and that's the War of Northern Aggression.) We are a family devoted not to forging a new utopia, but to remembering a lost one. This is our own Reconstruction--to build back, in imagination, all that Sherman burned. To protect our cedar trees, even when everyone else wants them cut down. To remember, remember, remember.

Last sumer, my grandfather died. He was a tall man who wore good English suits and stiff shirts, even when he had to use a walker. He had a great sense of humor: I remember him writing me that, at the old folks' home where he lived, they tried to get him to wear silly hats and sing "Happy Birthday." He made it into a joke but it must have hurt that they treated him, a dignified and brilliant man, as a child.

Like my grandmother, he felt himself not to be a solitary person, but a bundle of ancestors and histories and stories. He spent a few weeks of his life crafting a family history out of legend and letters and fact. He loved the out-of-doors, too, and could lead me through the woods reciting the names of all we saw: crow's foot, trillium, white birch, lady slipper.

There was something of the Indian in him. As a young man, he would disappear into the woods for weeks, living off what he found. He taught my sister and me stories he said came from the Indians. How Beaver got his tail. Why Wolf lives alone. When he married my grandmother, he refused to do it in a church. They got hitched in an open field at Rion Hall, before a worn millstone my grandfather loved. (Later the marriage in front of a millstone became a family joke.) Just before he died, he was struggling to read a weighty scientific book about the Greenhouse Effect.

As I see it, he studied his ancestors for the same reason he studied nature: He could imagine a sweep of time much longer than his own life, time measured by the shifting of mountains and peoples. He loved anything that made him feel connected to the past, like faded gravestones or prehistoric rocks. In fact, our family's gravestone *is* a rock, a venerable granite boulder that my grandfather and his father chose together and then hauled all the way from Sugarloaf Mountain to Arlington Cemetary. It sits there still, uncarved and moss-covered.

My grandmother said this about death: "A family really *is* a tree, that's what I've always believed. And each person on the tree is like a leaf. When the leaf falls to the ground, it decomposes and makes the soil richer. That helps the tree to grow and make new leaves."

Who are the people who came before me, really? Growing up in the groovy 1970s, I learned how my ancestors stole people from their homes in Africa, then whipped and tortured them. I learned that, before they were slaves, black people came from an enchanted land of a thousand languages, of Watusis and Pygmies. I became obsessed with African history and cultures; the first record I bought (when I was ten) was Olitunji's "Drums of Passion." And then there was *Roots*--in that miniseries I watched my ancestors portrayed, by the likes of Robert Reed and Lorne Greene and Sandy Duncan, as the villians. It all made me feel tainted; I wished I could invent a different history for myself. I wished *I* came from Africa, that continent shaped like a girl's head.

But now, looking through my family's Civil War-era letters, I am confronted by people nothing at all like the evil rascists I learned about on TV. The main fact of life for these plantation dwellers was not their ownership of slaves, but rather their lack of medical knowledge and antibiotics. "Sally has been quite sick with a rising breast, which, however, has been lanced," writes Virginia Brooke. And again, "Tell Puss her old freind Marion Roy died today--she had a baby and that horrible fever succeeded but she died a most triumphant, happy death." And again, "Henry, Ginny, Susan, Emily and Reuben are all broken out *full* with measles, or as Brother expresses it, are *measling*." And again, "[Jack Bryant went] out to Cousin Judy's on a visit, was taken ill almost immediately and died there day before yesterday. They called his disease Typhoid Dysentary."

Since Henry Brooke was a lawyer rather than farmer, he owned only a few slaves. Before the war he gave one of the slaves, Mammy, her freedom, but she stayed with the family. (Where was she supposed to go?) Like the white women in these letters, Mammy seems to spend most of her time tending to the sick and dying.

I admire my ancestors who loved so deeply, who cared for each other through plagues and fevers. The women--hovering by sickbeds, fretting, crying, yet knowing when to commend their dear ones to God--have much to teach us in the age of AIDS.

Still, there is the slavery. That haunts me, has always haunted me. As a child, I was taken to see one of the grand old homes of the South. Underneath the mansion ran a series of tunnels too low for an adult to stand up in, with shackles on the walls. The floors were mud and the doors were mouse holes. The lady giving the tour told us that this was where the slaves lived. I started crying. My parents got me out of there and bought me an ice cream cone, which I ate despite myself, guilty. For I was being bribed to forget, bribed into thinking of those shackles as normal and acceptable things.

If there is any image I could choose to represent the South, it would be that plantation of my memory. Aboveground, it spoke of gracious living, with its glass cupulas and dancing light. But below its floor, it hid a dungeon, a place where people were stabled like animals. How easy it is to live in a house built on evil. And the people who glide through the beautiful rooms of the house--one is continually surprised at how gracious they are, how humorous and kind.

1862 LETTER

art by Pagan

MRS. Virginia BROOKE to Mrs. Evelina LUCAS

13.

Richmond, May 11, 1849

My Beloved Line,

Your sweet letter found me stretched upon a bed of suffering illness, from which I have just arisen, though I am still so feeble as to be scarcely able to guide my pen, but my heart so longs for some commune with my precious Line, that I must scribble a little, even at the risk of my writing being scarcely legible. When I was taken sick, Mr. Brooke was in Washington presenting a sword to General Taylor, dining at the White House. The neighbors telegraphed him when I became dangerously ill.

I was so completely sunk that it was only by the use of strong stimulants that my life was spared. When brought to the verge of the grave, dear Line, how sweet is the religion that gives us peace, when with one's eyes fixed on the cross, we can resign all earthly cares. Oh Line! With such a Savior why need we repine at any troubles?

I had always had a shrinking from the "dark valley," the idea of passing through it alone was terrifying, but when I really thought my time had come, how sweetly did my Savior assure me that his ROD and STAFF would comfort me.

To anyone else, Dearest, I should consider it necessary to apologize for the egotism of this letter, but such is my confidence in my own Line that I feel assured she will forgive it.

Your devoted Virgin (Virginia Tucker Brooke)

back cover shows Mina's artistic interpretation of this letter

illustration: Mina Abbate

5

TEARING UP THE HIGHWAY

FOR YEARS, my group house, the part-time copyediting job, and fanatical devotion to writing had been enough to fill my life. And then it wasn't. I had just turned twenty-eight. For the first time, it was conceivable that someday I would turn thirty. Once I reached thirty, I could no longer consider myself a "promising writer" or a "postcollegiate group-house dweller." Real life would start, or should start. The question was, What was real life for me? I was pretty sure I didn't want marriage and kids, an office job, or even a car. So what did I want? Maybe risk. Maybe adventure.

I had enough money to take off for a month and a half. I wanted to spend that time exploring the highways and byways and thrift shops of this great nation. The trip would force me to get out of my rut, let go, give up all my rigid rituals. I wouldn't be able to write, or exercise regularly, or eat miso soup every night for dinner.

Of course, I wasn't entirely relinquishing control. I had big plans for this trip. At the time, I was still trying to finish my novel—a road novel. I hoped that traveling the country on an automotive adventure would help me flesh out the details in my book. After all, I had never been across the country in a car, so how could I describe the chill of the Texas desert or the souvenir shops that surround the Grand Canyon unless I experienced them firsthand?

But I also wanted to do more than collect literary material on my trip. I planned to become a literary character myself, to live out my own on-the-road novel. I decided to travel the country in the guise of Pagan[1]: wear crazy clothes, carry an outlandish suitcase, and whine all the way. I'd take pictures and collect artifacts so that when I got back home I could produce a lavish on-the-road issue of *Pagan's Head.*

All I needed now was someone who owned a car and shared my vision, a Lewis to my Clark. And sure enough, in a few weeks I had found her—a friend of a friend named Virginia who was planning to move across the country in her Ford Festiva. Shiva, the wise and merciful god of destruction, must have sent Virginia to me, because if anyone was going to kick my Eeyore-like butt, put an end to my complaining, and drag me through every nightclub in America, it was she. My exact and perfect opposite, the Ginster (as she is affectionately called) loves to part-ay, wear miniskirts and 1950s bras, smoke, drink, rock out, flirt, get lost on the highway while she insists she knows exactly where she's going, spy on celebrities, hang out at sports bars, and charm everyone she meets.

Our trip together, well, it was just what I needed. Of course it changed me—forced me to loosen up and adjust to the rhythms of the road. I had expected that. But I hadn't expected the whole world to change, too. While I'd been gone (or, rather, while I'd stopped reading the newspapers) the nineties had landed with a sickening thud. The new atmosphere of crisis, the busted economy, and the Gulf War changed me far more than any trip ever could have.

When I left Allston, I could pick up copyediting work whenever I wanted it. By the time I came back, the economy had collapsed and every publishing company in town seemed to be laying people off. It took me more than a month to find freelance work again—a job with my no-longer-so-glitzy employer *PC Week*. The magazine had moved to a trashy, failed office park in Medford. Back in the eighties, I would have refused to commute out there, but now I was glad to get any work at all.

And then there was the Gulf War. Just the phrase *Gulf War* brings it all back: the whirling video graphics that accompanied every report, Peter Jennings walking across a floor painted to look like a map of the Middle East, the yellow ribbons fluttering and turning gray as the winter progressed, the SCUD busters, the so-called smart bombs, and that particular despair I felt. This was was not a war, it was an ad campaign, a series of logos and slogans and puffy press conferences.

I have strange, flashbulb-lit memories from that winter. One night—it must have been twenty degrees out—I rode my bike to Boston Common for a demonstration. I joined a rag-tag band of leftists; they were marching in a circle over the ice and screaming, "No blood for oil!" The park was floodlit by TV cameras. Around us stood a threatening band of prowar people; one guy in an ROTC uniform shoved and screamed at the protestors. I didn't like mouthing slogans, merging with the crowd, chanting to the cameras. I'd done this so many times before—abortion, United States out of Central America, GE, nukes—and now all those marches had become in my memory nothing but a blur of Birkenstocks, bullhorns, and ethnic fabrics. I didn't want the Gulf War to turn into another in a series of protests. I didn't want to chant until the words sounded like gibberish.

A few weeks later, I rode down to the Washington antiwar demonstration on the *Luv Bus,* a vehicle for people loosely affiliated with a local, whacked-out radio station. From the moment I nestled into my seat, I sensed this demo would be different. The *Luv Bus*—equipped with awesome speakers—blasted technofunk while we black-clad hipsters regaled each other with conspiracy theories. As we pulled into the capital city, DJ Peter put on his captain's hat and roused us by prancing down the aisle singing, "The Moment I Wake Up."

The tribes had gathered. Hippies drummed in front of the White House. Vietnam vets stood by the Memorial, collecting signatures. A group of Korean musicians, clad in white, fluttered past. Bread and Puppet people carried flags with pictures of pans, toothbrushes, spoons, chairs—all that furniture of peace. Punk-rockers marched along chanting, "Blah, blah, blah, blah"; then they'd pogo in place, whooping, and run around screaming so the orderly crowd turned into a melee. I came in costume as Pagan[1], carrying a sign that said COPY EDITORS FOR PEACE: GRAMMAR, YES; GROUND WAR, NO.

There were so many people there (200,000 according to the European press) and so many of them were *freaks* that I came away full of hope. This hadn't been any ordinary protest. We'd flared up like fireworks. We'd become living examples of the other way, the other world we could have if America did not raze the Middle East with high-tech weapons. Who needed oil? We would ride around in our solar-powered dune buggies, eat algae, move into yurts, power this country with the flame of our own mad genius.

Well, I guess you had to be there to understand. You certainly wouldn't have learned anything about the demo from the *The New York Times.* The *Times* reported that only 70,000 people had protested, and the story didn't even make the front page. The *Times* also featured a large photo of a counterdemonstrator. Yeah, well, I saw those counterdemonstrators, all three of them. They were surrounded by TV cameras and reporters.

So maybe we didn't stop the war from trundling on. But surely those of us who ran alongside the peace punks through the streets of Washington—screaming, slam-dancing, spinning with rage—changed things in some intangible way. We refused to be soothed by news programs with their "Gulf War" video logos, by yellow ribbons, SCUD studs, or smart bombs. We refused to become numb. I did anyway. I went home with a lot of pissed-off political energy and kept fighting in my own ways.

Too bad it took a war to make me come alive like that. But, no, the war was just the jump start. What really happened was that I let Pagan[1], the Shiva inside me, take over my body. Adopting her devil-may-care attitude, I stopped writing every day. I gave up my self-improvement regimen. Why had I wanted to become perfect anyway? Better to make mistakes. Better to try something dorky like Step Aerobics, write a song, flirt with a stranger, let go, lose control. Better to do anything, no matter how dopey, than to become numb.

PaGan's HeaD

Formerly 'Back to Pagan'

$4 Because I'm broke

2 Copy Editors Tear Up America's Highways

This issue: No. 5
Pagan's issue: recycling

FRENCH FRIES

FRESH HOT COFFEE

IN A HAZE OF DOPE
AND DIET COKE,
PAGAN AND VIRGINIA
CROSS THE COUNTRY

PAGAN'S NEWS page 1

MY HAIR

Last you heard, I had cut off all my dreadlocks but one and had gone blond. But at some point, even that last dreadlock became onerous, so it went too. Now my hair's in a 1960s-style stewardess cut--a wedge with short hair in back, and a flap of hair on one side that gets longer towards the front and ends in one insouciant curl.

When it comes to the does-she-or-doesn't-she question of tinting, I'm torn. As an environmentalist and hypochondriac, I deplore hair-dye makers' use of lead and coal-tar (cold-tar?) derivatives that go on my head and then into the water supply. But as a narcissist, I feel naked without my bleached hair. I also feel it's my God-given right to be blond. There's a Miss Clairol hair-stripping product called, "Born Blond," and damn it, I was born blond. I was blond until I became a miserable, awkward pre-teen, at which my hair suddenly became limp and mousy brown to match my pale skin and thick glasses. It was <u>life</u>, not genetics that turned my hair brown, so who can blame me for trying to return to the golden innocence that--as the Miss Clairol ad people have suggested--is my natural birthright?

MY AGE

I've come to a decision: It's time to start lying about my age. I've decided that I'm 24 now. I made my new age official by announcing to my sister that she (26) is now the older sibling. She's an agreeable sort and didn't put up any fight, so it's official.

Actually, when I tell people my real age, I often feel like I'm lying. For one thing, I don't feel nearly as grown-up and together as I'm supposed to be. For God's sake, I don't even own a car (but that, of course, is for political reasons). And people--especially people down South--often register shock if I tell them my real age, saying, "I thought you were in high school." I want to be young, but not <u>that</u> young. This reached the point of absurdity when I was in Atlanta buying a ticket to a museum, and the lady asked, "Will that be an adult ticket or a children's?" The sign said children's tickets were for those under 12.

ADVERTISEMENT

EXPERIENCE FINE DINING IN ALLSTON...

INDIA ROYAL

your host, Pandit

...at the corner of Comm. Ave. and fantasy (near the Store 24), Pandit ushers you into the "ohm"-azing world of Oriental dining.

And here's some Hindi phrases to make Indian food more fun:

Call the wine steward.
baar-maiñ ko bu-laa-i-yé. बारमैन को बुलाइये।

Scented betel nut.
mee-THee su-paa-ree. मीठी सुपारी।

The food and service were excellent.
khaa-naa aur sé-vaa ba-hut ach-chhé thé. खाना और सेवा बहुत अच्छे थे।

And most important: Main (nasal 'n') Pagan Ko jānta huñ. मैं पागेन को जानता हैं
I know Pagan

WHERE IT PAYS TO KNOW PAGAN...

Tell Pandit that you're a close personal friend of Pagan's and receive a 15% discount on your Meal... India Royal, where Pagan's friends are treated like royalty.

Me with Mary in her San Fran backyard on Thanksgiving.

HOUSING

In September, I moved to the attic room in our huge (8 person) Victorian. My new room is absolutely giant, with angled eaves, two skylights (no windows), a ladder to the roof and a brick monolith in the middle that's part of the chimney. My room's really three rooms--a bedroom, a home entertainment center, and an office. When K-ROCK producer Bill Kates saw my spread, he said, "Wow, it's like Anne Frank's hideout redone in paisley."

CAREER

My novel's now out on the market. The first place I've heard from--a major publishing house--is interested in it, but not certain. However, I'm not getting my hopes up, because I've had so many near misses. (Crown Books almost bought my now-on-the-scrap-heap short story collection.)

These days, I'm in the strange position of living off my writing for the Village Voice, The Nation and other places. I thought, when I left for my trip (see story this issue), I could come back to my free-lance copy editing job at PC Week. Ha! In the past few months, lots of magazines in Boston have folded, moved or suffered major layoffs--out-of-work copy editors are as plentiful around here as failed banks. I'm still getting copy editing work, but it's sporadic. This has prooved a blessing in disguise, as it's gotten me off my ass. I'm querying new magazines, taking on more assignments, and starting to work on a book proposal. Look for an upcoming story in the Voice Literary Supplement about "personal magazines" like the one you're reading, as well as assorted book reviews in the Voice and Nation.

So blame the higher cover price of Pagan's Head on Boston's terrible economy.

2

OTHER

My pal Maggie (see issue #3), who I've known since we made trouble in high school, has just moved to Cambridge to attend the Harvard grad program in Sanskrit. Though we live a 10-minute bike ride from one another, we have a kind of stand-off going--both of us refuse to bike through the cold to get to the other's house. So instead we spend hours on the phone. (I have my own phone line--something Marsha Brady only dreamed about.)

Our other trouble-makin' high school pal, Saira, also lives in Cambridge. The three of us suffered through the WORST HIGH SCHOOL EVER DEVISED BY PREPPY MINIONS OF HELL, which I will name right here: [redacted]. Do not send your daughters there. (It's an all-girls' school. Like menstruation and sexism, [redacted] is one of the pestilences only suffered by females.)

I'm glad to have two of my best high school pals right here--it lends continuity to my life. What's also nice is that together we are a Jew, a Moslem and a Prostestant, providing a needed cultural bridge in these times of misunderstanding.

And speaking of that, Pagan OPPOSES THE WAR, and boy is it a big pain sometimes. I've been to demonstrations in subzero temperatures; I've been threatened by counter-demonstrators brandishing American flags, business-end forward. (Boston rednecks have a history of using American flags as weapons. A famous picture from the bus$ing wars shows a townie from Southie attempting to gore a black lawyer with a flag.) I rode 20 hours on the LUV bus to attend the Washington march, where I carried a sign that said, "Copy editors for peace: grammar, yes; ground war, no."

The Reagan years seemed terrible at the time, but now I just wish we could have Reagan back. Reagan wouldn't launch a real war; instead he'd just take on some tiny country that we could whup in three days. And while it was disturbing to have a sort of cartoon character running the country, it was better than having SATAN commanding his LEGIONS to do battle on the plains of Armageddon.

PAGAN'S QUOTABLE FRIENDS

Mike Broder's sister, insulting someone: "My Birkenstocks are two years old and they look it. Her's are two years old and they look brand new."

Mike Cronin: "You can never go back to a full-time job once you've been seduced by Lady Free-lance."

Maggie: "I feel like a work-oholic, except that I don't do any work."

Maggie, lying to the policeman who had her car towed out of the fire lane: "I couldn't move it. I was throwing up."

Lauren (laughing maniacally): "I don't know what it is. I just have this compulsion to lie to authority figures."

Sue McCabe: "The rays coming out of my computer made the orange in my desk shrivel up."

Mike Broder: "There was this episode of `The Patty Duke Show' where they introduced a third identical cousin. That shattered my world."

EVEN LARGE CORPORATIONS BOW TO THE WHIMS OF PAGAN! I submitted a proposal to the big-wigs at Ziff-Davis, which is the company that owns PC Week, where I am sometimes a copy editor. They approved the proposal, making recycling a policy at Ziff-Davis magazines all across the country. If you're interested in getting your company to pay for environmental sins, contact Pagan. Here are highlights from the interoffice memo:

TO	DEPARTMENT / SUBSIDIARY	OFFICE	
All Employees		Boston, Cambridge	
FROM	DEPARTMENT / SUBSIDIARY	OFFICE	PHONE EXTENSION
[redacted]	Facilities	Boston	
SUBJECT			
Recycling and the magnificent PAGAN!		9/10/90	

It's official...recycling has arrived! With full support from [redacted] ← wow! [redacted] himself!, all locations are implementing a program to recycle wherever possible. Here in Massachusetts, we have established a program to recycle both paper and aluminum cans.

We wish to acknowledge and thank a few people who felt strongly enough about recycling to influence the company's decision to implement an official program. Thanks first to Pagan Kennedy for submitting a proposal to Human Resources, which then found its way to the New York office for review. Pagan was also very helpful in providing input to [redacted] when she was putting our program together.

3

death cars! gambling! writers! rock stars! drugs!
voodoo

Wild in the Streets

puking!

Pagan tours U.S.A.

DEDICATED TO LAW ENFORCEMENT OFFICERS

As I finished up my novel during the Summer of Self-Improvement, I knew I had to reward myself with the cross-country car trip I've always dreamed about. I had decided that October 15 was my novel deadline, and the day I would leave on the trip. But who would go with me on this madcap journey, and where would I get a car?

Sometime in September, my awesome powers of networking yielded results: My pal Diane had a friend who was planning to quit her job as an editor at Little Brown and drive out to Santa Cruz to start a new life--and she wanted someone to drive to California with her.

Authorities at my free-lance job at *PC Week* assured me that there'd always be a place for me in the company, even if I did want to leave for a month on a whim. But my last day on the job, my generous co-workers gave me a going-away party, and I began to wonder if they knew something I didn't.

All told, I had three going-away parties. (By the by, I was also invited to three "Twin Peaks" season premier parties and three Bay Area Thanksgivings. Impressed?) Besides the work party, there was a huge blow-out that, admittedly, was really for my co-traveller, Virginia. Also, the day we left, my housemate Linda gave a brunch. I think she would have had the brunch whether or not I was leaving, but I chose to consider it part of the going-away blitz.

We Leave

At 5:00, Virginia drove up to my house in her overloaded Ford Festiva. She was only three hours late. At the end of my street, she screeched to a halt. "We have to get to the turnpike. Do you know which way it is?" Neither of us had any idea how to get to the turnpike: so, auspiciously, began our journey.

New York

We reached the city at about midnight. After a little tour of Harlem, we found my friend Anna's house at 102nd Street. Then began the parking odyssey. Like a modern-day Mary and Joseph, we drove from garage to garage begging for shelter. Finally, we found one a mere mile from Anna's house and lugged our suitcases past friendly gentlemen who said we could stay the night with them.

The next day, former New Yorker Pagan gave Virginia a whirlwind tour of downtown NYC. We made sure to stop in and use the bathrooms at the *Voice* and *The Nation*--my status as a free-lance writer allows me to pee in the offices of any leftist publication.

Dustin, signing autographs

Virginia (hereafter known as VV) was counting on Pagan to supply some celebrities for us to spot. When we were at the Voice, I pointed out Nat Hentoff to her, but I could sense her disappointment. She wanted to glimpse a Hollywood legend, not a first-amendment writer.

But, as fate would have it, when we got back to Anna's house, the street was blocked off and a film crew was standing around. Then we spotted him! It was Dustin Hoffman, looking a bit shriveled and puny, standing on the steps of a brownstone. Something came over VV. She ran up and down snapping pictures, and wouldn't leave the street. Pagan went upstairs and told Anna that Dustin Hoffman was standing below. Anna said, "Oh, Pagan, what do I care?" and I realized I didn't care either.

Next day, we dropped off my novel at my agent's office, and after several attempts to find the Holland Tunnel, left the city.

Washington

Coincidentally, VV and Pagan both were raised in the bucolic bliss of Maryland, the mall state. VV wanted to spend some time with her family since she was splitting the East, so I spent two days with my own family.

Pagan's mom has become obsessed with the idea that our ancestors have a deep, dark secret. I had trouble following Mom's explanation, but I think the upshot is that Mom's grandmother left her sons after her husband died and went off to start a new life. Somewhere out there is a lost branch of the Pagans, according to Mom.

This led to the most bizarre mother-daughter outing I've ever been on: We Drove to the Mormon Church to use their geneological library. First, we had to watch a filmstrip about how, if we joined the Mormons, we'd be reunited forever in heaven with our family. Then a rotund woman with a hairy face and no sense of humor showed us around. Mom kept giving me looks that said, "I know these people are stupid, but be polite." Together, as mother and daughter, we searched through endless microfilm and -fiche, with no results.

The next day, VV came to pick me up. WE WERE READY TO PARTY! We stopped in at a Maryland shopping mall, and among the silver-haired ladies, bought a lighter so we could FIRE UP A J! Whew, things were getting wild now. VV got a large Diet Coke and convinced me to drink some. I hate taht stuff and pot too, but during this trip, we were madwomen, downing gallons of Diet Coke and packs of Trident--a girl's version of *Fear and Loathing*. I was thinking, WE ARE TWO COPY EDITORS ON THE ROAD, so watch out America, you better not have a comma out of place.

But the caffeine and pot were to take their toll. In Culpeper, Va., we stopped at a restaurant with a giant pig out front. As I waited for my lemonade, I began to look around at the knick-knacks on the shelf by the cash register, and they were all cutesy pigs, some saying "Bacon" on them, all grinning like maniacs. Vegetarian Pagan began to have a fit of paranoia and could barely keep her composure when the lady came back with her drink.

North Carolina

We arrived that night in Chapel Hill, at the house of my long-lost pal Dan. He and I had suffered together through XXXX XXX's boot camp for would-be famous writers, and though Dan

← VV in front of pig restaurant in Culpeper, Va.

and I had kept in touch, I hadn't seen him for years. In the meantime, Dan had married Karen, who has two kids. He'd also won North Carolina's $8,000 writers' grant, and wisely used some of that money to invest in a cockatoo.

Dan, Karen, the kids, the cockatoo and two cats live in a beautiful house amid the pines, which rents for $750 a month. Karen makes jewelry; Dan works part-time.

As I traveled America, new possibilities began to open up to me. I began to see that, outside of major cities, this is a land of cheap apartments, great yard sales and only a marginal need for employment. Best of all, living in a smaller town gives you the perfect excuse to stay home and make your own fun (Pagan's favorite kind).

Dan with his pal Alice

We arrived on Saturday night, in fact, and Dan insisted we had to stay inside because tonight was homecoming weekend, and if we went out we'd be surrounded by drunk jocks. This made homebody Pagan elated, but saddened VV, a gal who likes to boogi-oogie-oogie the night away. It was the beginning of the tension Pagan and VV would feel with one another: the classic battle of morning person against night person.

So humans and animals alike, we piled into Dan and Karen's bedroom to watch "Twin Peaks." As luck would have it, VV and I did not miss an episode of the show during the month in which we crossed America.

As it happened, *The Nation* was having a party in Chapel Hill the next day to celebrate its 125th anniversary. Since Dan and I both work for the magazine, we decided we'd better haul our asses over there and network.

But once confronted with the crowd of earnest lefties quaffing vodka tonics, our crowd huddled together and talked about fashion. Lunch was a very non-vegetarian, non-p.c. fish platter, which upset both Karen and Pagan.

After the speeches, Karen regaled us with tales of her misspent youth, including her adventures traveling in a van with a hippie guy and a chicken. Just then, the *Nation* editor came over to schmooze our table. We all became very shy, especially when it became clear that the *Nation* editor had never heard of Dan or me--though Dan had gotten a letter from a big cheese at the *Nation* imploring him to show up at the party because the aforementioned *Nation* editor was just dying to meet him. It was a networking disaster area.

The next day, we took leave of this picturesque family of Southern intellectuals, Pagan swearing she was going to move to idyllic Chapel Hill.

It was Pagan who steered us out of the driveway--her first attempt ever at driving a stick-shift car. Karen and Dan stood guard to make sure the street was empty as the Ford Festiva rocked back and forth on its haunches and Virgina yelled, "No, push in the clutch." Pagan successfully made it to the end of the block before she broke out in a cold sweat and begged VV to take the wheel.

Knoxville

Those of you who read *Back to Pagan* issue numero uno know all about the joys of this former World's Fair site, to which I have traveled several times. My stay here, however, was less raucous than usual, due to poor weather conditions.

We stayed with the ever-hospitable Trevor in Knoxville's trendy Artists' Colony section (some old, broken-down houses with peace signs spray-painted on them). Trevor lives in a spacious bachelor's pad. I've forgotten how much he pays in rent or I'd report that.

Since Vatican Pizza (see *BTP* #1) was no more, we went to another pizza place and then home to watch selections from Trevor's extensive video library. VV picked a movie about Manson--the girls are sitting around with rifles on their laps saying, "Charlie shows us that death is groovy, that killing someone is like making love" made Pagan feel yucky and unbalanced. So did the Gwar record that Trevor played.

Next day, we planned to go for an outing in America's Wonderland of Cheesiness--Gatlinburg, Tennessee. However, the rain made everyone depressed, and all we really did was pose for photos outside the museum that contains Buford Pusser's death car. Actually, it turned

Trevor's probably not going to come out, but he's right there in a rebel cap.

Pagan + Trevor in Confederate regalia.

out not to even be his real death car--instead it was the one used in *Walking Tall*. We weren't going to pay four bucks to see that.

Georgia

Our first glimpse of Georgia was rather surreal. VV--ever the social one--got into a conversation with some old-timers at a gas station. Old Timer A, who lounged behind the register, was a pretty quiet fellow. But Old Timer B told us all about his adventures roaming around Texas, and about how his wife bought a car and now there's hell to pay, and warned us that when we go to LA, we musn't hobnob with those celebrities because they haven't got time for poor folks. He insulted VV in some way I've forgotten. Then he demanded to know how old I was. When I told him, he nearly fell off his chair. "I thought you was in high school," he said. "What's wrong with you? Why aren't you taller? Are you a midget?" This was to be only the beginning of my being taken for a high school student by Georgians.

VV made me drive out of the gas station, and as the little car bucked under me and stalled out, I just knew that old timer was looking out at us and saying, "By gum, those girls'll be lucky to make it out of Mississippi."

In Atlanta, we stayed with VV's pal Tod--a big-hearted surfer guy who's into speed metal and Gwar. That first night, we went down to Little Five Points

(L5P, as the natives say), Atlanta's sorry little hip neighborhood. We drove over with Tod and some of his friends, including Bob, a humorless economics major. On the way, we saw this guy walking really slowly, pushing a lawn mower ahead of him along the sidewalk--and all admired (I thought) this odd character.

We went to a bar and played darts. After a while, I heard a commotion outside, and there was the guy with the lawn mower, now seated on a bike with policemen gathered around him. He was insisting that he didn't steal the lawn mower. The policemen didn't seem to be mad at him or anything. One of them went over to try to start the mower; it

Whoops! That's not Atlanta: Pagan and Trevor dine in Knoxville.

didn't work. Then the police left, as if that somehow settled it.

Bob told us on the way back that he was the one who called the cops. "Look, I had my car stolen, and I'm sick of this. When I asked that guy if he'd sell that lawn mower, he said yeah, for ten bucks, which is exactly what a hit of crack costs." I wondered how Bob knew what a hit of crack costs and whether he would have called the cops if the guy had been white.

Next day, VV and I hung around in L5P. It was the beginning of my obsession with clothes. I already hated every piece of clothing in my suitcase. While I frantically thrift shopped, VV sat in a coffee shop and met a guy named Steve whom we later dubbed The Bore because it took us forever to escape him.

VV wanted to go downtown, to Five Points (which Pagan insisted on calling Big Five Points). We wandered around for a good hour trying to find the mysterious Atlanta subway. At one point, we asked a guy how to get to the subway stop and he gave us directions and said, "I'm walking there myself as soon as this clown shows up." I think we both pictured his friend the clown as dressed in a polka-dot suit and a red wig, and VV said, "Well at least he'll be easy to recognize" but the guy didn't get it.

As we walked to the subway, we were soon passed by the guy and the clown. But the clown didn't look like a clown. He was dressed in tux pants and a white shirt, and was carrying carrying a big bag. "He's not a clown at all," I said.

"Maybe his outfit's in the bag," VV said.

A girl with a shaved head in L5P had told us to go to The Underground, so imagine our surprise when it turned out to be a huge, horrible mall. Instead we walked around the streets of Atlanta in search of a wig for VV's costume. It was the beginning of her obsession with Halloween--she wanted to wear a full Viking costume and be in New Orleans on that special day. Pagan could care less, but tried to humor her.

Whew, that's better: VV and Pagan in L5P

Atlanta was wig city--wig stores galore. In fact, we thought the Georgia license plate should be changed to say "We Sell Wigs." (We'd decided that the Tennessee plates should be changed to "All You Can Eat" in light of the ample breakfast bars there.)

Atlanta seemed to have a huge black middle class: Most people downtown were black. This was the only thing Pagan could find in the city's favor--it was overrun by gross office buildings, every corporate plaza sitting on its own Peachtree Avenue or Peachtree Lane. As Tod said, "This is a city without a soul."

Next day, we drove out to Stone Mountain, an aptly named gray hulk with some Confederate generals carved on its side. As VV and I had been cultivating our Maryland accents, we preferred to call it Stay-in Maaooont'n. (To hear classic Maryland accents, watch any John Waters movie.)

Despite hurricane wind conditions, we climbed to the top of the mountain. I wouldn't go near the edge for fear of being

Shrine in Finster's garden

blown off, but VV, always a sucker for a photo op, gambled along the side of the mountain, her clothes whipping around her, yelling, "OK, take it now."

That afternoon saw the first major Pagan driving sprees, as we headed for Athens, Georgia, home of the B52s, more wigs and overly hip diners.

I had bought a Donnie and Marie 45 box--which I used for a camera bag--in Knoxville for $4. It was in Athens that the D&M bag began to open the doors of Southern hospitality. Our waiter in a diner examined it, and

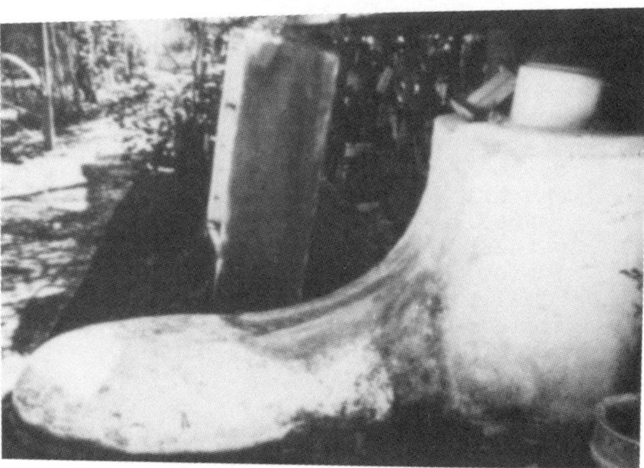

advised me that it could go for 20 bucks. It also started ladies in a card shop talking about their fave `70s shows.

Next day, it was destination Memphis, with a side-trip to Summerville, Georgia, to see the Reverend Finster's garden of weirdness. Finster is the folk artist who was "discovered" by Michael Stipe and who did the Talking Heads' "Little Creatures" album cover. People in Atlanta said the way to find Finster's house was to go to Summerville and then ask anybody. Sure enough, when we got to the town, a man at a gas station said, "Finster? Just take this here road a ways, then when you see two auto parts stores you turn off and go smack between `em."

Pagan and had been fascinated with Finster ever

since she saw the movie *Athens, Georgia*, where the Reverend tells how he began painting: The old man said that several years ago, he got some paint on his finger, and it turned into a face and began talking. It told him that the Lord wanted him to be an artist.

In fact, Finster does much more than paint. He makes huge, well, *things*: a giant shoe, a beehive of old bike parts, a wedding-cake-shaped tower decorated with pieces of aluminum cans that twirl in the wind, a wrecked car painted with exhortations to drive safely, a ten-foot-long Coke bottle. You walk around on sidewalks encrusted with marbles, colored glass, bits of metal. His garden must cover about two acres. Both of us ran around in ecstasy, but were also sort of dazed. There was now way to take it all in.

Memphis

Yes, we did Graceland. I'd already been there and I was bored. Even VV, who hadn't, was bored. I don't want to talk about it.

I insisted we go to Schwab's, the most amazing five-and-dime store ever. One floor of it is a Memphis "museum," with some dusty bottles, twigs of cotton plants and old yearbooks. The rest is dime-store voodoo books, polyester bellbottoms (sold as new clothing), and 3-D Jesuses. But Pagan couldn't concentrate on scouring Schwabs; she was too excited about visiting the 70s museum.

You see, I'd been trading BTP for a magazine based in Memphis called Kreature Komforts. The editors often talked about their museum, and the contributions people had sent them--a Charlie's Angels poster, a Welcome Back Kotter game, etc. The Kreature Komfort guys, I knew, also run a floatation tank and "brain tune-up" business and record store called Shangri-La, so I asked information for that number and called them up.

The guy who answered was none other than KC's Sherm, who gave us a warm, personal invitation to see the museum, and we headed right over. It turned out that Shangri-La was a big old house on one of the main streets in the hep section of town. Sherm and his friend Chiz--who had come down from Boston to help out with the store and the magazine--sat in the foyer of the house pretty much all day. People would parade in and out, some to look at records or float and some just to hang out. Memphis was the hanging-outingest city I've ever seen.

We had planned to leave that evening, but the folks in the foyer convinced us that we had to stay until the next day, Sunday, to see the Reverend Al Green ("Take Me to the River" and other soul hits of the sixties) preaching in the local gospel church. Sherm and Chiz said we could say at the house, so that settled it.

As for the seventies museum, it turned out to be the large, downstairs bathroom in the house. It was full of platform shoes,

David Cassidy books and bios, Fonzie paraphernalia, Kiss stuff and even the Donnie and Marie phonograph that matched the "camera bag" I'd bought in Knoxville.

That night, VV and I went on a mission to see the Memphis pyramid and Prince Mongo's. The KC guys had recommended the pyramid as the most hideous sight in Memphis. Apparently, the powers that be in Memphis are trying to link, in the minds of tourists, the Southern city with Egyptian one--so naturally

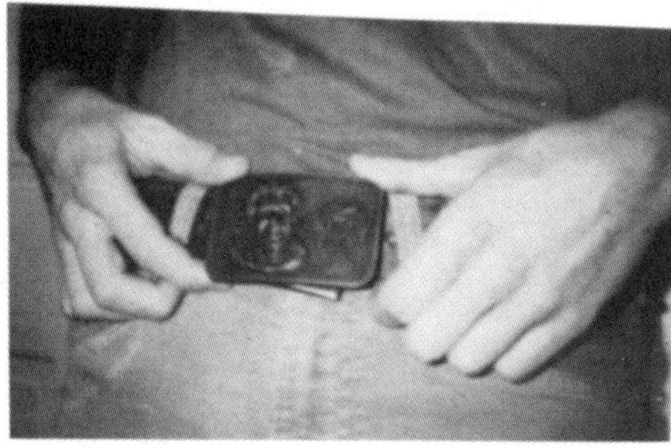

Sherm models fonzie belt buckle.

they're building a massive mall/astrodome shaped like a pyramid. Even unfinished and dark at night, the vast pyramid was an awesome sight--and like the original pyramids, a monument conspicuous consumption.

As for Prince Mongo's, that was Pagan's favorite place the first times she was in Memphis. Back then, it was called Prince Mongo's Spiritual Subs and Pizzas and one entered it through a long blacklight tunnel decorated with a skeleton riding a rocket. The menu was a manifesto about how Prince Mongo has brought love and peace to planet Earth. Instead of "green peppers" or "mushrooms" or "extra cheese," the pizza toppings were called by their names on Prince Mongo's native planet, words like "offo" and "trippo." The pizza was made by little kids and old drunk guys with yellow eyeballs. Prince Mongo--I gleaned from clippings hanging on the wall--was a rich kook who wore a sheepskin and a gas mask and was running for mayor.

When I asked Sherm what had happened to Prince Mongo's, he said the Prince had now declared himself King Mongo--and that he'd come in second in the mayoral race. So I wanted to go see whether Prince, uh, I mean King Mongo's place was still as groovy.

It had changed. First off, the word "Prince" in the building's neon sign had been replaced by "King." That was fine. But now there was a $5 cover charge, a giant video screen with MTV blasting, and the place was pretending to be a dance club. YUCK. Come on, King, what happened to your Zambodian ideals of love and peace?

The next morning, we went out to breakfast at yet another house that doubled a s a place of business. It was a groovy hippy crash pad with the menu written all over the living room wall. You go sit out on their porch and after two thousand years they bring you your blueberry buckwheat pancakes and soy-sauce hash browns.

At this time, I'd like to say something to those who make the health and zoning codes in Boston. Look, how the hell do expect any kind of wacky, unprofitable restaurants and stores to thrive in our town with your crazy laws and demanding health codes? Please mellow out guys and take a look at Memphis, where marginal businesses can breath free. C'mon, that hippy crash pad restaurant would be closed down in 10 seconds if it were in Boston, AND YET THE FOOD IS MUCH LESS LIKELY TO KILL YOU THAN WHAT YOU'D GET AT "SANITARY" PLACES LIKE RILEY'S ROAST BEEF OR CAJUN JOE'S.

Anyway, VV and I then headed off to see Memphis's most-touted attraction, the gospel church where Reverend Al Green preaches. We came in late, feeling guilty about looking rather disreputable, and slid into a back pew. A woman was preaching about the coming December 3rd Midwestern earthquake, and we began to worry that Al wouldn't show up.

But when she finished, a guy took the mike and started announcing church events. VV turned to the woman behind us and asked who the preacher was.

She gave VV a funny look and said, "Al Green. Didn't you see him on `Arsenio' last night?" Al began preaching and singing and jumping around on one of the organs (there were two organs, two electric guitars, a drum set and two choirs). He was absolutely great--joking and

At a diner in Memphis. "The Piña Colada Song" is playing on the juke box.

singing and having a blast. If I'd been raised with this Christianity, I might have stuck with it. What I especially liked about black Baptism (of the All Green variety, anyway) was that everyone seemed to be talking about Jesus as a support, someone you can always turn to. In my childhood Episcopalian church, the minister always talked about God as the judge--and I felt guilty, not loved, when I thought of church.

The best part of the service was when the Reverend christened two babies. He held each baby up and gave a little, off-the-cuff speech about it. Then he gave each one a big, wet kiss. Soon after, the service was over, and VV and I wiped the tears from our eyes, agreeing that this was the high point of our trip so far.

Our host in Mississippi was to be Paul, a friend of mine from *PC Week* days of yore. Paul had cut short his brilliant career as a computer magazine feature writer to attend the masters program in fiction at the University of Southern Mississippi, where the Barthelme brothers teach (older brother Donald, now deceased, is the most famous of this Southern shotguns-and-minimalist-fiction clan).

His bachelor pad featured a large living room and work space, a kitchen/dining room, a bedroom and a screen-in porch, all for about $200 a month. Paul proved the perfect host, offering us a deluxe fold-out sofa and an all-day bottomless pot of coffee. In fact, he begged us to stay with him forever--I guess Mississippi gets a little boring.

Of course, my one desire was to scour the thrift shops of Hattiesburg. This turned out be easy since there wasn't much to Hattiesburg *but* thrift shops.

The next morning, VV and I went downtown and found all the regular stores empty and boarded up; the only things still doing business were the Goodwill and the guns 'n' ammo store. I also noticed a strange hotel, with lion's head knockers and a grand foyer that was no longer so grand because there were a few shopping carts parked there as well as a dinosaur skeleton made out of wood. The lobby of the building also included a vintage 1940s barber shop, but locked and dusty. Paul later told us that this is the building where acid heads and old alkies live, and that there's a great party on the roof every year.

We followed directions the Goodwill lady had given us to the Salvation Army and discovered a semi-paved road lined with uninhabited, wrecked houses and thrift shop after thrift shop. I SWEAR TO GOD, THE ONLY STORES ON THE STREET WERE JUNK SHOPS AND USED-CLOTHING PLACES, AS IF NO ONE HERE BOUGHT ANYTHING NEW. I would have been in ecstasy if everyone hadn't looked so poor. VV went into a whitewashed hut of a bar to get lemonade and came out shaken. She said it looked primitive, especially because--instead of having neon liquor signs--they'd pasted up liquor ads from magazines all over the walls.

We'd decided to linger in Hattiesburg for two reasons. First, I wanted to sit in on Frederick Barthelme's fiction workshop. But most important, VV was in the throes of Halloween madness. By now, she had almost completely assembled her Viking outfit (complete with horned helmet, spear and miniskirt). In fact, all our travels up to this point had been choreographed so that we would hit Hattiesburg just before Halloween and could swoop down on New Orleans like invading Mongol hordes wearing blond wigs and plastic helmets.

The next day, the day before Halloween, we drove over to New Orleans as a sort of practice run. (Hattiesburg is only about an hour and a half from N.O.)

On the way to N.O. that morning, Pagan's prodigious consumption of coffee began to take its toll, and suddenly she had to pee, even though we were driving through God-forsaken swamps. VV had long been recommending that I pee outside, but I hate and fear nature and will not risk exposing my rump to the jaws of grass-dwelling creatures. The only bathroom we could find was a really horrible gas station one. When I came out, I said, "Uggh, that toilet seat was wet."

VV looked at me, horrified. "You sat on it?"

"Why yes," I stammered.

"I can't believe it. You're the one that's terrified of germs."

It turned out hat all this time as we used the most disgusting bathrooms of America, VV had been squatting over the toilets without actually touching any bodily part to them, while Pagan had been blithely and ignorantly sitting down on every one!

"But," Pagan said, "I thought the whole squatting-over-toilets thing was just something your mom tells you to do when you're a little kid like not drinking straight out of the milk carton. I didn't think that anyone really did it. You can't *really* catch anything from a toilet seat, can you?"

"I got crabs from one once in boarding school," VV nonchalantly commented.

As we drove the rest of the way to N.O., I huddled in an agony of fear. I knew I must already have crabs or something worse. How could I have been so careless? From now on I would squat over even the most pristine toilet.

And here I'd like to take time out to speak to those of you responsible for building roadside women's toilets. Look, if everyone's going to be squatting over them, why not make the toilets lower? Sure, it may be easy for a tall gal like Virginia to tower over a toilet without touching it, but what about those of us who barely reach the 5'4" mark? For us, squatting over a toilet means an agony of mid-thigh-muscle pain. Pair that pain with the desperation of someone who's been holding it in for hours as she quaffs Diet Coke in the care and you have a gal who might very well say, Oh what the hell, and sit on the toilet.

I don't want to talk about New Orleans. I'd already been there, and the second time around, the French Quarter just seemed touristy and gross. However, our day trip to N.O. was important because of two purchases VV made. First, she finally found the perfect blond wig for her costume in a store that catered to transvestites. Second, in a cheesy voodoo shop she bought the Little Death Guy, a skeleton holding a sword and riding on a horse, which thereafter hung from the rear-view mirror in our car. The Little Death Guy was actually pretty big--maybe five inches high--and made out of springs and clay, so that the sword in his hand swung back and forth as if he were a horseman of the apocalypse cutting down souls. I was terrified of the Little Death Guy, and whenever he turns toward me and bobbed his sword--as if telling me I was doomed to die any minute--I'd scream until VV pointed him at herself. She said she preferred having him shake his sword at her to having his horse's ass in her face anyway.

On Halloween, I went to Fred Barthelme's workshop with Paul--FB actually knew of me somehow (maybe because I sent some stories to the *Mississippi Review*) and was very hospitable. It was strange to be in a workshop after so long away from that scene--it made me miss the companionship and competition of the academic writing world.

When we got back to Paul's apartment, VV was wearing her Halloween costume and dancing around to loud music. My heart sunk. I really didn't want to run around the dangerous streets of New Orleans behind a Viking woman hell-bent on having fun. "Come on, Pagan," VV kept saying. "Aren't you going to wear a costume? I'll lend you something." Though I didn't want to be a spoilsport, I drew the line at wearing a humiliating costume in a strange city where people murder you (this was all that the Mississippians would say about N.O.--"Watch out for those crazy Louisianans, they'll kill you as soon as look at you).

Our plan--or rather I should say, Virginia's plan to which Paul and I had resigned ourselves--was this: The three of us would go to a club in N.O., party the night away, and then get a cheap motel room. Next morning, VV and I would take off for Texas, and Paul would go back home.

So I got in Paul's car to keep him company on the drive to N.O. while VV followed us in the Festiva. As Paul drove, he got more and more sullen, and then finally he admitted that he didn't want to go. I told him not to feel guilty, that if there was any way he could get out of this hellish night of fun, he should do it--even as my heart sunk at the though of being alone with a Halloween-crazed VV in the city of swamp gas and Pat O'Brian Hurricanes.

So finally Paul signaled to VV and we all pulled of f the road. WE bid good-bye to Paul--he giving my pitying looks--and I climbed back into the Festiva. Virginia the Viking and I discussed the new plan for fun. First we'd find a motel, then we'd go out to dinner and a club.

"You're not really into this, though, are you?" VV asked, as we approached the city.

"No," I admitted. "But I know how much it means to you." I was driving through the city now.

"Maybe we should just go out to dinner," she said, her Valkyrie eyes gazing off into the distance.

My heart leapt. "Okay," I said, "but decide quickly which exit you want or we're going to go right through the city."

Virginia swiveled her helmeted head this way and that, as she gazed at the city. "You know what?" she said. "You're not into it. Paul wasn't into it. No one ever gets as excited about Halloween as I do. Maybe we should just skip New Orleans and keep pushing west."

"All right," I said calmly. But inside I was shouting the joyous words of Martin Luther King, "Free at last, free at last, thank God Almighty I'm free at last."

And so we pushed on to a small town in Louisiana and had our Halloween dinner at a Pizza Hut, just as it was closing up. Then I drove us through the swamps of Louisiana, along a highway flanked by burned-out cars and the twisted outlines of trees. A heavy mist swirled in the road in front of us, scudding and eddying on the asphalt and disappearing in tendrils all around the car. I imagined that the swamp steam was the souls of slaves who'd had their children sold from them, or the ghosts of Confederates whose bodies lay under the soil of Chicamauga or Antietam.

We were pushing west into the unknown, the souls of all the dead who'd lived here--blacks and whites and Indians and Spanish and French--swirling around us, a crazy gumbo of American mojo mixed together in death even more than life, so all their sadnesses and joys became one milky white vapor. You couldn't see those swamp ghosts without thinking that maybe that's why the dead linger--it's not life they want to hold onto, but the land they farmed and fought for. And I began to think America is not a geography of identical malls and highways and Pizza Huts. On this land, the ashes of the dead lie thick as gris-gris--the voodoo powder with the power of good and evil. Their souls link every place you can name like a vast silver cobweb: history. Suddenly, it had become my best Halloween ever.

Baton Rouge

We stayed in a motel just outside Baton Rouge that night; the next morning it was 90 degrees out, and we headed into town to see the Mississippi and find a piece of wire for the Little Death Guy, who'd fallen off the rear-view mirror. Baton Rouge, while not a ghost town like Hattiesburg, seemed inordinately quiet and empty, the Mississippi like a gray haze behind the buildings. We walked up and down the pretty, unpeopled streets until we found a crafts studio that made stained-glass windows. We walked in, and as there was no one around, went right into the back, where two guys were working on long tables with beautiful pieces of glass scattered around them.

VV asked one guy for a piece of wire and of course he wanted to know why. "It's so we can hang our little voodoo mascot guy on the rear view."

"Well, here, here," the guy said, giving her some wire. "Just don't put a hex on us."

Then we went to explore the Mississippi, where two men stood on a river boat, bored, and two women fished. We watched one of the women pull in an eel. "I don't like 'em," she said, "but my brother does." As she reeled it in, the guys ran off the river boat to watch.

I began to get the feeling we were in a town where everyone was very friendly simply because they were dying of boredom. Thumbs up for Baton Rouge.

Cotton field

We drove a long way that day, through some of the strangest country I've seen. In lower Louisiana, the highway was raised on stilts over the swamp. When I looked down beneath us, the water glanced between the tall grass and the funny, stumpy trees with leaves like seaweed. It seemed as if we'd passed into prehistoric time--except for the highway, you could easily imagine a woolly mammoth standing knee-deep in the water.

As we neared Texas, we passed through cotton towns, where the fields had just been harvested and the cotton sat in huge rectangular heaps that looked like trailer homes. In places where the cotton had been blown around, whole towns were flecked with white, like sea foam clinging to houses and bushes and lying thick on the side of the road.

At a Texas gas station. Note dead bugs in "Out of Order" gas pump. Little Death guy hangs from rear-view.

By nightfall, we were under the big sky of East Texas, with lush fields that rolled out to the horizon. Our destination was VV's grandparent's house in a town that is known as the rose capital of the world.

Her grandparents are Baptists and ultra-conservatives. Her Grandpa ran a big Southern company; her Grandma was a deb and now a member of the DAR, the Daughters of the Republic of Texas, and a bunch of other ladies groups dedicated to reviving the memory of elite ancestors. (Pagan, having to been exposed to the Southern aristocracy thing in her youth, slipped into an easy familiarity with VV's grandparents.)

We had long ago decided that during our stay in East Texas, my name would be Peggy, since her Baptist grandparents might not see the humor in the name Pagan. So when we finally walked up to their house and VV's grandma opened the door, she said to me, "Oh, you must be Virginia's friend Peggy." I smiled and nodded and called her ma'am.

Her grandparents ushered us into the kitchen where they'd prepared a grandparently feast for us of nothing but cake, cookies and ice cream. It turned out this was pretty much what they lived on. In fact, her grandfather--a man with a heart condition--said, " I want to show you girls a little trick. Now get me my cereal," he called to Grandma. When he had his cereal and milk and a carton of frozen Cool Whip before him, he said, "See, you make a bowl of cereal and then after the milk you add a spoonful of whipped cream."

The next morning for breakfast (muffins, candy, cereal with whipped cream), Grandpa had to take all of his medicine. He held up one bottle of pills-potassium--and said, "This cost fifteen dollars, and you know what it is? Dirt. Dirt I could go dig out of the yard."

Then it was off for a whirlwind tour of the town in the grandparent's Caddy. Grandma drove and twice swerved into oncoming traffic. We had a tour of a campus, while Grandpa held up a shaky finger at each building and said, "I built that." Then it was off to the rose gardens to see the pictures of rose queens--each year, a society gal is crowned queen of the famous crop. (VV's mom was a rose duchess in the fifties.)

When we got back to the car, Grandma was still excitedly telling us about the roses. Grandpa broke in, saying, "Can I just have three minutes to tell the girls something?"

"Of course, dear," she said, "but first I have to tell the girls about..."

"No, I want three minutes."

So they fought for our attention. Finally, Grandpa got his three minutes and said, "I want to tell you girls about the invention of the hamburger. It was introduced at the 1906 World's Fair, just a few towns over from us." He fell silent.

I couldn't believe that was all there was to it, so I plied him with questions. How did the hamburger get its name? Who thought of the bun?

But he said that was the end of the story and there wasn't any more.

A few hours later, we climbed out of the Cadillac and back into our Festiva, and bid goodbye to those two old roses of the South. VV had to smoke a J immediately and we whooped it up as we headed out onto the open road.

Austin

We stayed with my ex-roommates Eric and Lesley, who just moved down there this fall. They say that Austin and Allston are very much the same, except of course Texas is cheaper and warmer. How cheap? Well, they had their own cute house with a living room, kitchen, garage, music room, ugly room, bedroom and backyard for about $300 a month.

Pagan rates Austin an A number 1 city for marginal living. Fact 1: There's a food coop. Fact 2: one of the richest state-college systems in the country. Fact 3: cheap Mexican food. Fact 4: A great rock and roll scene. Fact 5: The best vintage 1950s neon signs I've ever seen. Fact 6: THRIFT STORES.

We stayed at Eric and Lesley's for a few days, during which time we saw Austin's awesome city park, which has a spring that's been dammed up to form a gigantic swimming area (the size of several pools put together) and lots of ducks to feed. If you *still* think Austin's scary because it's in Texas, get this: The park also has "moon lights," giant towers topped with lights that cast the same eerie bluish glow as the moon.

Despite their change of locale, Eric and Lesley seemed to have gone right back into their groove. Lesley was tackling frightening craft projects, like making a bed with a slatted headboard. Eric was still studying classical guitar. And to top it off, these two, who served as high officials in the Boston-area census effort, were now back at work for the bureau!

The last night VV and I were there, we played a "friendly" game of poker, in which Lesley lost $30. Then we went out to dinner with Kathy, another ex-roommate, who's studying architecture at UT, and who had just come back form romantic Mexico.

→ Should it be called "Native American Poker"?

West Texas

People had warned us that the drive would be tortuously long and boring; it was long, but I wasn't bored. Sometimes the highway would run right through a butte. As you get near the two high cliffs signs warn about heavy cross winds (which were all too easy to feel in the Festiva) and then you're shooting between walls of rock, with the bright blue sky overhead. It's weirdly silent, except the sound of the wind.

VV, Lesley and Eric play Indian Poker.

As night fell, I began to feel awful--cranky, sick to my stomach, headachy. After a while, the only way I could drive was to listen to one of the "talking books" my mother insisted we take. Finally, I couldn't drive at all, and moaned and groaned in the passenger seat. I wanted to stop, but VV was hellbent on making El Paso that night (and there were no motels in sight anyway).

The Compassionate One said, "If you're going to throw up, just tell me and I'll pull over."

After maintaining a tortured silence, I yelled, "I have to puke. Hurry, pull over!"

Like a "Dukes of Hazard" star, VV braked the car into a tailspin, skidded past the other cars on the highway, and jumped our Festiva onto an exit ramp. Like another "Dukes of Hazard" star, I was out of the car before it stopped.

I puked and puked all over that exit ramp somewhere in Texas, leaving a monument to our trip there, the way the astronauts planted a flag on the moon. You'd think that when you puke your guts out, you'd feel better, right? But a few minutes later I was groaning again. We were almost in El Paso now, and so we pulled off at the first motel. It cost almost 40 bucks for the room, there was a dead fly on VV's bed, the bathtub had cigarette burns all over it and the tap water tasted like chalk. This was the room where I spent the night of my illness. No sooner would I puke than I'd need to puke again, for hours and hours, until my back ached with the strain of retching.

Finally the sun dawned over polluted El Paso like a wad of flem splattered across the sky. I was weak but at least I'd stopped vomiting. Now, I have to admit, VV did become very sympathetic, and even offered to stay in this hell hole another night if I couldn't stand to be in the car. But with the aid of Gingerale, I was able to ride in the car and even smile wanly.

Arizona

We were headed to Tucson to stay with a friend of VV's. But when we got into the city that night, we found it impossible to follow the friend's directions because about half of Tucson had been blocked off for the making of a Mel Gibson movie--our second brush with Hollywood. To complicate things, VV's friend lied in a "guest house" off an alley and behind another house--VV ended up ringing a doorbell and forcing the inhabitant to lend us his phone to call her friend Sara (?). (I've forgotten the friend's name because we saw her for a total of about ten minutes.)

So finally we found the house we wanted. Sara? Wasn't there (she was in the middle of final exams), but her roommates and their three cats and giant dog Betsy greeted us at the door. Betsy was the best dog in the world--she'd look at you with big goo-goo eyes and wag her tail constantly. When one of the cats swatted her in the face, Betsy simply wagged her tail in a

Pagan worships Betsy the dog, while Sara(?) and cat look on.

confused way and backed off. In the course of my stay there, I decided that Betsy was a Buddha who'd been reincarnated as a dog--how else could you explain so much kindness? So I declared her my goddess and began to worship her.

Tucson is another place that wins Pagan's highest laud: the Summertime-and-the-Livin-Is-Easy, I'd-Move-There-If-I-Could City Award. For one thing, it's small enough that you can get around by bike or by foot. And the streets are paved with thrift shops! There's even a huge, department-store-style place where everything they sell is used. I found lots of 1960s shirts with the tags still on 'em! Tucson also had a food coop and a college--two indispensables in Pagan's book. And if you drive for about 15 minutes (as we did our last day there), you can hang out in beautiful, cactus-laden deserts--a lot of the land is protected from development by the state. What I liked most about Tucson was its laid-back, groovin' feel; it seems like a town where people drink iced herb tea and play backgammon, where

you could thrive on ten hours of work a week, where you can have a dog and three cats and your roommates won't mind.

One of Sara?'s roommates was a female firefighter who carved bowls out of tree burls. She suggested that on our way up to the Grand Canyon, we check out Sedona, Arizona, which is supposed to have a "vortex," out of which flows all the good energy for the Western world. "I don't know if I believe it," she said, "but I'll tell you this: You can feel something when you go there."

We drove that day through Phoenix--which must have a vortex of evil, because it sucked us in as we tried to pass it by on the highway. Then we wound our way through the high mountains of Arizona, where the air is thin and the sky ethereally blue.

Sedona was up in this high country, a little town among the red canyons, where breathing the air feels like drinking the clearest spring water. I have to admit that I felt high there too--but maybe just because Virginia's nail polish remover had leaked all over the car.

One of the first things we saw in Sedona was a house and garden that had been decorated with Finster-style kook monuments. Out front was a huge no-war assemblage; a wooden structure that could be turned like a prayer wheel, from which chili peppers hung; and a tiki god. The roof of the house had an exercise bench and a toilet nailed to the shingles.

"Stop the car!" Pagan demanded, and we went in to visit.

We were greeted by a hippie in a sailor cap who looked just like Bruce Dern. (He's the washed-up actor who used to have cameo roles in drug movies. He plays the acid-head artists in *Psych Out*, Peter Fonda's LSD mentor in *The Trip* and the environmentalist gone psycho in *Silent Running*.)

When VV asked him if he was Bruce Dern, he said, "Yeah," grinning as if he meant, "if your trip is that you want me to be Bruce Dern, I can go along with that, man."

"Well, congratulations on your daughter's career," I said.

The hippie showed us around--it turned out that we'd stumbled onto a gallery of sorts, and he wanted to sell us art. There were some terrible water color landscapes, even worse Indians sculpted out of tree trunks (how demeaning!), and the obligatory crystal jewelry. We pretended to like it, and also plied him with questions about the vortex, which

Anti-war monument

he evaded.

But he did pass on some wisdom. "I want to give you a special message, four words," he said. VV and I leaned forward. Bruce paused dramatically, then said slowly, "Love works. Fear don't."

I was disappointed in his message, which made me argumentative. "I agree with you," I said. "But the problem is, it's easy to know that intellectually, but it's almost impossible to really go around not being afraid and loving everyone."

← VV poses with Bruce Dern.

"I'll tell you how to do it," Bruce said, holding up a finger. "What's your favorite color."

"Black," I said, thinking he'd give me shit for that, but he didn't.

"What's your favorite shape?"

"Circle," I said.

"OK, whenever you're having trouble, just meditate on black circles," he said, as if he'd just revealed the secret of the universe.

"Well thanks," we said, "bye now, gotta go." But before we left, he insisted that we must all hold hands and ohm. I'm humiliated to say that the vortex had so affected our minds that VV and I ohmed our little hearts out.

Only later did I realize the full significance of what Bruce had told me. What is a black circle? A coffee cup seen from the top. So when I'm depressed, I must head for the coffee maker. Hey, I knew that.

Flagstaff

Not far from the vortex is Grand Canyon town. Flagstaff is actually more than an hour from the canyon, but its the closest place to get a shower and a cup of joe.

We arrived there after dark and I insisted we stop at the first motel we saw because it was so beautiful. The Auto-Lodge was painted mind green and had a carport--and in every other way looked exactly as it must have in 1962.

That night we glued ourselves to the TV set in our room, hoping to see "Babes," a show we'd heard was about three fat women who sleep in the same bed. But the magic TV in the Auto-Lodge could only tune in shows from its own era.

The next morning, as we drove through town (it took three minutes), we found that the Auto-Lodge was no anomaly in Flagstaff. THE WHOLE TOWN LOOKED LIKE THE SET OF "TWIN PEAKS," FOR GOD'S SAKE! Most buildings were circa 1965, with a heavy emphasis on he hewn-pine-tree-with forest-green-trim look that reminded me of the nature center I used to visit when I was five.

As we drove through silent forests with snow on the ground, the air crisp and bright, Virginia gushed about the beauty of nature while Pagan sulked. I was visiting the Grand Canyon under duress. I get bored looking at nature; so I consoled myself by insisting that the

Grand Canyon is actually kitsch, the ultimate roadside attraction.

I perked up when we stopped in Bedrock, Arizona, where someone had erected a Flintstones theme park (Bedrock, U.S.A.) that as bordered by a stone-age wall made out of giant bones and pink rocks. We took advantage of the

many free photo opportunities and visited the (unheated) gift shop, but due to arctic wind conditions, were not able to tour the theme park itself.

It costs ten bucks to get into the Grand Canyon, and it's not worth it. We spent several hours hiking around the perimeter of the canyon as I tried to summon up some awe, even though the view just kept looking flat as a postcard. I was trying to be a good sport, but when VV wanted to hike down the ice-covered trail that goes eighteen miles into the canyon, that's where I drew the line.

"You go ahead; I'll wait for you in the gift shop," I said. We ended up hanging around and reading the historical-marker signs for grammar and punctuation errors.

Then, thank God, we left, heading back down into the desert. Our drive that night was particularly surreal. For instance, we happened to pull over at a rest stop the size of a small city, where every store was designed for truckers. It's the only place I've ever seen where you can buy those mud flaps with chrome naked ladies on them. And as we neared Las Vegas, a series of road signs decorated with fifties graphics (like an X-ed out champagne glass) warned us not to drink, sleep or speed.

Weirdest of all was the Hoover Dam. It was lit up as brightly as a stage in the middle of the black desert, and the thing was so huge--with its giant towers and massive girders sinking at an angle into the water--that I felt as dwarfed as as character in the movie *Metropolis*. The architecture is that 1940s Federal style that looks like it comes from a Communist country. As you drive along, madly negotiating your way through the curving bridges and locks and mountains, you glimpse one tower with a clock on it that says, "Arizona Time," and then another--set an hour earlier--that says "Nevada Time." At that point, the dam seemed to me a creation of a government that was so powerful it could not only bring an ocean into the desert, but control the very nature of time.

Las Vegas

We'd heard that hotel rooms and meals are cheap--and drinks are free as long as you're gambling--in this city where they'll do anything to keep you losing money. True enough, a hotel room with two beds in downtown Las Vegas only cost us $30. Bu what a room! The windows had metal gratings on

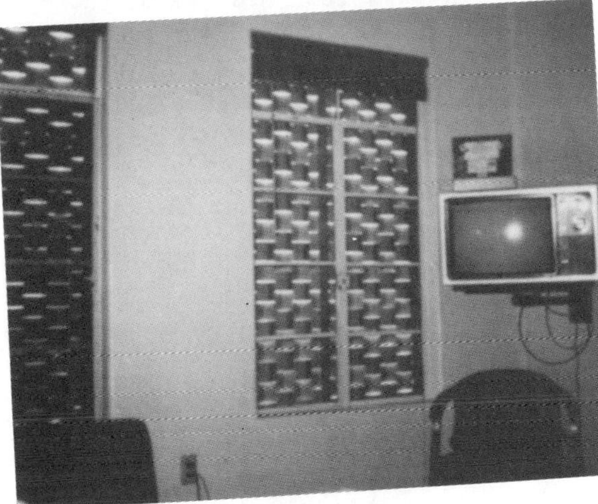

Our hotel room

them, to block out the light from the giant "Nudes on Ice" neon sign across the street. Likewise, when we went downstairs for dinner, we found the restaurant to be incredibly cheap--dinner specials were about $3. But though the food look delicious in a junky way--French fries and jumbo shrimp and iceberg lettuce--it tasted like rancid cardboard.

← lucky lady

Everything in our hotel had this air of false elegance, of barely disguised decay: The hotel clerk looked like a prostitute. The lobby (a casino, so you could go down and play slots in your pajamas if you wanted) was full of black-jack dealers wearing polyester tuxes. The rug looked like it had two tons of cigarette ashes rubbed into it. The women wore too much make-up; the men had their hair combed over their bald spots; and everyone had shifty eyes.

We went to gamble as The Golden Nugget--a hotel a few doors down--which was glitzy and tacky instead of just plain scummy.

VV sat down at a table with a dealer and four serious gamblers. She'd bought $20 worth of chips and slowly her pile dwindled. However, as promised, she did get free drinks. A cocktail waitress with poofy hair in an outfit like a bathing suit brought her watered-down whiskey sours.

Meanwhile, I got bored and went over to the slots. I've never been interested in gambling: Maybe it's my Puritan upbringing, but it doesn't seem possible to make money without paying for it with hard work. While this turns most Puritans into workaholics, it's taught me to be lazy: I'm happy to live without much money or much work. Even gambling is too much work for me--working a slot machine seems as boring and repetitive as doing some wage-slave job like data entry.

I'd said I wouldn't gamble in Las Vegas, but there was nothing else to do, so I put a few quarters in the slots to watch the clowns and bells and cherries roll by. I won. Then, I felt I had to keep playing the slots until I got rid of the pile of quarters I'd accumulated. But

I kept winning. I ended up with a huge pile of quarters, $15 worth it turned out. VV, who'd lost her pile, said I was lucky. But my winning streak only made me hate and fear gambling all the more; it's like dealing with the IRS. They may give you a rebate once and a while, but you know it's only to lull you into submission so they can take all your money later.

The next day we decided to split Las Vegas. But no sooner were we past the city limits than it became imperative to stop, because a huge sign promised Bonnie and Clyde's Original Death Car. Astute readers will remember that VV and I had run across another death car, in Tennessee. That death car turned out to be a fake, a movie prop. When it comes to death cars, I accept no substitutes. I want to know that real bullets passed through the holes in the fenders, and that real people's heads crashed through into the windshield. I go with the hope that some brain tissue or blood from a famous person's body might still cling to the broken glass. Only then will a death car make history come alive.

←Clyde mannequin lurks in background

The Bonnie and Clyde Death Car met those criteria. There was a bullet-ridden, beat-up Ford; there was as historic plaque; there was a lack of security that made it easy to touch the battered sides of the car; there were even mannequins--with ugly, uncombed wigs askew, plastic machine guns and K-mart versions of twenties costumes--to represent the famous couple.

This magnificent display was right in the middle of a casino called Whiskey Pete's, which was amazing in itself. Built to look like a castle on the outside, inside Whiskey Pete's is a huge warehouse of slot machines, whores, bars, drug addicts, and good-for-nothing youths--and all of this before noon. I felt like I'd stumbled into one of those dens of sin so lavishly illustrated in Jack Chick's scathing Christian comic books. I've always thought sin had a sort of dignity--Mick Jagger wearing a velvet robe and quoting Nietzsche in *Performance*. I had never realized that sin could shoddy. But maybe I'm confusing sin with being down and out.

We stopped for lunch in the middle of the Mojave Desert, at a diner where everyone knew each other. Next to this diner--in the middle of the most barren desert you can imagine--was a duck pond. A strange ecosystem.

Outside the diner, a government-type sign said, "Early Man Site, 3.6 Miles." So, always ready for educational tourist spots, we took off in search of prehistoric man and woman.

The signs led us through the desert along a road that was nothing but packed-down sand. The little Festiva chugged along bravely for miles. Finally, we came to a broken-down shack, and our efforts were vastly rewarded, because we had stumbled upon the MOST BORING TOURIST ATTRACTION IN THE USA! On view inside the shack were copies of some rocks that had been chipped at by long-ago tool makers. The guy behind the desk gave us a map of the site: You can spend the entire day touring the pits and mounds from which these rocks were excavated. You won't see any remains of early man, but you will see lots of remains of the archeologists: Dorito bags, big holes in the sand, net fences, piles of dirt. Appropriately, the early man site offered the most boring postcard ever--three rocks lying next to a ruler.

California

OK, now I'm going to have to speed things up, otherwise I'll never finish this stupid magazine.

Next stop was L.A.--we stayed with the sister of a friend of VV's. Lee lives with her guy Patrick and their baby Sam right off Montrose--the sorta hep, sorta too-trendy main drag in West Hollywood. (Correct me if I'm wrong, L.A.ers.) Pagan and VV went to visit Mann's Chinese Theater and the street with all the stars embedded on the sidewalk. When Lucy and Ethel visit these tourist traps on "I Love Lucy," it all seems kind of swanky. But the truth is, Hollywood is like a little strip of sleazy New York on the West Coast--complete with street hawkers, con artists, guys who try to touch you and bored prostitutes.

At night, we went out to dinner with VV's friend Gary. He revealed that VV is actually a countess in Germany (East). YES, THIS IS REALLY TRUE. Obviously she can't go back and reclaim her throne in these unimaginative modern times, but she does still retain the title which is so long I can't remember it. All this time I had been traveling with royalty! It gave my cross-country trip a new cachet.

Though I wasn't supposed to, I like L.A. Lee makes a good living writing the blurbs on the back of videotape boxes, and many of her friends are screenplay writers or script readers. I liked what I glimpsed of her high-powered world of schmoozing and writing and networking.

Along the way to Santa Cruz (VV's final destination) we stopped at the fabulous Madonna Inn. No, it's not a hotel where they show banned Madonna videos in every room. It's more like a place where your grandma takes you when you're ten, and you eat three slices of German Black Forest cake and throw up when you get home.

Everything at the Madonna Inn is pink--from the sugar on the tables to the cash register slips on which they ring up your souvenirs. The decor is a cross between "Falcon Crest" nouveau riche and mad Kind Louis: wacky stained-glass windows; a "cute" doll on a swing, which rocks back and forth near the ceiling; gooey pink luv seats; a golden tree that spreads its branches across the formal dining room. And of course each hotel room is decorated according to a different nutty theme--like the caveman room and the Indian room.

DISCLAIMER

This story contains graphic depictions of people using up precious oil as they drive long distances--thereby contributing to the Greenhouse Effect and a perilous world situation. Pagan does not endorse car ownership or driving in general, except as a means to discover America. For local travel, she uses her bike, public transportation or her own two feet. She strongly suggests you do the same.

As we neared Santa Cruz, VV began to eat huge meals--whole pizzas and Pad Thais disappeared into her skinny frame. She was terrified: Soon we'd pull up at Willie's house. Willie was the real reason she was moving to earthquake-torn Santa Cruz. The two love birds had only spent a few weeks together in Boston after they'd been introduced by mutual friends, but they knew it was much more than a hunch--they could somehow form a family (OK, not a family, gut that's how the song goes). At the time, VV had been wanting to quit her job and move out of Boston, and when she met dream-guy Willie, she went for it.

Poor Virginia. She was facing a new relationship and the prospect of finding a job and a place to live in a strange city;

everything in her life was an unknown, and the girl was a mess.

Late that night, we pulled up in front of a run-down house with four VW hippie buses in the yard, none of which appeared to work. There was no street number on the house, but somehow we knew we'd come to the right place. And we had, because soon Willie appeared in the door and they had a tearful reunion--after Virginia rushed around looking for her cat Spud, who had preceded us to California.

Santa Cruz is unrelentingly groovy: Even gas station mini-marts carry carrot juice, and

WILLIE: DREAM GUY
A PAGAN'S HEAD EXCLUSIVE

Description: Tall with tousled brown hair and groovy amber eyes that pierce into your soul.
Ambition: To make YOU happy.
Occupation: Part-time janitor at a Jewish temple. Sensitive guy Willie has also written a novel.
Turn ons: Brazil, gymnastics, soy cheese, sleeping on the job.
Turn offs: Kids who attend the Temple's youth group. They make a big mess and Willie doesn't dig that because then he has to wake up!
Sign: Unknown, but I'd guess Leo, 'cause he's a guy who goes for what he wants.

every street has a bike lane. Even though this was sort of annoying, after a few days I was talking about moving to The Cruz as well. Happiness seemed so simple there. Everything's in walking distance; vegetarian food is plentiful; there's a college I could teach at; all the women in the aerobics classes have hairy armpits too; it's sunny; life is slow and easy. Life seemed especially slow and easy at the home of Willie and his roommate Lou. Due to an insane landlady, they have a huge house with a great view for about $150 a month each. (Santa Cruz rents tend toward $300 or more per person in a group house.) Pagan stayed more than a week in an unused wing of the Willie/Lou mansion.

I normally hate nature, but couldn't help falling under the spell of Santa Cruz's empty beaches echoing with the barks of sea lions. One sunset, VV and I played Frisbee on a beach where the waves were as thin as veils, and all the pinks of the sky showed through them. I know, I know, it sounds like a scene that would be air-brushed onto a seventies van, but the colors were so beautiful that I felt like I was on drugs.

High in the redwood forests near Santa Cruz, trees grow backwards, golf balls roll upwards, and a cabin leans at an insane angle on a steep hillside. This is the famous Santa Cruz mystery spot. VV and I, still in tourist mode, insisted that Willie escort us to the Spot. As it turned out, we were the only Americans on the tour; everyone else was Japanese. Our tour guide, the spitting image of Larry "Bud" Melman, tried to communicate with them in their own language, but they just giggled.

Once inside the mystery cabin, Willie and Pagan clung to the walls while VV and the Japanese cavorted in the twisted gravity that made us all lean wackily to one side. Both Willie and I felt awful there, like we had terrible hangovers tinged with an acid paranoia. I was pleased that Willie was a fellow stick-in-the-mud, and that he and I could whine together, dampening the spirits of the ever-enthusiastic VV.

VV and Willie had to drive a lusty teen to San Francisco (it's a long story) so I got a ride with them into the city and began my own adventures. After a month of traveling with VV, it was weird to be alone. I missed her.

San Francisco

Everyone told me I'd love SF, but I HATED it. I don't have the energy to explain why. I'll just say it seemed as dangerous as New York but without the compensating career opportunities--though maybe I got that impression because most of my friends lived in scary neighborhoods or had jobs they hated.

However, it was great to see so many long-lost friends. I stayed in the Mission with the Buck Boys, a household of computer hippies who are developing some kind of on-line library.

Then it was off to Berkeley, where I stayed with my younger sister (now my older sister because I've changed my age), who's in the grad school there for Latin American studies. I liked Berkeley--a town where a great cup of coffee is never more than ten feet away--much better than the bewildering SF.

I was now using the Donnie & Marie 45 box I got in Knoxville as a purse, which made it impossible to get down the streets of Berkeley without notice. People stopped me, wanting to fondle the bag, and I was forced to point out to each of them the two sides of the bag--showing the Polyester D&M and the Rockin' D&M. I was also obliged to pontificate on how half of the body of the youngest Osmond, Jimmy, appears on one side (the young boy looking like the forty-year-old Elvis) as if he is half in and half out of the show-business world. One of my D&M admirers told me that his mom owns a store on Haight Street, and that she sells boxes like mine for hundreds of dollars!

I spent Thanksgiving with the Famiglia Purpura--my college pal Mary's new family. Since I'd last seen her, she'd married an Italian writer named Paolo--or come to think of it, are they married?--and had two beautiful boys, Ely or "the bad seed," and Alissao (sp?). Full of bravado and gumption, Mary had decided we'd make ravioli from scratch for our Thanksgiving feast. After five hours, we had about twenty tiny, perfectly formed pieces of ravioli, two screaming children covered in flour, and a kitchen that looked like the ceiling had fallen in on it.

Thanksgiving was like a scene from a Fellini movie, as Russians, French and Italians drank wine and gabbed about literature and life. The Thanksgiving party also saw the reunion of three of the original members--Mary, Johhn and me--of the greatest band in the solar system, Planet Love (this was a cheesy psychedelic band that we formed in college).

I'd visited Johhn earlier in his Oakland digs, where I tried to convince him to continue his music career--he does banjo renditions of seventies songs now. However, he seems content to be supported as a gentleman of leisure by the Berkeley sociology department.

The Mystery Spot: Shouldn't someone tell NASA about this?

Thanksgiving day, I walked over to the Buck Boy's house to return their key and was treated to a surprise appearance by the famed Nietzsche Woman. I'd dubbed her that because she was in my Nietzsche seminar in college. After that year, she left Wesleyan to go off and live in Allston (!), which I'd never heard of at the time, and meet everyone I would later become friends with. The NW has caused me no end of confusion because she's a Wesleyan person who knows my non-Wesleyan friends. This leads me to introduce people to one another only to find out that, because of the NW, they already know one another, or indeed have slept together. The NW valiantly tried to call the guy who runs the Unknown Museum [illegible]) so that I could see that wonderful kook house; however, the Unknown Museum was still in transit to a new site at the time.

After much gabbing and networking, and after I'd finally figured out the dualistic SF subway, it was time for me to bid goodbye to the golden coast and make my way back to recession-wracked Boston.

On the plane, as I looked down at the white expanse of the Sierras and nudged the fifties-styled airplane silverware into my pocket, I thought about all I'd seen and experienced. How could the country I crossed now, gliding over it in six hours, be the same one I'd covered in a month of sleeping on floors, seeing old friends in new towns, eating Southern-fried tofu burgers, crossing rivers and driving into the fine blue expanse of sky? The truth is, we create a new America each time we travel it.

← What a lame conclusion!

Diary of a Boy Chaser

by Ingrid

← This means Ingrid wrote it

Pagan's note:
Ingrid is my pal and colleague—she's also a free-lance copy editor. We produced these pages one day when work was slow.

For me, as for most suburban teenagers, 1975 was a watershed year. At Peachtree High School, in Chamblee, Georgia, I ran with a pack of good, straight, middle-of the road girls, and what we ran after was boys. In 1975 I was 15 and held a learner's permit. Some of my friends had their actual licenses, which extended our boy-chasing period from school hours to all night long. The following passages are uncensored excerpts from my desktop diary. I feel compelled to add that this diary contains only facts and figures. My real, intimate diary disappeared that year. (My brother remains the prime suspect.) Please, reader, judge me not harshly.

General note: All the boys noted here were high-school jocks three to four years older than us. Except where noted, we never spoke a word to them. —Ingrid

18 JAN. 1975

game-Joe Horton, Carl Cutena

Monical's - in parking lot Joe Copeland, Mike Campbell Lee Autrey + Dave Hewitt pulled up next to us + drove around looking at us - we could have followed them but the car wouldn't start

18— SATURDAY, JAN. 18, 1975 —347

25 JAN. 1975

after meet followed Steve C. and Kenny over to Sheraton Inn - they met Jim, Tom Shehan & Tom Rosemond there (party) then to Monical's - Steve & Kenny got there at the same time as us & left. Then we ran David Dayton off the road & he blew his tire out. Went to his house + settled everything.

Whew!

25— SATURDAY, JAN. 25, 1975 —340

Jim, Tom, & Tom knew we were after them (went in circles to see if we'd follow them.

Red-haired girl on the periphery of our crowd. Would do anything.

28 JAN. 1975

At the game, we dared Beverly to ask Gary King how Tom was and she did!! He said, "I don't know, all right I guess."

We saw Mike Bailey drive by & he waved!

TUESDAY, JAN. 28, 1975 —337

Tom Calvert, class of '74. I considered him the love of my life and knew that someday we would speak and perhaps date. He was a tall, lanky basketball player with dark-rimmed glasses who drove a white VW bug and had once lived in my subdivision. I babysat for the new people in his house and stole a little knob from a kitchen cabinet to keep at home in a box.

12 FEB. 1975

← Tom was at school 5th period - I didn't see him but Christy and Teresa did.

Ken's picture in paper!

library with Shelly and Gerri - John was there!

Mike Bailey at school during our lunch period - I don't care.

MONDAY

1975	FEBRUARY					1975
SUN	MON	TUE	WED	THU	FRI	SAT
« »	« »	« »	« »	« »	« »	1
2	3	4	5	6	7	8
9	10	11	12	13	14	15
16	17	18	19	20	21	22
23	24	25	26	27	28	« »

17

FEB. 1975

WASHINGTON'S BIRTHDAY

WQXI started the "Get the Beatles Back Together" campaign the first station in U.S.A.!

TUESDAY

1975	MARCH					1975
SUN	MON	TUE	WED	THU	FRI	SAT
« »	« »	« »	« »	« »	« »	1
2	3	4	5	6	7	8
9	10	11	12	13	14	15
16	17	18	19	20	21	22
23/30	24/31	25	26	27	28	29

11

MAR. 1975

Chap. 20 questions and maps due

Evel Knievel on Mike Douglas

Eng. questions and essay due

I was a dutiful student.

TUESDAY

1975	FEBRUARY					1975
SUN	MON	TUE	WED	THU	FRI	SAT
« »	« »	« »	« »	« »	« »	1
2	3	4	5	6	7	8
9	10	11	12	13	14	15
16	17	18	19	20	21	22
23	24	25	26	27	28	« »

25

FEB. 1975

flag

Reference unknown.

George Harrison's 32nd

Renay said that she heard on WQXI that they might get back together and ~~do~~ an album and then tour the U.S.!

Tom was up at school but naturally I wasn't there.
I'd already gone home

Naturally. Fine sense of irony, even at 15.

TUESDAY

1975	APRIL					1975
SUN	MON	TUE	WED	THU	FRI	SAT
« »	« »	1	2	3	4	5
6	7	8	9	10	11	12
13	14	15	16	17	18	19
20	21	22	23	24	25	26
27	28	29	30	« »	« »	« »

29

APRIL 1975

saw Tom!!!

Just for a split-second. He was sitting in his car, outside school & we drove by (on way to dentist, 5th period) when I came back his car was there but didn't see him. Looked all over the school (Kate & I) but we never saw him.

TUESDAY

1975	MARCH					1975
SUN	MON	TUE	WED	THU	FRI	SAT
« »	« »	« »	« »	« »	« »	1
2	3	4	5	6	7	8
9	10	11	12	13	14	15
16	17	18	19	20	21	22
23/30	24/31	25	26	27	28	29

4

MAR. 1975

got lit. books in English - I got Ralph Clark's old book! (just by accident.)

Wore a dress to school - 1st time all year!

TUESDAY

1975	APRIL					1975
SUN	MON	TUE	WED	THU	FRI	SAT
« »	« »	1	2	3	4	5
6	7	8	9	10	11	12
13	14	15	16	17	18	19
20	21	22	23	24	25	26
27	28	29	30	« »	« »	« »

1

APRIL 1975

Wow! Wonder if that serve made it over the net!

I SAW TOM!!!

at volleyball practice - we were playing and I was just about to serve and I heard someone behind me and it was Tom! I only saw him for a second, he was leaving the gym. 1st time this year!

Pagan apologizes to the physically challenged for the contents of this page.

The Boston Globe

THURSDAY, NOVEMBER 1, 1990

Silber, Weld renew debate on the stump

This cartoon by my pal Diane requires a lengthy explanation: Crazed Neo-Nazi Silber was running on the Democratic ticket in our state. Though Silber had one arm, the press discretely avoided this issue. Pagan thought it should be a major anti-Silber rallying point. To wit, in the event of a nuclear attack on Massachusetts, would Silber be able to push the button? The above suggestive headline made Diane think of Silber's stump and Pagan's poem: "Hitler had one testicle, Silber has one arm. The only difference between them is Hitler had more charm."

6

THE BIG CAR

ONE NIGHT in April 1991, my mother called. Dad had lung cancer. He would die within six months. The news was so horrible, so sudden, and yet it hit with the dull thud of an expected tragedy. Ever since I was a kid, he'd worked like a maniac, getting up at 5 A.M. and coming home late. And then a few months ago, he'd admitted he couldn't take the pace anymore. "I'm so tired I forget people's names," he'd said to us—my mother, my sister, and me. His first admission of frailty opened a crack in our lives, a slit through which we glimpsed what would follow.

Even living under a death sentence, Dad remained capable and sensible. He planned to travel, enjoy himself, and when the end came he would resort only to painkillers. Instead of checking into a hospital, he would stay at home, his death supervised only by us and by a hospice organization. (Hospices are private companies that provide nurses, medical supplies, painkillers, and counseling to patients who have chosen to die without medical intervention.) There would be no life-support systems or last-ditch operations, no useless tests, no denial.

But the doctors—with their promises of a few more weeks of life, a little less pain—eventually talked him into several harrowing lung operations and a round of chemo. Not only did those procedures fail to stop the advance of his cancer, they sometimes amounted to torture.

I visited him often, and his decline shocked me. For a while, he remained the hearty man I knew. Then, after the chemo, he became bald and frail. After the lung operations, his hair grew back steel gray instead of brown, his cheeks sank in, and his eyes seemed pathetically large. Only when he spoke did I remember the powerful man he used to be, the one who started his own company and sat on city planning boards. "The way this hospital is run is very interesting," he'd say, listing the hierarchies he'd noticed among the doctors, the habits of the nurses. A part of him could float out of his wasted body and watch the world with as much intelligence as ever.

I stopped working on *Pagan's Head* when I heard the news about Dad. I also stopped working on my novel, which—weirdly—was about two sisters whose father had just died of lung cancer; I felt haunted and guilty by the way my book had predicted my father's illness, and didn't touch it for a long time. I did keep on writing for magazines and newspapers; in fact, I asked for, and was allowed to have, a column in the *Voice Literary Supplement* about 'zines.

I thought that I didn't want to publish another *Pagan's Head* because it seemed too silly, too out-of-key with the hell I was going through. But then, I don't know, after a few months I got so tired of being *sad* all the time. So I started working on the 'zine again. It seemed like a happy refuge from the stomach-churning Tilt-A-Whirl of my life, those wrenching phone calls and visits. Pagan[1] never concerned herself with death—the big issues for her were hair and gossip. In Issue Six, I discussed nothing more traumatic than my search for a used car.

Meanwhile, I kept myself busy and diverted with yet another crazy Pagan project. A few months after Dad got sick, my friend Peter had suggested we put *Pagan's Head* on TV—he would produce "The Pagan Show" on community-access cable. I took him up on this offer; the show seemed like another way to distract myself. So we agreed: I would supply the content; he'd do the music, filler sounds, cheesy video effects.

Even more so than my 'zine, the TV show became an all-consuming project that summer. We created an opening bit, very much like the opening of a sitcom. In it, I'm walking down the streets of Allston, waving and smiling. At the last moment, I throw my headband in the air and the shot freezes, just like the opening credits of "The Mary Tyler Moore Show."

We made a video spot about my ex-roommate Linda, following her around as she picked through garbage and expounded on the history of Allston group houses. We planned to show some footage we'd found of William Shatner reciting "Rocket Man." We also lined up a bunch of nutty guests who I would interview.

Creating a TV show—even if it was only for a community cable station—was a trip. How many times, strolling through Allston, had I imagined myself as a character in a sitcom or movie, credits rolling and theme song swelling as I walked? How often had I, as a kid, imagined myself hanging out with the Mod Squad or exploring the Banana Splits' mansion? The line between TV and reality—between fantasy and life—had always been very thin for me, and now I'd crossed over. I would step through the looking glass into a TV Wonderland where Pagan[1] was as real as any sitcom character or talk-show host. For the hour-long program—which would be shot live, except for a few video clips—she would control my body, speak through me. I'd been inhabited by Pagan[1] before. Sometimes at parties or among strangers, I'd find myself adopting a bratty, self-assured personality that came out of my 'zine. But this would be different. Now Pagan[1] would have her own theme song; her world would be documented in video segments; she would speak on live TV. She would be real.

Two weeks before the show was supposed to air, my mother called again. Dad had suddenly gotten worse. I flew home the next day. Aboard the plane, I looked down on a tumble of clouds below me that lay in ugly heaps, like dirty laundry. The silver wing outside my window glared in the sun, hurting my eyes. The airplane smelled like a hospital.

When you are deep in grief, that is all you are. You can't remember what foods you used to crave or why you loved them; you can't imagine going for a bike ride just for the joy of it, or calling up a friend to tell her something funny. There is only the sickening twist of your stomach, the ache of your chest. On that plane, I wasn't Pagan or Pagan[1] or any of my selves. I was just a woman hanging several miles high in the air, with nothing underneath.

It all happens in...
THIS MEDICATION NOT TO BE USED AFTER Dec. '91
PAGAN'S
HEAD #6
The Big Car Issue
Plus...
NETWORKING IN NEW YORK
GOSSIP
DAVID CASSIDY
MY WRITING GROUP
A more happiness for Planet Earth production
$2

PAGAN FOR BEGINNERS

Pagan's Head is the official publication of Pagan Kennedy, who is a person, not a religion. Pagan Kennedy was nicknamed "Pagan" in high school by her friend Saira after Pagan tried to instigate a protest against the prayers they were forced to say in assembly.

Pagan, who is a struggling fiction writer, started this magazine as a way to procrastinate. Over the six issues that now exist, the Pagan character has evolved into someone more flamboyant, fabulous and frivolous than the real Pagan. This character she created--with the same name and physical attributes as herself--suggested to the real Pagan an unexplored avenue of literature. She would write about her own life in such a way as to transform it into a parody of itself; she would become a living parody of herself.

Winterized Pagan sticking out tongue by mistake

Pagan is now officially a columnist for the Village Voice! Twice a year, she'll do a report about fanzines and marginal publishing for the Voice Literary Supplement. And after much pleading on the part of the Voice staff, Pagan finally agreed to do over 10 articles or book reviews a year for the VLS--so subscribe today.

Pagan Classic®

What's the biggest advertising word of the last few years? Classic--as in Coke Classic, Macintosh Classic, Citibank Classic Checking Account, and on and on. What a perfect word to assuage our anxieties and at the same time make us feel, well, classy. "Classic" simultaneously implies old money snobbishness and no-frills thrift, a melding of the time-worn and familiar with the new and fashionable.

Thus Pagan announces her latest image: Pagan Classic. It's the Pagan you've come to love without the grungy hair-styles and frightening fashion statements. Gone are the dreadlocks, horn-rimmed glasses, ripped tights and combat boots. Say hello to a simplified, sleeker Pagan--a Pagan who's gone from hip to timeless.

The elements of this statement? First, an insouciant red page-boy to frame the Pagan head you've already come to know. Next, barely-there wire-frame glasses with rectangular rims that are a little bit Ben Franklin and a little bit Mrs. Beasley. And her clothes sum up the simple elegance, too! Black jeans or ski pants paired with the basic white T--what could be easier? We think you're going to find a lot to love in the new Pagan--without the fuss and muss of the old one!

Yes, it's true! Pagan will have her own talk show on TV--Somerville Cable TV, that is. See all the pals you've read about live and uncensored as they sound off about Q-tips, careers, the weather and their hobbies. The pilot is scheduled to air Dec. 3.

↑ this landmark no longer exists.

PAGAN'S MAIL BAG

People rarely send letters to Pagan's Head, the magazine. Most send letters to Pagan as an entire gestalt, and therefore to publish the letters I'd have to give lots of background info about the writer and it would be a big pain.

Of course, when people do send letters to the Pagan's Head, the magazine, I usually lose them anyway. All this is to explain why there are only two letters in the letters column.

The following is from Phil Milstein, famed Boston recluse, collector and Forced Exposure writer. He's also working on putting out an album called "The Beat of the Traps," which anthologizes songs made at vanity recording studios (the kind of place where you send in lyrics and money, and they turn it into a song(!)). Phil and I have several friends in common, so when he ordered my magazine as if I were a stranger, I blasted him for pretending not to know who I was.

Here's his response:

Dear Ms. Kennedy:

While it is true that I have been aware of your existence, I surely would not know who you were, even if our cars were to collide and we were forced to exchange papers. (In fact, come to think of it, even then I probably would not know who you were, since parents didn't start giving their newborn daughters names like Pagan prior to 1966 at the very earliest).

It's odd how the puzzles sometimes come together very abruptly. For instance, in the past week I received correspondences from both Virginia [see Pagan's Head #5] and the people at Kreature Comforts, each referring to this Pagan character as if it's someone I'm supposed to know.

As per your request, here is your copy of the Beat of the Traps. I've finished out the tape with another album that might be to your liking, The Dream World of Dion McGregor. It was released in 1964, and is an honest-to-god recording of a man who not only talks in his sleep, he actually narrates his dreams. His "roommate" would record these sessions. [Next, a list of everything on the tape he sent me]

In this ever-changing world, I remain,
Phil Milstein

The final letter comes from an ex-co-worker who now works a reporter at Ad Week:

I was in Primal Plunge and I saw Pagan's Head. At first I thought it must be about post-Christian dieties--boy was I wrong! You are onto something and I like your efforts better than other self-named magazines such as Forbes, which doesn't even have a 70s page. Pagan's Head is a literary work equaled only to Joan Didion (in her morose phase) and certain Star Trek episodes (the one with the Horta).
Peace, Dave G.

NC NJ NY SC V NE G M P
UNITE OR DIE

Pagan salutes...

Pagan salutes old people, whose wealth of memories and wisdom make them a national treasure. She especially salutes our elders for meticulously keeping up old cars so that young hipsters can buy them for a song and run them into the ground.

Pagan salutes America's veterans for risking their lives to defend our freedom (sometimes wrongheadedly, but let's not quibble). She especially salutes our veterans for founding AmVets, the best and cheapest damn thrift store in all of Allston.

Pagan thanks...

Thanks to Max for saving about $200 worth of Letraset from being thrown away and putting it into the hands of Pagan. Thanks to Ingrid for medical clip art, and Jason, Tony and all the Typotech copy professionals for their dedication to making my slip-shod layouts look as good as possible. Thanks to Leslie B for Lava Lamp press packet.

Pagan confesses
I Was a Slant-Six Slut

Okay, ridicule me, call me a hypocrite. Though for years I've railed against cars as the ultimate evil, a few months ago I decided to get one.

First of all, the magazine where I most frequently free-lance, PC Week, moved out to the Mystic River--an hour and a half by public transportation or 40 minutes by bike. And what a bike ride! I pass through the most hipster-hating neighborhoods of Somerville, negotiate some major highways and finally cut through the mystical wasteland of Medford, where shopping carts poke out of the river and smokestacks loom over abandonned train tracks. I just couldn't imagine that commute in the cold.

In fact, the whole biking thing has been cramping my style the past few winters. Forget going to a party when it's 20 degrees out--a night of fun is not worth frostbite. Even when I do manage to get somewhere, I arrive in five layers of wool instead of a fashionable ripped dress and tights. I'm sick of the black policeman's socks, the sweat-pants over pants, the three layers of gloves, that make winter biking possible. Moreover, I'm really sick of being trapped in the house while all the car owners are out whooping it up (or so I imagine).

Also, I had a revelation, of sorts. A car isn't just a fossil-fuel-burning hulk of environmental poison; it can be an indispensable fashion accessory, too! What I needed was the automotive equivalent to one of those 1970s polyester button-down shirts that have shiny photographs of waterfalls or autumn trees on them--a car so mass-produced and ugly that it hadn't yet become over-priced, the kind of bold fashion statement that comes cheap. Even if I had to attach a rope to my new car and drag it behind me, I was determined to have a nutty early '70s Valiant, Dart, Polera or something.

How would I get the car--look through the paper? Go to used car lots? No, of course not. I'd network: I told everyone I knew to find me a car.

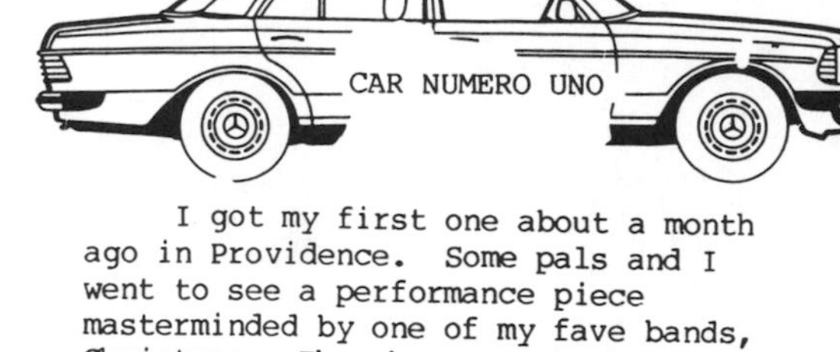

I got my first one about a month ago in Providence. Some pals and I went to see a performance piece masterminded by one of my fave bands, Christmas. The show was the best I've ever seen in my life--sort of like if Gwar had brought a tiki lounge to the stage, complete with a smoking volcano, a comedian in a Suffering Bastard costume, and an orchestra playing Herb Albert-style cocktail music. It was also a game show, and at the end of the night, they awarded the contestant a thrift-shop TV. They were supposed to give away a car, I'd heard, but its battery had been stolen just before the show.

That car--I kept thinking about it. Where was it, and how could I wheedle my way into getting it? After the show, we went to the exclusive party at Liz Cox's house. Out front, among many, many cars was parked a Plymouth Scamp--white interior, vinyl top, "Scamp" written in nutty letters. It was my dream car, and I knew in an instant, with an intuition honed after years of combing through thrift stores, that it could be mine.

I was too awed to even speak to Christmas' lead guitarist, Michael Cudahy, so I found his brother Nicholas (who's also in the band but seemed more approachable). Nicholas politely deflected the screeching enthusiasm of a hell-bent Pagan: Though the car I'd spotted was the right one, it belonged to his brother, and I'd have to ask him.

I would just have to overcome my fear and talk to Michael. This proved to be easy, since I found him in a drunken stupor. Sure, he slurred, you can have it--the only problem is the brakes are mushy and there's a spring that's about to cut through the fuel line and cause the car to blow up.

A few days later I called a now-sober Michael to firm things up. Much to my surprise, he turned out to be a long-time Pagan's Head fan. In fact, he was thrilled to think that his vehicle might now cradle the famed Pagan buttocks.

"I can barely speak, I'm so intimidated to be talking to a real writer," he said.

At which point Pagan minced, "I'm even more intimidated by you!"

This embarrassing L.A.-style banter went on until arrangements were made for Pagan to visit her new car.

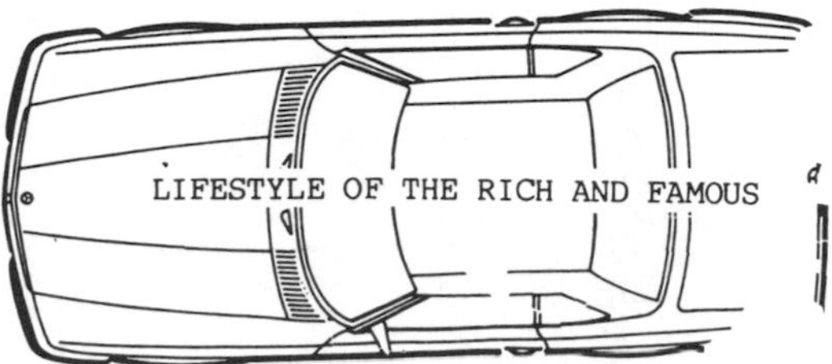

Michael, I'd found out in the coarse of our conversation, calls himself "The Millionare" because he is heir to the famous Cudahy fortune--left to him by his great-aunt, who invented the Q-tip. No job for this guy; he spends his days lounging around in a silk smoking jacket.

He met me at the train station and drove me to his luxurious penthouse. I was wowed! A wall of glass looked out on the fabulous Providence skyline; you could see the river winking between the Biltmore and the Fleet buildings; hell, you could see all the way to Boston. Michael flipped a switch and wall slid back to reveal an entertainment center; another flip of a switch, and Jackie Gleason's band played on the stereo.

The phone never stopped ringing--Michael's accountant, his band mates, his publicist. So I had time to snoop through the vast rooms of the penthouse, finding everywhere the hush of thick carpets and the sheen of fine fabrics.

"I've had a special air-filter system installed," he said. "Germs. I can't stand germs!" he moaned, wringing his hands. So that explained why he'd made me don a white spacesuit before he'd let me enter the apartment. I guess all millionaires have a thing about cleaniness.

We walked over to look at the car--more beautiful than ever in full daylight. However, when I opened the trunk, I saw the problem. The whole suspension spring had burst through the rotten trunk floor. Rust never sleeps.

But Pagan's enthusiasm was undimmed--I got a tow truck to take it to the nearest garage. The mechanic could see it was no use to argue with a crazed Pagan, so he told me to leave it there.

No sooner had I gotten back to Boston than Diane called. Her roommate was giving away an old car (Datsun B210) and the lucky recipient was me! In the space of week, I'd accomplished with networking what most people slave a lifetime for--I'd achieved the middle-class dream; I was a two-car family!

Diane dropped the Datsun over at my house, and I drove it around for a day. Very early on, I realized this was not the car for me. First, as a brown, rusted-out Japanese car, it was a fashion debacle. Second, it was a stick-shift--the broken kind that requires you to double-clutch--and Pagan hates to drive in anything but automatic comfort. I consider the luxury of not knowing what gear I'm in to be one of my inalienable rights as an American. So I gave the car to my housemate Tony.

THE EXPERTS COMMENT
ABOUT PAGAN'S DRIVING

Maggie: "You drive like Rickie does on 'I Love Lucy,' you know, moving the steering wheel back and forth in that exaggerated way."
Marcus: "Wow, you're going to drive? That's taking Pagan into a whole new dimension."
Virginia (on our cross-country trip, her voice dripping with irony): "Of course, the car will run a lot smoother without the emergency brake on."
Patrick: "You're going to own a car!?" (Laughing and sputtering, emphatic hand gestures) "Are you sure this is wise?"
Jay, on hearing I'm getting a car: Puts his head in his hands and moans.

Soon after I came to my senses about the Scamp. After all, white-vinyl bench seats and chrome trim do not a car make. A car needs a suspension system. When I called the mechanic, it turned out he'd been stalling me, knowing that it would take days before I woke from my automotive dream world.

So now I was back to square one and zero cars. Networking, I realized, would only yeild duds. It was time to look in the Want Advertiser.

The Datsun, looking better than real life

I went through two weeks of car hell. I'll spare you the details, except to say that I spent an entire afternoon getting to Braintree only to find a smoking rust heap, and I nearly bought a purple car that turned out to be held together with nothing but Bondo and black magic.

Pagan the romantic, who believed that every beautiful car she saw was meant for her, had become Pagan the hard-bitten cynic. Now every used car seemed like a mound of misery. So when I saw a Want Ad that said, "1974 Plymouth Valiant. Gd running. 40K mi. $600," I sneered.

"140 thousand miles is more like it," scoffed the jaded Pagan. "It will probably burst into flames when I test drive it." I was so sick of the search I nearly didn't go. But something--call it fate or kizmet--helped me decide it was worth the effort to bike all the way to the old Irish people's section of JP.

As I approached the house, I glimpsed it. In the driveway of a modest middle-class home lined with shrubs and blooming flowers waited The Car. The clouds parted and a ray of sun shot down and illuminated its gorgeous boxy olive body, its cat-eye tail lights, the round side-view mirror and chrome fenders, the hood that modestly covered six cyclinders of pure power. Little birdies chirped in the trees, songs of driving pleasure. A teensy faun teetered over on unsteady

IT'S ALL IN THE NAME

Some '70s cars are named for places--take the Dodge Aspen and Chevy Malibu. These represent the two poles of late '70s culture. On the one hand, Aspen calls up images of exclusive ski resorts, the perfect setting for a miniseries--starring, perhaps, Morgan Fairchild or even midget singer Paul Williams. You, the name suggests, are an executive who rents a hot-tub-equipped chalet in order to romp with your latest mistress. Meanwhile, "Malibu" hints at another sort of hedonism; you're a drop-out surfer. You strap your board on top of your car, slide your bronzed body behind the steering wheel, and you're off on a carefree whirl. In "Aspen" we sense the first stirrings of the dress-for-success culture of the '80s; in "Malibu" we hear the last cough of the counterculture.

Perhaps the ne plus ultra of late-'70s car names was Renault's Le Car. Add "Le" in front of anything and you make it '70s--a cheap American product masquerading as something French and upscale.

Call me an old fogey, but my fave car names are late '60s, early '70s Dodges and Plymouths. "Scamp" suggests that your car is a cute little pet and/or the star of a Disney movie. Perhaps the cartoony quality of the name derives from the era's obsession with pop art. "Duster" (with its Tasmanian Devel-style logo, supposed to be a whirl of dust, I guess) also suggests a cartoon character. It sounds kinda wacky, like the car is a carefree, knock-about vehicle for driving through the back roads.

But Pagan's best-name-ever award goes to the Plymouth (?) Swinger. What a perfect car name for the early '70s, the era of singles' bars and skyrocketing divorce! But the real brilliance of the name is its double shade of meaning. First of all, of course, it suggests a guy in gold chains speeding down the highway to a wife-swapping party. But it also implies a madcap innocence, like that old camp song, "Swinging Along the Open Road." And the ultimate irony is that you never see anyone younger than 80 driving a Swinger.

legs, nuzzled the car and then gamboled away. Pagan kicked up her heels, sang a chorus of "Chitty Chitty Bang Bang" and ran over to fondle her new friend.

Pagan rang the bell and after a long 20 minutes an aged man came out. He had such a thick Irish brogue that he seemed like a bad character actor from a TV show: "Sure'n yall wanna warm 'er up ferst." I just couldn't take him seriously.

Though my Irish heritage is tenuous (my last name is actually Scottish), I tried my best to act like Pageen Kennedy, a lass from Old Eyre. This included driving the car at a creeping pace as he gave me directions. Still, I didn't go slow enough for him. "Now, no need for hotroddin'," he'd say, "Easy now," as if we were screeching around corners rather than going 5 miles an hour. This test drive did more to test Pagan's sanity than the car's prowess.

When we got back, I asked if I could take the car to a mechanic--I even offered to leave the cash with the guy to prove I'd come back. But he couldn't conceive of leaving the neighborhood. He kept clucking that his mechanic (a retired policeman) lived three houses away, so why did I want to go to some stanger's gas station? Finally I gave in, and went through the charade of asking his neighbor questions about the car. Mr. Car Owner wasn't trying to pull one over on me, he was just, as his wife later said, "confused."

I came back the next day to get the car (part of his confusion involved making me return in the morning). This time I was invited into the house, which was just as you'd expect: lace on dark wood tables, statues of saints in various attitudes of suffering, a pearlescent Last Supper and plush-covered chairs. I did a real Irish jig for them, talking about my relatives from Limerick and my dear old great aunt.

The very sweet wife of Mr. Car Owner took me aside and said, "Now I wanna give you some things to keep you safe." She proceeded to hand me a beautiful medallion for the dash with a picture of Jesus ripping his heart open and the inscription, "Sacred Heart Auto League." She also gave me "The Driver's Prayer" to put in the glove compartment. My thanks was sincere. Then Mr. Car Owner slipped me $50 of the $600 cash I'd given him, saying, "Naa go get yrrsilf a cold one."

As I drove off, neighbors came out to see what was going on. Everyone had a last word of advice for me: "Put some Vaseline on the battery connections" and "remember to warm it up" and "don't drive to fast." Waving and smiling, I eased my way out of the crowd and took my baby home.

THE VALIANT, UP CLOSE

It may be a '70s car, but the dashboard is vintage '50s. There are gadgets like a map light and a remote-control side-view mirror; every label is in an old-fashioned typeface. At night, the dash lights up with a tentative glow the faint greenish color of a luna moth--very ornamental but no help at all when it comes to seeing.

The seats are green quilted naugahyde, bench-style of course. There are three seat belts up front and room for 20 pals in back. Green nubbly carpeting adorns the fabulous floor. Best of all is the smell: like a hardware store in a small town, an odoriferous blend of rust, must and old man's cigar smoke.

There are two rules in Pagan's car:

1) The radio must at all times be tuned to the "Music of Your Life" station, which plays only soothing songs like "Born Free," "To Dream the Impossible Dream" and anything by Johhny Mathis.

2) Gas is smelly and disgusting. Therefore, Pagan refuses to pump--any pal who happens to be in the car has to do it for her.

So far the car's been performing fine, though it does stall out like crazy if not warmed up. This led to a bizarre episode that says more about Pagan than her car.

OK, first I have to explain that because the PC Week offices are on a major interstate highway, getting out, turned around and headed back to Allston is a nightmare. You have to first go away from Allston, negotiate a circle full of lights and exits, and then get back onto the right highway. My first night driving home, there happened to be pouring rain and a flood warning, just to make things more exciting.

Of course I'd failed to warm up the car and of course it stalled out at the first light. At the second light, it stalled and did not come back to life at all--no coughing from the ignition, nothing. The traffic light turned green and mean, horrible Boston drivers honked at me as if I'd done this just to annoy them.

Well, I flipped out. My car was dead in the middle of an interstate highway. I left the keys in the ignition, put on the flashers and ran to the nearest restaurant, where I called a tow truck.

Then I ran back out into the hurricane, hair whipping all around my face, to find my car. I darted in and out of traffic, sobbing and cursing myself. I was so disoriented, I couldn't figure out where I'd left the it, and ran around like a chicken with my head cut off until finally a police car stopped and the guy asked me what was wrong.

"My car died somewhere around here, and I panicked and now I can't find it," groaned Pagan.

"It's over at the station," he said, referring to the police station that I suddenly remembered was nearby.

And there it was, looking a bit guilty and contrite. I went in and they gave me the keys, advising me to pump the gas pedal next time--I guess it had started right up for them. I still don't know exactly why the car just went dead like that, but I think maybe I didn't have it perfectly in Park or something.

I stood over my car and said, "Bad, bad car. Never do that again." And it hasn't.

PET UPDATE

My housemate Sid just got a Vietnamese pot-bellied pig, which has been named by The Globe as the trendiest pet for the '90s. Though I love dear Bianca, I have to say that for a trendy pet, she's awfully messy. She likes to dump her water onto the floor and then lick it up. Hell, she just likes to eat the dust right off the floor, smacking her lips loudly.

She's still a baby--about the size of a cat--and is pure black, right down to her snout. If you squint your eyes, she looks like a tiny, noble bison roaming the plains, but when you un-squint your eyes she looks disturbingly like a pig with a giant head.

We can't wait until she's big enough to scare off the cats from downstairs, who treat our half of the house like their personal litterbox.

Bianca licked this page

Bianca the Pig

More than a gossip fest, less than a literary salon, it's...

My Writing Group

One day in 1987, I met an old classmate from a Wesleyan writing workshop on the inbound B line. I remembered Elizabeth as the quiet gal who wrote a wonderful story about people combing the beach for blue glass. Anyway, she and I got talking and she said, "Some women I met at Breadloaf [a hoity-toity writers' conference] are starting a group where we'll critique each others' fiction. Do you want to be in it?"

The historic first meeting of this writers' group was held at Elizabeth's apartment--which was right next to the park that is home to the Somerville "Led Zep" castle, where good-for-nothing youths go to get stoned. From her window, we could watch under-age teenagers make out in the bushes. But of course we didn't do that, because we had important writer business to attend to.

Pagan arrived at the first meeting eager to impress the others, whom she pictured as a roomful of snooty Breadloaf ladies. In fact, the group turned out to be just me, Elizabeth and Audrey--a redhead who wore army fatigues and read a novel excerpt about a shark ripping someone to pieces. [Editor's note: Audrey has since updated her image. She now wears beautiful antique clothes and writes about women killing men.]

Later that summer we were joined by a third Breadloaf gal, Lauren, who upon hearing I was in the group said, "You mean, THE Pagan Kennedy?" You see, she'd read one of the short stories I'd had published in The Quarterly. From the story--about a girl riding horses with her father--she expected a statuesque, proper preppie. Lauren was surprised to meet the very non-statuesque Pagan, dressed in combat boots and a ripped dress, splattered with mud from riding her bike through the rain.

At first, I saw the writers' group as a professional, rather than social, link in my life. That is, while we all meshed as writers, I felt like the weird Allston cousin to these Cambridge gals. They lived in more-or-less normal apartments and had dishes that matched and clothes they'd bought new. At the time, I was living in the E Ranch, a punk-rock house with graffitti-covered walls; a floating population of scary, armed occupants; and a back yard with a 14-foot fence covered with "Danger" signs, because on the other side was an acre of transformers owned by Boston Edison.

At the end of that summer, I went off to a fiction-writing graduate program at Johns Hopkins. It was a dream come true--I was paid to study with John Barth [a famous writer, in case you don't know, author of The Floating Opera]. I also got to hang out with 9 other ambitious writers who'd been picked for the program--a ready-made writers' group--and to teach my own class. (Can you imagine the wacky Pagan teaching a group of straight-laced pre-meds how to construct a short story? I'll have to write about that disasterous experience someday.)

While I was at Hopkins I desperately thought of ways to forstall my re-entry into the real world. As it turned out, Elizabeth and I both applied to the program at Washington Univ. in St. Louis, and both were offered huge sums of money to go to that wealthy school. Elizabeth decided to go; I decided not to. I'd found it hard to pick up everything, go to Baltimore and make new friends; I just couldn't bear the thought of doing all over again, in the Midwest, no less.

So now I was back in Boston. (1988, for those keeping count.) With Elizabeth off at a two-year program (and later at Cornell), the group was just Audrey, Lauren and me. It was at this juncture that writers' group began to evolve into its current frivolous form. I think the first lapse of professionalism was "thirtysomething": We met on Tuesday nights, and if we finished business on time, we'd watch the show--not because we thought it was any good, but because we wanted to drool over the clothes and apartments. All of the writers, including punk Pagan, lusted for expensive, understated suits and homes full of architectual details.

The next lapse was when dinner became part of the evening's festivities, and our attention veered from things literary to arguments over what kind of ice cream to get.

Then came Jimmy, the one man who dared to enter the feminine halls of the writers' group. Jimmy Guterman is a rock 'n' roll writer (author of "12 Days on the Road: The Sex Pistols in America" and "You're No Good: The 50 Worst Albums of All Time" among other books); but he wanted to write a novel. Strangely, though he was the one who desperately tried to keep writers' group all business, it was during the Jimmy Era that we never missed an episode of "thirtysomething," that we plunged headlong into whiny arguments which of us (gals) had less money, and whose life was more depressing. I don't know what accounted for our decline--maybe it was Jimmy's large-screen TV or the low-cholestoral snacks his lovely wife Jane offered us, or maybe it was just the atmosphere late '80s, you know, one of those zeitgeistish, weltanschauungy kind of things.

Jimmy dropped out last year (?), and we entered a new phase. Now we usually met at Audrey's apartment, renowned for its excellent laundry facilities. Pagan and Lauren began bringing their dirty clothes. Maybe we'd do a little criticism of each others' work, but it had to take place between spin cycles.

This summer, our long-lost member Elizabeth (still at Cornell) had tremendous success: She won the coveted Drue Heinz prize and had a piece in "Best American Short Stories." Meanwhile, the rest of us were beset by depression, too much work and free-floating angst. Thus began the current, most decadent stage of the writing group. Now we just flop around on the floor whining about our lives and about how Elizabeth's successes make us jealous. Writing? What's that?

The writing babes: Every man's dream

AUDREY

This carrot-topped lass does Macintosh programming for a living--and, say, what a living! She has a swank garden apartment in fashionable Cambridge, where the speciality of the maison is curried tofu stir-fry.

Auds hails from Canada--thus the wool hunting cap she always wears in the winter. Her best quality is her generosity; somebody's always borrowing her car, her coat, her TV, or eating all the food in her fridge. Auds never seems to mind.

Strangely, this gentle native of our Neighbor to the North loves to write about violence: "The bear reached slowly down with its mouth and pulled off Butler's face, started to chew."

ELIZABETH

The most academic of the writing gals, Elizabeth hails from Williamstown, Mass., where both her parents are English professors. She's now off at Cornell, getting her own PhD.

With her raven tresses, blue eyes and porcelain skin, this Fulbright French scholar has a real savoir faire. Until she has a neurotic fit. Then she's likely to start obsessing: "Oh my God, do you think this sweater is too black? I mean, I want it to be black, but not black black, like some kind of grease stain. I mean is it like dull, understated black?"

Elizabeth tends to write about preteen girls coming of age. ("Oh my God, are all my stories about 13-year-old girls? Do you think that's all I can write about? What if I never write about anything else, wouldn't that be pitiful?")

Her details are exquisite: "Folding [sheets] with her was like a kind of dance--leaning back to pull the wrinkles from the fabric, stepping, then, toward each other, arms upraised, faces almost touching as the two sides of the sheet embraced. Backing up again as the fabric caught a swell of air and lifted in a puff."

LAUREN

Pint-sized Lauren is the shortest of the short writing gals. This five-foot-tall cutie wears prim flowered dresses and pumps, but don't let her composure fool you. She's so neurotic that she has to keep rifling through her purse every few minutes to check that she hasn't lost anything--comfort to her means curling up in a fetal position, clutching her keys.

Lauren works as a therapist for addicts and alcoholics; she's also getting a graduate degree in psychology from BU. Asked if she thinks therapy is helpful, she says, "Oh, it's very helpful for the therapist--I'm learning all about human behavior. I'm not sure if it does my clients any good, though."

She writes essays about her childhood, growing up in a pathologically perfectionist Jewish family--and about when perfect facade crumbles. "The horse snorted, backed up, and before I could turn him towards the jump, lifted his tail and took the most elegant, stinking dump I'd ever seen from horse or human before."

A TYPICAL WRITERS' MEETING, by Lauren

7:30 Lauren arrives at 14 Farrington in her vehicle. Pagan, still in various of undress in her room, starts to screech. It may be that she's having difficulty color coordinating or that she's discovered a potential tumor.
8:00 They arrive at Audrey's place loaded down with laundry and death anxiety. Audrey is amazing. She works sometimes 50 hours a week and still manages to write reams. Audrey has the best apartment--five rooms, silk pillowcases, VCR. Her brass fixtures are awesome. She is maybe the most awesome of us all...
8:05 The competition is building. Pagan, statuesque, stands in the middle of the living room, rolls up her pant legs, baring muscle, and flexes. The subtext here: "Well, Audrey, you may have nice things, but can your calf compare? You may be a poet of place, but I, I am a poet of heart, lungs and limb."
8:06 Audrey defers for now. Dinner is served.
9:00 Arm-wrestling match. Championship titles stolen or won back. Muscle conditioning exercises. Existential complaints.
10:00 TV time. Pagan puts laundry in the dryer.
11:00 Chapters, short stories, articles read aloud and critiqued.
11:20 Literary exercises closed. Laundry folded. Good night.

Once I read a cartoon about Barbie where she goes to New York City on vacation, heads out on a fabulous shopping spree, is discovered by a modeling agency and awarded a huge contract, and ends up dining at Windows on the World with Ken.

I've always longed for a glamorous New York trip like that, and this summer I got it! You see, back in June (?) the Village Voice held a party to promote a book I'm in ("Disorderly Conduct: The VLS Reader" an anthology of Voice fiction put out by Serpent's Tail Press). The party was planned to coincide with the week of the American Booksellers Association (?) convention, when every editor, book-store owner, author and agent in this great land gathers to hobnob at the Jacob Javitts (sp?) Center during the day. Then they network during the night at a round of upscale parties held in rooms with wood paneling.

Enter Pagan in a tattered dress, too much makeup, old-lady glasses and jewelry made out of chicken bones.

The night of my arrival in NYC, I met Cliff--a roommate of mine from days of yore--and we headed downtown to attend the Voice party at Limelight.

Now here's where I have to take a moment to assess my readership. Are you jaded hipsters who think, "Limelight! That club was out in 1986. Geez, am I supposed to be impressed?" or are you country bumpkins who say, "Shucks, Limelight, what's that?" Well, you city slickers skip over this description; this is for my small-town pals: Limelight is an old church that's been renovated to make a club. Bret Easton Ellis had his publication party for Less Than Zero there in the early '80s, and no doubt snorted coke with Jay McInerny in the bathroom. Nowadays the club's full of nerds from New Jersey who pay $18 to get in and 4 goddamned dollars for a Rolling Rock. (Whereas, at the far more commodious Model Cafe in Allston, beers are $1.50.) However, I will say this for Limelight: It's fun to walk through it once and discover all the elaborate decorations, like the "Alice in Wonderland" room.

Anyway--since I was one of the authors in the book--I hoped heads would turn as I entered the club, people would whisper, fans would crowd me. This is what happens (sort of) when I go to Primal Plunge events, because (if I may flatter myself) I'm a wacky Allston character almost on the scale of Xanna Don't.

But instead, I cowered with Cliff in the corner as fabulous women in lycra tube dresses and men in designer suits whirled around us. Where were the Voice people I knew? Why didn't anyone look like a nerdy writer? In fact, many of these people were probably sleezy publicists and sales directors from minor publishing houses, who'd somehow gotten ahold of a free invite. These people were vapid club-hoppers and I was a PUBLISHED AUTHOR, and yet here I was feeling like a complete social reject wearing rags. It was high school all over again, when I felt both envy and disdain for the airheads who snubbed me.

Then I heard someone yelling over the music, "Pagan, there you are. I've been looking everywhere for you!" It was my agent, come to the rescue. She hugged me and said, "I've got so many people to introduce you to." Oh, why didn't I have an agent in high school?

She led me off to where a friendly crowd was hanging out--some of her other clients, people who'd taken Gordon Lish's workshop, people I knew from The Nation, and Voice people. Suddenly, I was in my element! I was a networking machine!

Cliff took one look at the networking Pagan, giving her friends air kisses and talking a mile a minute about contracts, and he fled.

I left at about 1 a.m., when the club had opened its doors to the general public, and the place was filling up with the Bridge and Tunnel Crowd. In order to get out, I had to snake my way past a long line of them, all waiting with surly expressions to pay their $18. One of these people yelled at me in a horrible sarcastic voice, "Hey, can I have glasses like yours?" If I had been brave enough, I'd have yelled back, "At least I got in here free, but losers like you have to pay. Hey, one of the nose pieces from my glasses is cooler than you are, Asshole!" (Yikes, it's the return of the annoyed New York Pagan, my personality before I became the World Love Groovin' Allston Pagan.)

The next day proved to be a non-stop networking whirl. I had a lunch appointment with an editor from Houghton-Mifflin, ostensibly to hype my book. You see, I was writing a proposal to do a non-fiction book about the worst fads of the '70s. (I've since written the proposal. It came very close to be taken by Houghton-Mifflin, but at the last minute the deal fell through. However, look for my piece on the '70s in the December issue of the VLS.) The Houghton-Mifflin editor, a loyal Pagan's Head reader and all-around cool person, took me into her office and offered me all the free books I wanted! Then she took me out to lunch at a restaurant made up to look like a cheap diner that was actually fabulously expensive!

The editor at Houghton-Mifflin humors me by looking busy so I can take her pic.

Next it was off to the Voice, where I visited my editor Stacey and friend Polly. I also used the bathroom. Then I called on my editor at The Nation, who gave me more free books. I used the bathroom there, too. (The coffee I'd quaffed at my expensive meal was taking its toll.)

A word about bathrooms at leftist magazines: They're uniformly grungy. And as you might expect, the bathroom at The Nation is significantly more shabby than at the Voice. The Nation's bathroom is

Stacey obliges me by posing with her snack.

the type where the mirror has fallen down and forever after remains propped against the wall, as if it's about to be fixed; the graffiti tends toward quotes from Fourier. In general, there's an atmosphere that says, "Hey, we're in this bathroom meditating on social injustice in Sudan, not the peeling paint."

Meanwhile, the bathroom at the Voice is institutional and inelegant, but clean. The graffiti tends toward slogans, gossip and conspiracy theories. "Feminine" pads and tampons are provided free! There is an atmosphere of no-frills comfort that says, "All people--male or female, gay or straight, white or black--are equally entitled to a decent bathroom experience!"

At 5:00, I scooted West to meet an editor from Ballantine for drinks. The bar at which we rendezvoused was decorated to look like a roadside barbeque shack down South--with red-and-white-checked tableclothes and scrap-wood walls. It was also fabulously expensive. I hyped my book to her, we gabbed, and soon it was time for my next appointment.

My editor at the Nation had apprised me of several parties that night, the most tempting of which was the Atlantic Monthly Press party at the Grolier Club. My editor had said, "They're not going to be taking invitations, so just walk in like you know what you're doing."

As I approached the club, a swank townhouse in the East 30s (I think), I became apprehensive. I was sweaty and my accessories were made of animal bones--surely they wouldn't let me in.

In fact, the doormen did stop me, asking, "What are you here for?"

"The party," I sang, and walzed between them.

Inside was four stories of thick

carpeting, mahogany paneling and oil paintings, crowded with glittering people in crisp suits. Thank god I soon spotted a pal, JD, and we made our way to the nearest bar for a free drink. We saw famous editor Garry Fiskejohn (sp?) and famous swami Shirley MacLaine (sp?). Later I heard that Bret Easton Ellis was there, too! I had just written a piece condemning his American Psycho for The Nation, so it's a good thing I didn't see him in the flesh. A fist fight might have ensued.

JD: Writer, editor, bar-tender.

It was at that party that I got my most intense Hub-of-the-Lit-Scene feeling. For one shining moment, with the middle-aged, bespectacled editors all around me, I soaked up the atmosphere of pure publishing power.

After I left the party, I'd wait on a subway platform pocked with the black circles of stepped-on chewing gum, my skin getting sticky in the heat. But the Important Editors would leave the party in cabs, floating in air-conditioned calm through the dirty, hot, hairball of a city. The Important Editors live in an entirely different New York than I know--well-appointed apartments on the Upper East Side, expense-account dinners, and the power to create or kill books. They, I'm sure, feel they are shut out from a yet more powerful and moneyed group. New York, like Dante's Inferno, is a series of concentric circles--though in the case of the city, the circles are social.

Barbie may have capped off her trip to New York by dining at Windows of the World, looking out at the throbbing skyline. For me, the culmination was eating free food supplied by the Atlantic Monthly Press while surveying my own imagined New York, a place where ideas and eloquence are celebrated on the surface, but where the marketplace always throbs below like that grimy dynamo, the subway.

A Guided Snoop Through Anna's House

Her bathroom sink is always full of leaves and twigs: beautiful, yes; practical, no.

The living room. Anna decided she hated the color of her couch (foreground), so she simply painted the fabric.

Anna in park.

While I was in NYC, I stayed with one of my dearest friends, Anna, a painter and eccentric heiress* who's in her 60s. Anna has lived in Mexico; been through several "husbands"; raised two kids (who are now a doctor and lawyer, though she urged her son to be a ballet dancer and her daughter a weaver); written a column about nuclear energy for the Voice; published many short stories; and befriended bakery owners, jazz musicians, electroshock patients, Southern aristocrats and street people. Now, Pagan's Head takes you on an exclusive tour of Anna's rent-controlled apartment on the Upper West Side.

READ THIS FIRST!

*She's a very poor heiress, actually

By Anna: carved, painted wood with pressed tin.

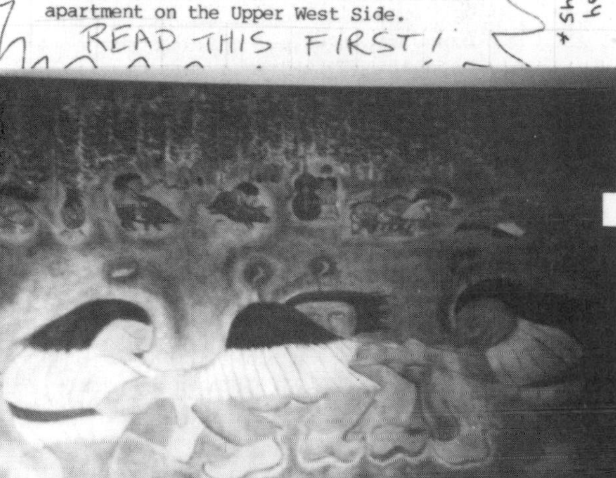

This is Anna's painting of the place she'll go when she dies.

The fridge is covered with clippings that prove her conspiracy theories.

The walls in her kitchen are lined with pictures by famous friends.

One room is walled with funhouse mirrors.

David Cassidy Concert Points Pagan in Direction Of Alka-Selzer

Recently, my co-workers presented me with a very thoughtful gift for my birthday: two tickets to the David Cassidy concert.

If I thought about the concert at all before I went (and God knows I tried not to) I imagined that the crowd would be full of smirking hipsters suffering as David showcased his new hits. David's comeback album--how can I explain how utterly bland it is. If you heard his hit "Lyin' to Myself" on the radio in 1981, you might think it was a particularly lame cut from Foreigner.

Still, maybe the concert would be OK. Maybe when David played "Wa Think I Love Ya," the hipsters in the crowd would lose their jaded expressions. We'd tap our feet and smile at each other, just like people do on TV when they hear the P Family. The 200 lonely, lost people who had walked into Citi that night would become one generation: Partridge Nation.

Oh, how wrong I was. Besides my co-workers, their buddies and Maggie, no one in the audience seemed sane, much less hip. Maggie and I made the mistake of standing up front, where we were jostled by big-haired women wearing David T-shirts and whining, "Oh, Gawd, he was so cute when I saw him at the Philadelphia concert." I heard a fat man regaling someone with a tale about hiding on a hotel fire escape and (I missed a lot of the story) finally holding open a door ~~open~~ for David.

The show was introduced by some smarmy DJ from WZLX, who tried to turn the whole thing into a promotion for his bonehead "classic hits" station. That pretty much set the tone for what followed.

OK, actually Danny Bonaduce, who opened up with a comedy/freak show, would have been pretty good had not the audience screamed with laughter at his dumbest jokes. Also unbearable was the running commentary of the woman beside me; for instance, when Danny joked about David beating someone up, she said, "He can beat me up anytime."

The best moment for me was when Danny first walked onto the stage. I thought, "Here I am, yards away from the guy I lived and died for when I was 8 years old." Just being near Danny was enough to send me into some kind of psychedelic state where I was simultaneously young and old. But that wore off quickly. Thank God Danny had the sense to make fun of himself and his full-time job as an ex-child star. At one point someone yelled, "Is the Partridge Family going to have a reunion?" He said, "Don't look at me; I'm not the one whose standing in the way of a reunion. I'm so desperate for work I'd play all six parts if I had to."

After Danny, the serious jostling began. A huge woman tried to push between Maggie and me, claiming she just wanted to put a rose on the stage. The Big Hair Squad got out tape recorders and cameras, and hunkered in position. Maggie suggested we move back but I stupidly insisted on standing our ground.

David came out dressed like George Michael, in leather jeans, white T and

silver-fringed motorcycle jacket. The latter hung pitifully around his puny frame (granted, though, David's arms are far buffer than Pagan's). His band looked like a random collection of MTV clones--keyboards played by a metalhead woman, two puffy-haired guitarists, an Allston Beat-attired bassist and drummer. Sorely lacking in this false P Family was the brilliant tambourine-manship of Tracy. I was also sorry to see Laurie's flimsy Farfisa replaced by a stack of Yamaha keyboards. And while I'm griping, why didn't the band wear matching velveteen outfits?

Where's Reuben now? 'Cause these guys are sorely in need of some career advice.

At least David had the sense to play mostly Partridge hits. But unfortunately, the songs had been given new arrangements--a kinda Vegas, disco sound that undercut any emotion they'd once had. Amazingly, David still acted like a TV version of a rock star. He must have thought he was Eddie Van Halen for a moment, because he ran over to the other guitar player and they made scruched-up faces at one another as if they actually cared about what they were playing. At one point, David yelled out, "Boston, are you ready to rock? You're the best audience we've ever had." His insincerity was so obvious that no responding roar came from the crowd.

As David whipped into a medley from The Partridge Family By Numbers, I had a disturbing revelation. Suddenly I became terribly aware of myself standing in that crowd of salespeople and secretaries; I was not separate and hipper ~~and~~ but the same. All of us had now

entered a new stage in our lives--we were a target audience for oldies. Soon they'd be selling us Preperation H and Geritol between P Family cuts, Village People songs and the theme from "Welcome Back, Kotter."

For all his babble about artistic integrity, David Cassidy is poised to make much money as he can from our lust for lost youth. Medleys, for Christsake! Vegas versions of pop anthems! He was as shameless as Elvis launching into the "America The Beautiful" medley.

Before the thing was over, Maggie and I fled, feeling used and disgusted.

ABOUT THE BACK COVER

The magazine where I free-lance as a copy editor, PC Week, gives out a "Ben Franklin" award every so often. The award—a cheesy, computer-generated plaque and a $100 bill-goes to the journalist, researcher or production person who exhibits the most dedication, zeal and company spirit. Last time they were about to give out the award, Pagan insisted she would try to win for "Best Free-lancer." Thus, she made a big show of beating the other free-lancer when it came to reading proofs, initialling stories and showing enthusiasm for her work. For the week, Pagan staged a sophisticated parody of her job—while getting more work done than ever! Nonetheless, PC Week did not see fit to award Pagan a Ben Franklin. So her friends in the art department consoled a crushed Pagan by making her a "George Washington" award. When they presented it to her, she stood on her desk and shrieked, waving the one-dollar prize.

Be it known that

Pagan Kennedy,

having demonstrated junior high school spirit, astrological foresight and owning groovy attire, has earned this prestigious award. Don't spend it all in one place baby!

PW WEEK

this 17 day of May, 1991

Witness Copy Editor

Witness Freelancer

7

MEN

THE DOCTORS had promised Dad he'd be given drugs that would shield him from the excruciating pain of lung cancer. But the medication they prescribed him at the end—orally administered morphine—was a joke. Dad would be comfortable for a few hours and then suddenly, without warning, the drug would wear off. He would yell, "I can't breathe!" and then my sister, my mom, or I would run to get the vial of morphine, unscrewing the top as fast as we could, and drop some of that brown liquid into his mouth. Dad's horrible state would last twenty more minutes or so—oral medication does not hit the bloodstream right away. "Do something. More," he'd gasp, struggling for breath, holding the oxygen tube closer to his nose, tossing his head. And we'd say, "You just have to wait. It will work. Just wait." Until the morphine kicked in, he could feel the slow deterioration of his lungs; his panic was the reflex of a drowning man.

My mother kept calling our hospice organization, hoping someone would tell us what we were doing wrong. Well, we finally got an appointment with a registered nurse, but she wasn't much help. "Just make sure you give him a dose every four hours. That should cover him," she said. "Don't hesitate to up the doses if they're not working."

We explained that we had been raising the doses, and sometimes this tactic worked; but other times, Dad would suddenly snap out of his medicated calm after two hours or three. Our doses were all guesswork, didn't the nurse understand that? Didn't she understand what it was like to see someone grasping at his sheets, struggling out of bed, suffocating, and not be able to help him? "Just keep doing what you're doing," the nurse said.

So this was it. This was all they had to offer Dad after promising him no pain. We kept on the best we could, began raising the doses so quickly that Dad frequently nodded out or talked nonsense. But it didn't work. In the middle of the night, he'd wake into pain, crying out and struggling to draw breath. So we took turns sleeping in the room with him.

And then the day came when we kept giving him drops of morphine and it didn't work at all. For more than an hour we circled around his bed, changing the position of his body, putting on music, taking it off, giving him whole squirtfuls of the drug. It was no longer we who ruled the room, who brought him back into our world. Now we had entered his panic state. We couldn't think. "Turn up the air. Give me more air," he kept saying. We'd answer in high, shaky voices, "It's up all the way."

And then someone noticed his oxygen tube. Nothing was coming out of it. We had been given a defective oxygen tank; it's meter read Full when it should have said Empty. Once we figured that out, we hooked Dad up to another canister of oxygen. Gradually he calmed and fell asleep.

But now we had no spare tank of oxygen. Still panicked, my mother, sister, and I held a meeting in the kitchen and decided we needed to get another one right away. My mother called the company that supplied the oxygen. They refused to bring us a canister—even after Mom told them what had happened—because it was Sunday and they were only delivering on an emergency basis. My mother threw a fit. I'm not sure what she said, but that oxygen guy pulled up in front of our house within a few hours.

It hardly mattered. We'd turned some corner that afternoon. Whatever happened, we wouldn't let Dad suffer; we were determined to find some new solution. I called a friend of mine, a woman who'd just begun practicing as a doctor, and asked her what to do. "You need a morphine drip," she said. "They have these little machines that deliver intravenous doses of medication, constantly pumping it into the bloodstream. If that's not enough, you can push a button and it's like giving him an injection. What you should do is call your hospice organization and threaten to take him to a hospital. Say you'll pull him out unless you get a morphine pump right away."

I imparted this information to my mother, and she immediately began calling people and throwing scenes. Though nobody at hospice had ever mentioned the existence of a morphine pump to us, apparently they had had access to the miraculous machine all along. In a few hours a man came to our house and hooked one up to Dad's arm. He slept peacefully and died the next day.

I wrote a speech to read at Dad's funeral. I didn't talk about his work as a city planner or even say much about what he had been like as a father. Instead I talked about Dad and his relationship to bees. He used to put a drop of honey on the tip of his finger, walk out into the yard, and wait until a honeybee landed to suckle there. Then he would delicately stroke the fur on its fat body, patting the bee with one finger as he talked to it. I wanted this image—my father as he was before the cancer, unafraid of any sting—to blot out the last memories I had of him.

Later, at home in Boston, I began to write about his sickness. I felt that I had to produce an article detailing the failures of hospice, had to warn other families what could happen when they signed up with an institution that—as we'd found out—cared more about the bottom line than the needs of the dying. I'd never written about medical issues before and I was in way over my head. Nonetheless, I finished the piece and sent it to *The Nation.* They actually considered taking it, but finally suggested I rewrite it as an Op-Ed piece and send it to the *Times.* At that point I gave up. If I had kept on revising the piece I'm sure I would have gotten it published somewhere. But I just didn't have the strength to do that. I didn't want to rewrite and rewrite Dad's death anymore. I wanted to move on.

It was time to bring myself out of shell shock. My own echoing room in the attic of our group house seemed strange, lonely after the closeness of my family in crisis. So I plunged into life. Now I never missed a party, booked my calendar solid with social engagements, signed up for a cartooning class and got myself a job at an on-line service called Ziffnet. And I changed my attitude about dating.

When I was in college, nobody dated. We all just sort of floated into relationships—it was so easy to meet people when everyone was borrowing each others' clothes, bikes, records, rooms. If you had a crush on a guy, you could just go over to his house, walk through the unlocked door, and lie on the sofa gabbing with his roommates. You became friends with a guy, and then, after a drunken night, might find yourself in a relationship with him.

I'd clung to this style of courtship even after it no longer worked. By the time you turn twenty-five or twenty-six, it's hard to float in and out of relationships; people don't hang out anymore. If you want to spend time with someone you barely know, you've got to (gulp) make a date with them. *Dating,* yuck, yuck, yuck. Those of us who came of age in the seventies think of it as this very corny ritual. When I was growing up, only people on TV dated; cool teenagers met each other by sitting in front of the 7-Eleven or by getting stoned together in the woods.

Well, one of the painful things about emerging from your postcollegiate years is that you finally accept the necessity of owning a car, getting Pap smears, cleaning hair out of the bathtub drain, and dating. At least that's how it worked among my friends. Even some of my rabid feminist buddies had begun reading the Personals in those late-twenties crisis years.

I had taken my first tentative stabs at dating long before, but now I decided to follow the example of my housemate Sid, who once said, "I'll date anyone, anywhere, anytime." I think Sid was able to reconcile himself to dating because he expected so little from his evenings out.

I fostered a similarly Zen attitude by deciding that I wasn't *dating,* I was staging a series of performance-art pieces. As performance art, the whole business of having dinner with someone I barely knew seemed highly amusing. However, after a few meetings with any given collaborator, I found that my performance pieces invariably became so complicated and messy that they resembled life rather than art.

I spent a year in this frenetic, show-offy mood—Pagan[1] to the max. You'd think my father's death would have made me hunger for deep relationships, but no, I wanted adventure. I got it. Let's see, I had a fling with this Latino ska boy; he was so young he was still deciding what tattoos to get. Then there was the African intellectual. After I went out with him a couple of times, he became obsessed with the idea that the two of us had to move to a cabin in Vermont together, where we would write sarcastic novels. He began to call me late at night to discuss our imaginary future in the wilderness.

By far my most performance art–like of dating experiences was my brief courtship with Jack—a guy who had a public persona almost as elaborate as my own. He published a fanzine, too, only his was about the fringe music scene: interviews with obscure but incredibly cool Japanese bands, gossip about ultrahip Boston personalities, reviews of old LPs.

This might seem like a match made in heaven, but early on I discovered Jack had some serious problems. Every night he had to go to *the* cool party or show in town—which of course meant that that's what we always did on our dates. When I suggested we spend a quiet evening together, he trembled with neurotic terror at the idea. "If I disappear from the scene, for even a moment, it's like I'm dead," he pronounced. The whirl of cool friends around him was the only thing that kept him from falling apart.

I went out with Jack (not his real name) for only about two weeks and the only bodily fluid we exchanged was saliva. During that time, he admitted to me that he hadn't slept with anyone for five years—a fact, it turned out, that was well known to the general Boston-rock community. Things got even more interesting after we stopped seeing each other. Hearing a rumor that I might write about him in *Pagan's Head,* Jack threatened to write about me in *his* fanzine.

I had never had anyone sink to my own level before—so unabashedly turning life into performance art. Suddenly I realized this whole thing had gone way too far, and I sent word through a mutual friend that we should call a truce. I'm glad I did, but those anti-Pagan, anti-Jack fanzines might have made great copy.

My three male housemates and I established this rule: Anyone who went on a date had to dish out the details over coffee the next morning. We'd talk about our romantic adventures in this very guy way; we weren't concerned with lasting relationships, we only cared about scoring. "Hey, did you get lucky?" or "Did you move in for a kiss at least?" we'd demand of the hapless dater.

They egged me on, I guess, made me crazier. I mean, how could I come home and tell them nothing had happened? With those guys around, dating really *was* performance art, and half the fun was turning it into a story I could spill later.

It was great to feel like one of the guys—and at the same time like an observer, a woman who'd stumbled into the locker room to hear all the secrets of the male psyche. Now I see that my need to be around men during that year had a lot to do with losing my father; I was trying to figure out some new way to relate to guys, to get from my male friends some of the love and support I used to get from Dad.

PAGAN'S HEAD

PAGAN FOR BEGINNERS

Pagan's Head is the official publication of Pagan Kennedy, who is a person, not a religion. Pagan Kennedy was nicknamed "Pagan" in high school by her friend Saira after Pagan tried to instigate a protest against the prayers they were forced to say in assembly.

Pagan, who is a quasi-professional writer, started this magazine as a way to procrastinate. Over the seven issues that now exist, the Pagan character has evolved into someone more flamboyant, fabulous and frivolous than the real Pagan. This character she created--with the same name and physical attributes as herself--suggested to the real Pagan an unexplored avenue of literature. She would write about her own life in such a way as to transform it into a parody of itself; she would become a living parody of herself.

UPDATE ON MY LIFE

MY HAIR

I'm trying to grow it out. I don't want to talk about it.

MY IMAGE

Lately I can't decide who or what I should be--so I've asked my readers to help. See "Pick Your Pagan" to cast your vote on which personality I should adopt, and help me save the thousands of dollars I would otherwise have to spend on therapy.

MY RELATIONSHIPS AND EMOTIONS

I put this section in just so you wouldn't think I'm a cold, image-obsessed jerk--and so you'd know that I DO deeply value caring and closeness.

But, come on, I'm not going tell you anything about my emotional life. Do you think I'd actually reveal anthing REAL in Pagan's Head? Geez, I could get sued -- or, at the very least, really offend someone.

MY CAREER

Boy, this is one area of my life that's swell. I GOT A BOOK CONTRACT! I GOT A BOOK CONTRACT! And maybe another one on the way.

Yes, I got a contract with the editor at St. Martin's Press who bought Generation X--he's now putting out a whole line of books aimed at the 20somethings. My book will be about the political pop culture of the '70s (ie, Earth Shoes, blaxploitation movies, working-class van culture). I've already written about the '70s in a piece for the Village Voice (it was reprinted in the Utne Reader) so I'm firmly establishing myself as a '70sologist and spokeswoman for my generation (see "Battle of the Spokespeople," also in this issue).

Meanwhile, I'm waiting to hear whether my short story collection will be published by an eminent and as-yet-unnamed small press.

Oh my God, and (as a result of the '70s piece) I was interviewed on Australian radio. It was a pre-recorded interview, unfortunately, because on the same show they were having DANNY BONADUCE in the studio! I ended my interview with, "Give my love to Danny" and the radio announcer guy seemed confused. Maybe when my book comes out, Danny and I can do a stand-up comedy/nostalgia act together and then I can marry him and visit him in prison--the culmination of a life-long dream.

OH YES, and don't forget the Pagan TV show on Somerville Cable (actually, I keep forgetting it myself). We're planning our third show for the end of summer--we do a show every few months, because each one is such a pain to put together. It's a talk show. Maggie is my Ed McMahon and we have goofy "commercials" and interview people like my housemates. The whole thing is sorta like those TV shows you pretended to have when you were seven years old, playing down in the basement and using soup cans for microphones. Actually, The Pagan Show isn't much more technically sophisticated than that either.

WHY AN ISSUE ON MEN?

First of all, the media has just discovered men. Suddenly, the male psyche is THE hot topic for magazine articles and there's references to Robert Bly, drumming and male initiation rites everywhere you turn. Well, I've never been one to resist getting caught up in a full-scale media barrage (ie, my obsession with disease-carrying ticks last summer). So Pagan's Head is jumping on the writing-about-men bandwagon.

Meanwhile, my own life seems to be mimmicking the media. Men, men, men everywhere (oy! what's a girl to do?). I now share my half of the Farrington mansion with three guys, making our apartment a non-stop "Three's Company" laff riot, in which I am eternally the befuddled Jack Tripper caught in compromising, yet secretly innocent, situations with my housemates. And suddenly it seems like at least half of my good friends are men.

But most importantly, my attitude toward men changes as I mellow with age. There was a time when I felt that perhaps men were responsible for the world's evils, that any relationship I had with a man was a temporary truce in the war they waged on our gender. Women, I thought, should depose men in an armed revolution, taking over all governments. If only the sisters were in power we could eradicate war, liberate the oppressed, and provide government-subsidized Tampons.

Now I see the foolishness of my youthful idealism. For one thing, if we killed all the men (only keeping a few to put in the museums), who would we get to change our car batteries when we were really grossed out by all the scary fluids dripping down the sides? Who'd reach the top shelf? Who'd finally give in and fix the

* Why should I ever learn to draw better when there's Clipart like this?

doorknob? It's not that women can't do these things, but it's so much easier to get a man to do them.

Then, of course, if women did take over the world, you just know that the all-female government would be as oppresive (OK, ALMOST as oppresive) as what we've got now.

But most of all, if we killed all the men, I'd really miss 'em--and not just for prurient reasons. They're fun to have around, with their talk of sub-woofers and silk ties, commitment and full-court presses. So in this issue, I say, hail men! The nasty ones among them may have kept our gender enslaved for thousands of years (and still do!), but for a moment, let's let bygones be bygones. And Pagan especially hails the tryin'-not-to-oppress, nutty, gossiping men who are her friends, colleagues and dates.

PAGAN'S QUOTABLE FRIENDS

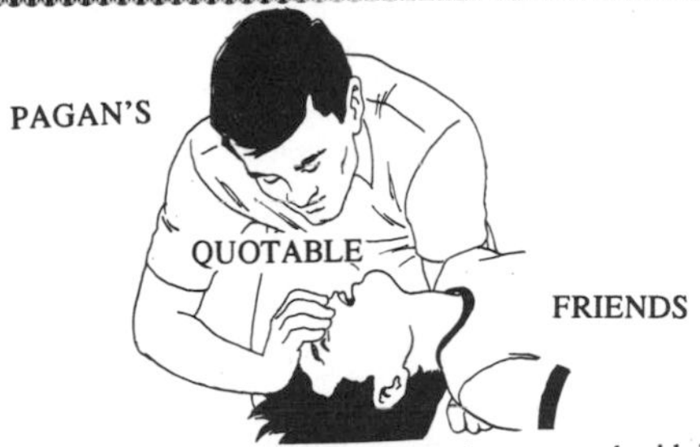

Maggie and I were walking somewhere around midnight when we heard a bird singing. I said, "Why is a bird singing this late? I thought they only sang during the day."

Maggie said, "Maybe it's rabid."

Mike Cronin (after attending the Inc. 500 conference for work): "Wearing a suit and tie for four days on end is grueling."

Elyse, my editor at Inc., cracked her professional exterior to talk about her wild hippy days back in the '60s: "I wore that colored paint stuff on my face once, but I washed it off right away."

Willie (when he was a telemarketer): "I have a new fake name I use to sell these real-estate magazines that really capatilizes on peoples' inner fears. I call up and say I'm 'Lucifer Die.' Then they say 'Hold on a minute, Mr. Die.'"

Maggie: "I wish I had a car phone. ... But I don't want a car."

Diane: "Really, you like this dress? It was 49 cents at Value Village in Bladensburg, Maryland. I saw it in this huge pile and I grabbed it. I also got this incredible velvet dress there for three dollars and this girl scout uniform that just fits me for a dollar and a ... "

Maggie: "I found my G-spot after I read this article about G-spots in Penthouse. But now I don't even know where the article is."

ABOUT MEN

Nowadays I live with three male housemates, and I'm here to say that this whole men-not-talking-about-their-feelings thing is a lot of media hype. For God's sake, my housemates won't shut up about their feelings. They blab to anyone who'll listen about bruised egos, therapy sessions, dates, relationships, fashion dilemmas and "secret" crushes.

In fact, this tendency is so pronounced that all of us are in danger of getting absolutely NO work done, ever. Instead we gravitate to the kitchen table--dubbed the Relationship Table--to talk about intimacy. It is around this simple wood slab that the men gossip shamelessly, under the guise of being "senstitive."

Other times we bond by talking starter motors, master cylinders and ground wires. This, I've learned, is not mere mechanic talk, but a complex code for our deepest feelings. And of course, there's nothing that brings us closer than sweaty athletic play, as we rollerblade around through the hallways of our house, or challenge each other to skateboard a 360 in the kitchen.

In the past months, Pagan has become initiated into the deepest mysteries of the male psyche--as complex as the duel-carb system you find on some foreign cars. Pagan's pronouncement? There's no difference between the genders at all, except that women are perfect beings while men are merely twisted puppets of their libidos.

THE HUNKS OF PAGAN'S HOUSE
(soon to be a calendar)

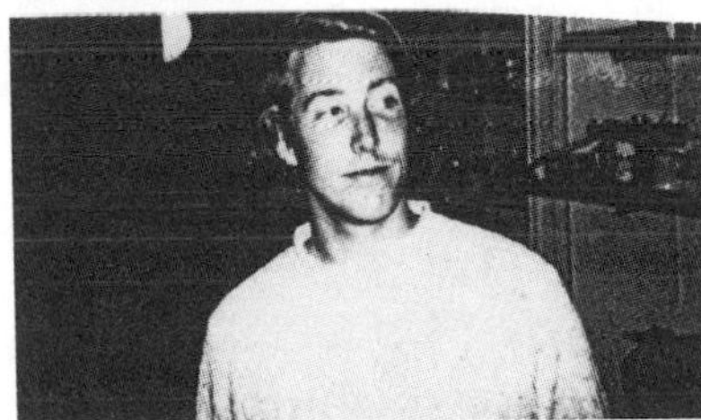

Sid's Come-hither look

Blond and WASPy, Sid is an all-around go-for-it guy. By day he's a dressed-for-success editor at a market-research firm, working on reports about phones in the Third World. By night, he's a wild man, crooning in karioki (sp?) bars, networking long-distance with execs in Pakistan, drinking to excess (how preppy!) with his co-workers or borrowing some chick's car to drive off to a ski resort.

Your dream date with Sagittarian Sid? How about dinner in Chinatown? Sid will converse with your waiter in the Chinese he picked up while he lived in glamorous Taiwan. Or how about Indian food? Global Sid speaks a smattering of Hindi, too! When he drops you off at your house, he might even whisper a gentle namaste as he nibbles your ear.

Tony's a hard-hitting Scorpio, and African politics is his thing! This hunky grad student knows how to network to get financial aid and cushy jobs--and he's also the Farrington guy voted most likely to save the world. He polished his Portuguese by documenting human rights violations in Brazil--what an awesome way to get a tan!

Pagan suggests that before your date with Tony, you shoot some speed so you can keep up with this manic guy. Where will you go? How about taking him to Lambada night at Molly's? You can shake it with him on the dance floor, and after a few beers, he may tell you his dreams. The bike factory in Angola, the p.c. coffee plantation, a new U.S. trade policy with Africa. Let him talk, because it's

TONY: DOCTOR OF LOVE (hey, what do want? He's in Angola right now. How am I supposed to take his picture?)

only after he's figured out the world's problems that this guy will be in the mood for love!

Wille maintains proper dental hygene.

Willy, a tall grad student who tones his body with martial arts, is a real cassanova: a while ago, he was asked out on four dates in one week. But all the attention hasn't given him a swelled head. Willie has a self-esteem problem that sends him running out of the bathroom screaming, "Uuugh, I hair's so ugly. I'm never going to go out in public again." The groovy Californian has a love/hate relationship with his previous home state: One minute he'll make fun of dolphin worshippers and the next he'll be offering to rolf you.

Your date with this Leo guy? How about if Willy comes over to your house, cooks up a delicious tostada for you, and then lies on your floor and whines about his anxieties?

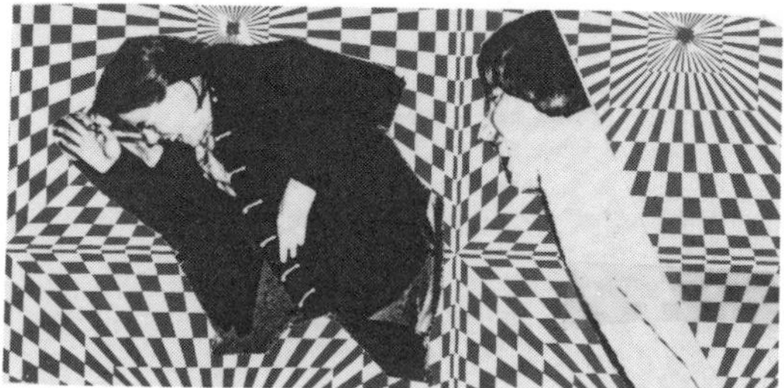

Are these guys sensitive or what?

LIFE WITH PAGAN

By Willie, housemate to her eminence

Mornings are a peaceful time in the kitchen. Sunlight streams in the windows, birds chirp and the hippies next door are crashed out on their porch, recouping from a night of smoking pot and acoustic jamming. If not for the occasional car alarm, one might think this was a rural setting.

Then, around 8:30, the tranquility is shattered by the baleful sound of leather boots descending the stairs. An imposing, bathrobed figure clomps in the kitchen, seizes the largest of three espresso makers and snaps, "Whose dishes are these?" Crashing dishes ensue: Mistress Pagan is up.

It is no coincidence that Sid works the early shift at the office. And Tony, our other housemate, has fled to Angola under the thin excuse of a job.

As she loads the coffee maker, she notices the recycling is piling up. Without turning from the sink, she kicks the box with a mighty boot, breaking bottles. "Someone's gotta do recycling and it ain't gonna be me!"

"If you check the chore wheel," I venture, "you'll see it's Tony's job."

"~~Your~~ You're the one who drinks all the juice. You should do it."

For a crazy moment, I consider telling the MP that the bottles are hers, that I just cleaned the bathroom. But caffeine-infused sanity calms my brain. "Yes, Mistress Pagan," I say.

I escape into the bathroom and pretend to shave, trying to think of a way to leave the house without the recycling box. Upon returning, I find the lady of the house seated at the table, thumbing through a VLS.

"Here's another article of mine that the Voice printed. You'll want to read it now." As she shoves the paper in my direction, I notice a copy of the Nation underneath. "There'll be a test on that article this afternoon. I'm also in the Nation. You can recycle between readings. Oh, and that car of yours has been in the driveway for months. Unless you give it to me, you'll be responsible for finding a place to park my car."

"But we can shuffle the cars and ..."

"We'll go to the DMV tomorrow. The quiz will be in five minutes."

I look out the window, at the hippies next door. They're still sleeping. The hammock on their porch is vacant and I decide at that moment to go get an acoustic guitar. Joe Friday always said that drugs and hippie music were an escape. I hope he was right.

← Looking like a Pez dispenser, Sid tries to hug Pagan.

PICK YOUR PAGAN

It's been so long since the last issue of Pagan's Head that I've gone through several image changes after the one I announced then (Pagan Classic--All the Taste of the Old Pagan, but Less Filling).

How am I to decide which of the many new Pagan images to be? Well, the Elvis stamp gave me an idea--you know, how you could vote for either the rockin' '50s Elvis or the peanut-butter-and-quaaludes '70s Elvis?

I love the idea of being able to create our own pop icons by voting (soon we'll be able to decide which JFK and James Dean we want, too--in the '90s, this is what passes for political power). So I thought to myself, "Why not give my reading public a choice of several Pagan images and let THEM decide who I should be." Isn't this exciting? You, the reader, can help me through my constantly evolving identity crisis.

Below are four images I've been experimenting with. Send your vote to 14 Farrington Ave., Allston, MA 02134 (but don't come by in person and try to kill me because I have seven housemates who will throw themselves in front of me rather than see me harmed).

photos by Willie

THE GROWN-UP-HIGH-SCHOOL-REJECT, NERDY PAGAN
The look: Cat-eye glasses, pedal pushers, a stack of books under one arm.
Marketing concept: This is a non-threatening version of intelligence that the American public can relate to. Like the professor on Gilligan's Island or Andrea on Beverly Hills 902.10, tne GUHSRN Pagen will be both intellectual and innocent--a sexually inept genius. The American consumer normally feels threatened by intellectuals, therefore it is crucial to make this Pagan seem vulnerable and bumbling.

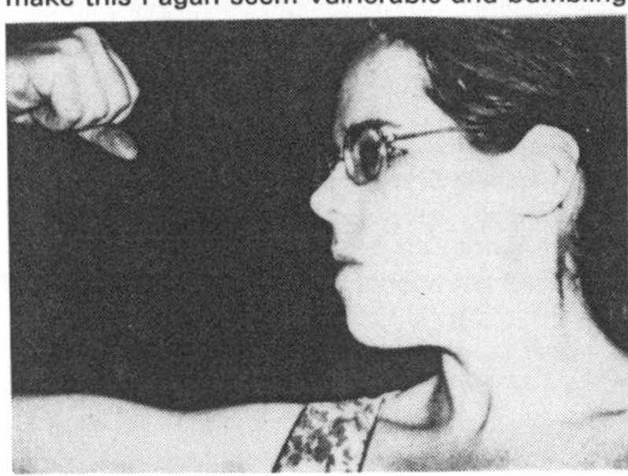

THE CARDIOVASCULAR, IRON-WOMAN PAGAN
The look: Spandex, spandex, spandex.
Marketing concept: Granted, when you think of Pagan, "athletic" may not be the first word that comes to mind. But the advantages of this image are manifold--like, for instance, skimpy outfits. Not only will the emphasis on athletics boost Pagan's male audience, but the chance for spin-off products is unlimited. We are currently investigating the possibility of putting out a Pagan exercise video,

THE FUNKY, SHAKE-YO'-ASS PAGAN
The look: Fabulous hair and generic MTV-clone clothing.
Marketing concept: We're worried that the audience for Pagan is too narrow--a small subculture of disaffected, urban adults in their mid to late '20s. By making Pagan seem "black," we can widen her target market to a variety of ethnic groups and to a younger audience.

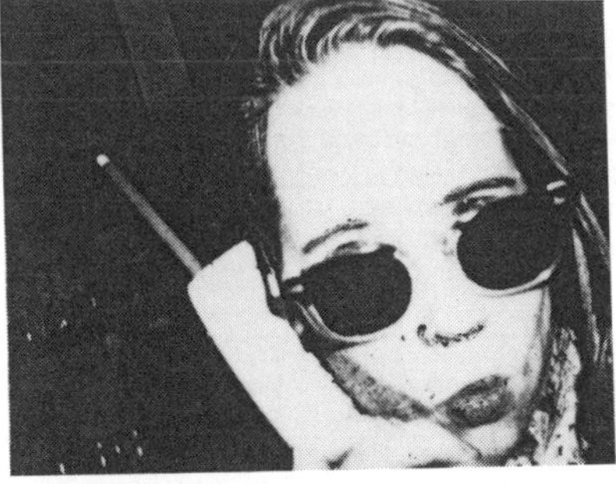

↑ photo had to be retouched because it came out barely visible.

THE L.A. PAGAN
The look: Cordless phone; white silk suits; 1965 Swinger convertible.
Marketing concept: Power. This Pagan is always on the phone making deals, always networking at cocktail parties. She is nothing but a whirl of celebrityhood--a death-dealing Shiva of fabulousness. We see her from afar, drinking a martini poolside or practicing Tai-Chi on a California cliff. The American public will buy this Pagan for the same reason they bought "Dallas"--the chance to vicariously enjoy wealth, fame and great clothes.

Pagan Confesses:

How I Slept With A Famous Editor And Never Even Knew It

Scene: New York in the mid-'80s, a time when every publishing house was hot to discover young writers--if you were 25, you were too old. During the flurry to find the authentic voices of Youth Today, major houses snapped up the fiction of David Leavitt, Jill Eisenburg, Brett Easton Ellis--pushing into the print some fledgling writers who weren't ready to be published and some who never would be.

Chief among the editors looking for the Fountain of Youth was one Dudley Pish[1]. He'd become famous for his ability to spot talent in the '60s. By the '80s, Pish had moved to a major publishing house, where he wielded considerable power as a senior editor. He also taught a famous class at Columbia (it had been written up in various glossy magazines), a fiction workshop renowned for its harrowing intensity.

Enter Pagan: I was 22 and more than anything I wanted to write brilliant prose. (Thank god I've since given THAT up.) Pish's workshop, I decided, would be my trial by fire. So one blistering day in June, I walked up to 116th Street to register for his summer session. I clutched a short story in my hand--my ticket, I hoped, into his class.

The story was something special, magical, to me. I'd taken workshops in college and had written fiction pieces as assignments. But this story was different. The beginning had come to me, unbidden, the summer after I graduated from college. Every few days or so, another bit of it would take form in my head; after a several months, the story had completed itself. I say "completed itself" because it seemed as if I had nothing to do with the creation, except transcribing the words.

But after that story, there had been silence--no more sentences unfurling before me like secret paths. I desperately wanted to find the source of that voice again; and Pish, I was sure, would know how.

At the Columbia University English department that day, I waited in line for an audience with him--there were almost 30 others who'd come clutching their stories and we watched the door tensely as each person went in to speak with the master.

When it was my turn, I found myself in a tiny, cramped office, sitting almost knee-to-knee with him. He was in his 50s, with thick silver hair, tanned skin, and an outfit that I can only describe as painstakingly preppie: denim shirt, khaki pants and mahogany-colored boots.

"So what is it? What have you got for me?" he said. I handed him the story, and he glanced at it. "All right, all right, it's terrible, throw it away. But it has promise. I can see a little glimmer. Look, will you give up all this crap and do what I say if you join my class?"

I nodded vigorously.

[1] I changed his name because he's notorious for his litigious anger.

"All right Here's a card. Give it to the registrar," he said, and dismissed me.

I think everyone who showed up got into Pish's class. So why did he interview each of us, act as if he'd only select a few? The tension of waiting to meet him, the humiliation of having our stories insulted, the exaltation of being chosen--this was his first lesson. In a way, every class was a repetition of the drama he'd put on in the English department. Each week, he'd scrutinize us, humiliate us, pit us against one another, and send us away blessed.

The first class: Stifling heat of an unventilated Columbia classroom at night with two dozen people packed together, anxious as animals. Pish announced that every week we'd go for six hours, though the class was only scheduled for three--and he'd appreciate it if we didn't get up for any reason during that time. If he could last 6 hours without "pishing," so could we.

Artist's conception of Pish. Artist was too lazy to try and draw him herself.

Then he explained what truth is. All great fiction is truth; it is the baring of the soul, the admission of our deepest secrets. We know truth when we hear it because all our secrets are the same. Now, he announced, we were going to go around the room and each tell a terrible truth about ourselves. He'd start.

"Well, you see," he said, shuffling his feet a bit and going into his vaudeville parody of himself--the aging Jew who feared death, the nebbish neurotic. "My wife has three diaphrams. One is in the bedside drawer and two are in the bathroom cabinet. Every time she goes on a trip, the moment she's out of the apartment, I run around and check that all diaphrams are there. I never tell her I do this. I think she knows I do it, but I never tell her."

So we went around the classroom. One guy stammered, "I'm gay."

"So what?" Pish said.

"And, well, I have constant fits of hypochondria about AIDS." He detailed his anxieties, which finally satisfied Pish.

The truth-telling proceeded around the circle as people admitted to showing false emotion at funerals, lusting for strangers, sadistic urges. As my turn came closer, I realized that what Pish really wanted--and no one seemed to have grasped this--was not truth so much as a magnificent falsehood.

And so I spun a tale about how I'd been invited to a party at the apartment of a very rich kid, whose parents were away, and in this apartment was a genuine Whistler. I'd been carrying a smoke machine (the story was very elaborate, I won't give you the whole thing), and I'd bumped into the Whistler and knocked off a chip of white paint from the canvas. And so, I said, I'd run into the study, found a vial of White Out®, and--when no one was looking--dabbed some onto the chipped canvas.

Though this wasn't soul-baring, it was an amusing tale that involved wealth (Pish's obsession), and he loved it. While I told my story, I'd been fanning myself with an antique Chinese fan, and he said, "Kennedy, that's wonderful. I'm in love with you. You're a woman from the 1930s. You're a mystery."

But I had yet to get in his good graces as a writer.

Next class, we were supposed to bring something--a sentence or a story. It was supposed to be new: "You may not be reborn in Jesus," he'd said, "but you'll be reborn in Pish."

So I'd labored over a sentence, trying to make it as weird and intriguing as possible. When it came my turn, I read it and Pish seemed rather to like it, but said, "Okay, okay, fine, but where's the rest?"

"There is no rest," I said, and I lost him.

The routine we followed then and for every class after was this: You'd bring in a story; he'd let you read the first sentence; usually, he wouldn't like the sentence; usually, it would launch him on a lecture about some way in which bad writers falsify experience. Pish had a terror of the cliche.

But if Pish liked your sentence, the earth moved. You were praised, petted and flattered. You were allowed to read your next sentence--and keep on reading until some word or phrase offended him. Then he'd stop you short, saying, "So close, so close, but you lost your courage. I'm disappointed in you."

If you were really in Pish's favor, you'd get to read a whole story; usually only two or three people had this privilege bestowed on them.

So what happened during the six hours of class? Someone would read a sentence and Pish would criticize it--going off on a half-hour-long speech about greatness. This happened over and over all night, but that class was never boring. For one thing, Pish the showman had a flair for the perfect bon mot, the entertaining anecdote. For another, he set up a horrible yet irresistable dynamic by pitting us against one another. After hearing a story, he might announce, "Brilliant, Winslow, that's genius. Now I think you've outdone Wallace; you're the best writer in the class--unless Wallace outdoes you next time. Look, look, he's already planning how to do it." So while I read my piece each week, I always had sweaty palms and a stomach ache, waiting, waiting for the verdict.

At first Pish lavished his praise only on these two guys (I'm still in touch with both of them). But in the fourth class, I finally cheated and brought in an old story--violating Pish's law. He let me read the whole thing and then raved about how I'd bested everyone in the class.

"And how old are you, Kennedy?"

"22."

"You see," he looked at Winslow and Wallace. "She's young, young, young." He really knew how to hurt a writer.

And so--aided I'm sure by youthfulness and probably by femaleness--I became his pet. He tantalized me; he toyed with me; he said, "Kennedy, you're going to be famous. You're going to go down in history" in front of the class, tormenting the others. He talked about me in his other classes. I knew it was all a load of crap but I loved it.

I'd always wanted to write about underground culture for the *Voice*. But as soon as fiction writing seemed like a practical alternative, and Pish made it seem so, I had no other ambition. By the end of the class, I think I almost believed that I'd be the next famous young writer, that Pish might publish me or recommend me to another editor and I'd be wafted aloft into the glamorous world of *Vanity Fair* interviews.

He did publish me, actually, but not in the way I imagined. Soon after our class ended, he started a magazine and published a couple of my stories in there, but never took my collection.

Cut to two years later, when my stories show up in this perfect-bound, slick lit magazine in all the bookstores. I'm not so young anymore--pushing 25. I've moved to Boston. One day I call an old friend, Lisa, who lives in New York.

She says, "Pagan, is there something you aren't telling me? Did you sleep with Dudley Pish?"

"No," I say, "in fact, maybe that's my problem. Maybe he'd have given me a book contract."

"Are you SURE you didn't?" Lisa says. "Because I just went out to lunch with X and his mother Y. Y knows everyone in publishing--in fact, she wrote that scandolous book about her affair with Z [famous hipster]. Anyway, Y says that she knows someone who works with Dudley Pish and that he borrowed her friend's office so he could have a tryst with you. She said that's how you got into Pish's magazine. And I said, 'If Pagan slept with Pish, she would have told me.' I defended you. But then hours later, well, I began to wonder, you know?"

"Lisa," I say, "I went over to see Pish at his office ONCE, and that was only to talk about whether I could get an editorial job there."

But I knew it would do no good. Lisa might have believed me, but the publishing gossip mill had already started churning. And once something becomes gossip it eventually turns into truth. So unknowingly, unwittingly, I HAD slept with Dudley Pish.

Now I need a punchy ending to this story, but I don't have the energy to think one up. You see how my standards have slipped since my youthful days of idealism?

BATTLE OF THE SPOKESPEOPLE

There's a bunch of trendoids out there vying to be the spokesman (spokeswoman? spokesmodel?) for the 20something generation, and Pagan is no better than the rest, clawing and scratching her competitors for the coveted title. But though many will write trenchent essays about our generation's angst, only one will be annointed by the media as the spokesperson. Here's a rundown of some of the candidates.

BRET EASTON ELLIS
General assessment: We're all cruel and amoral.
Quote: "The comedy that audiences responce to wholehearedly is in blockbuster crash-and-burn epics and horror films, usually after a body has been bloodily dispatched and the hero or villian (twentysomething audiences often root for both) gives us a knowing wink."

DOUG COUPLAND
General assessment: We--hit by a rotten economy, AIDS, the ozone hole--yearn for the innocent, stable world of the 1950s.
Quote: "[Generation X] formats its world in top-ten lists and game-show banter. ... The X inner world is one of perceived loss and perceived unmet promises."

PAGAN
General assessment: We're all a bunch of crazy kooks!
Quote (from the July/August *Utne Reader*): "Is it any surprise that those of us who grew up in the '70s are now obsessed by pop culture? ... Our social status depended on whether our bell-bottoms dragged in just the right way under the heels of our Olaf Daughter clogs ... in that era of ever-shifting fads, fads that came at us so fast we couldn't hope to keep up."

LETTERS TO PAGAN

From Scot, my California boyfriend (OK, so we've never met, but that hasn't stopped us from dating in other dimensions).

Dearest Pagan:

Having known you by removed but romantic proxy [through our mutual pal Willy], every time I see another of your articles in the Village Voice Literary Supplement it's like glimpsing another tantalizing morsel. You have become in my eyes like an aromatic, succulent steak, dangled by monofiliment just inches before my quivering snoot. But though I lurch and lunge and my gastric fluids rumble and I strain at the ropes, foaming at the mouth, and though I snarl and yap with unrequited anticipation, still the perfect flank of flesh is not allowed to graze my hungry lips.

So I raise my eyes to the open beams above and try to envision your manifestation on this coil of clay we call home. Is she venus in furs? Is she box-like or amorphous? Is she a train or a rocketship? Or must such unfathomable grandeur be embodied in some truly alien form, which cannot even be beheld by mortal eyes?

Your obedient slave, Scot

And on a very different note, here's a letter from Jay, my quasi-housemate (he lives in the other half of the Farrington mansion). I met Jay five years ago when I moved to Boston; at the time, he was the housemate of my pal Max.

Pagan, you slimeball:

All my favorite musicians started out pure and eventually sold out to the corporate oligarchy--now not only Mick Jones but, horror of horrors, Johnny Rotten are foisting watered-down crap on the public. But I thought you were immune to big-business whoredom, that you had indestructable artistic integrity.

Then you announced in your last issue that you had adopted a new image: Pagan Classic. It was like Jesus saying he'd decided to do a Pepsi commercial.

Now I see that you can be bought and sold by The Man just like anyone else. I wish I could cancel my subscription to Pagan's Head, but any Pagan is better than no Pagan at all. Barely.

MY Pagan wouldn't dream of polluting the air with an old gas-guzzling bomb of a car. The OLD Pagan was an environmental Nazi, who mocked cars and would have never owned a cordless phone.

And MEN .... The old Pagan would be as likely to go on a standard '90s date as she would to sit out in the sun's harmful rays for eight hours.

[editor's note: This is but one angry man's opinion--a man who jumps on top of Pagan and pants while she's innocently watching TV. Pagan's dating rituals are beyond the ken of philistine primates such as the esteemed letter writer.]

To sum up: Old Pagan, 8-tracks; new Pagan, compact disks. What's next? A DAT player? The horror, the horror ...

So I'll just sit here and nurture my memories of the pre-sell-out Pagan, the Pagan you were when you moved to Boston. For me, you'll always be the Shy Neurotic Bag Lady Punk Writer Girl in your cat-eye glasses, huge overcoat, droopy dress and Frankenstein boots. Maybe you can't SELL that Pagan to masses of teeny boppers. Well, I hope you profit big on your new image.

With regrets, Jay

Pagan welcomes open and frank letters to the editor.

Pagan thanks the copy professionals of Typotech for all their help and support.

PAGAN'S CULTURAL ANALYSIS KORNER

Cheesy movies and TV shows are particularly prone to stereotyping when they portray teens. In fact, after long study, I've come to the conclusion that there are only five different teenage personalities--each movie or show merely recycles the same characters, giving them new names, clothes and slang.

TV Show/ Movie	Cute Girl	Cute Guy	Loner, Stoner or Reject	Rebel	Brain
Scooby Doo, Where Are You?	Daphne	Freddie	Shaggy	Scooby	Velma
Beverly Hills 90201	Brenda	Brandon	the radio station guy	Dylan	Andrea
The Breakfast Club	Molly Ringwald	Emilio Estevez	Allie Sheedy	Judd Nelson	Anthony Hall
Welcome Back, Kotter	various	Barbarino	Horshack	Epstein	n/a (Kotter?)
Happy Days	Joni	Richie	Ralph Malph	Fonzie	Chachie (smart ass)
St Elmo's Fire	Allie Sheedy	Judd Nelson	Rob Lowe ← whoops reverse these →	the blonde prep	Andrew McCarthy ← he's really the cute one
Say Anything	Ioni Sky	~~Michael~~ John Cusak	John ~~Michael~~ Cusak	the guitar girl	Ioni Sky

It should be noted that most "teen" TV shows are about large families (P Family, Brady Bunch, Waltons, Family, Eight Is Enough, Cosby et al). The characters in these shows do not fit the Scooby-Do-ian archetypes because the characters are differentiated by age more than by personality type.

What does this confluence of teen stereotyping mean? Well, the whole thing seems to revolve around the popularity issue. The rebel, reject and brain may be cool or canny, but none of their accomplishments stack up to the good looks of the Cute Guy/Gal. Actually, this is a pretty fair portrayal of high school reality. Nonetheless, it's too bad that message goes no deeper than that--few directors hint that the Cute Guy/Gal is headed for a life of suburban boredom.

Anyway, if someone wants to write their PhD. dissertation on this, they're welcome to it.

KARMIC KOMIX PROUDLY PRESENTS
FATAL FUNNIES
PART III DEPRESSION
BLAME JIM KENDALL ©1992
CHAPTER XI
"NO HOPE, NO HOPE, NO HOPE AND STILL NO HOPE."
DO NOT EXPECT ANY PUNCHLINES. I'VE BEEN SOMEWHAT DEPRESSED.
IT'S HARD TO KEEP UP APPEARANCES.
FANS OF "FATAL FUNNIES" REMEMBER THAT I WENT THROUGH CLINICAL DEPRESSION IN CHAPTERS V-X. TODAY WE START THE MORE ETHERIAL GLOOM OF EVERYDAY DEPRESSION.
IT TOOK ME YEARS TO AQUIRE SUCH AN EXTENSIVE COLLECTION OF MASKS. MOST OF THEM AREN'T EVEN SKIN-DEEP. ULTIMATELY, ALL ARE USELESS.
WHAT MATTERS MOST IS WHAT'S INSIDE YOUR HEAD- Y'KNOW.
USUALLY MY BRAIN IS ON FIRE. BUT SOMETIMES IT SIMPLY OVERFLOWS WITH WORMS AND SNAKES.
I WONDER IF THE GLASS IS HALF FULL OR HALF EMPTY? -WHATEVER.
REAL CRAZY PEOPLE HEAR VOICES ORDERING THEM TO DO MANY UNSPEAKABLE THINGS.
LUCKY ME, I'M ONLY DEPRESSED.
ANYWAY, WE'RE ALL GOING TO DIE SOON.
RIP
YOUR NAME HERE
AND MOST OF US WILL DIE IN HUMILIATING AND PAINFULL WAYS. DEPRESSING, ISN'T IT.
Pagan's note: This was done by college pal Jim. He was depressed then but now he's really happy.
Jim's a famous Soho artist now with a goatee. We met at Wesleyan when we were both tripping.

8

BOOKS, BOYFRIENDS, OOPHORECTOMY

ON THE SECOND DAY of the new year, 1993, I found out I'd won a grant from the National Endowment for the Arts for my fiction; it would be enough money to support me until 1994 and beyond—freedom from copyediting!

That same week, I fell in love. The guy, Bill, lived on the Cape. We'd spent a romantic weekend together, but weren't sure if we wanted to get serious. So when he got four days off for New Year's, he decided to stay with me, just to see how we'd click. Well, a few hours into our vacation together, we both became drugged-out, drunk, high with love—it was that teetery moment at the top of the roller coaster just before you plunge down into the wild ride of a relationship.

We spent the weekend staring into each other's eyes and subsisting on chocolate chip cookies because we couldn't be bothered to leave the house. This intense period coincided with the January thaw. The sun glared on the wooden floors of my room and flashed across the windows of passing cars; everything seemed too bright to look at. I felt the way you do when you've been laughing hard. Too much happiness hurts. It's scary. In the back of my mind, I knew something bad would happen to balance all this out.

By the spring it did—in a way I never expected. I got sick, found out my ovary had swelled up bigger than a grapefruit, and lost it in surgery. Because the cyst turned out to be a rare, borderline malignancy, I would now live with the shadowy threat of cancer.

As I dealt with my illness and fought to get decent care, I knew I had to turn this experience into a comic book. Friends urged me to write a serious article about what had happened. Well, I'd already tried that. After my father died, I'd worked on a fact-filled indictment of the health industry. I tried to argue against the medical establishment using its own language, frequently making reference to studies in the *Journal of the American Medical Association* and the *New England Journal of Medicine*. But that hadn't worked; I lost my own message among the medical mumbo jumbo; trying to sound reasonable, I held back my anger and outrage. And then I'd grown weary of the whole project and never published the article.

This time, I would do things differently. I would not try to argue against them, the doctors, the world of reasonable people. Instead, I would speak in my own most primitive language, a childlike mixture of words and pictures.

It took me months to finish the comic book. My drawing skills came and went, and I screwed up a lot of good sketches with some terrible inking. Sometimes I'd start crying with frustration as I worked—especially when Bill got involved and gave me pointers.

It was because of the comic book that I decided to put together another *Pagan's Head.* After all, where else could I publish an extended cartoon about women's health? Besides, I wanted to do one final issue, for old times' sake. All the issues of the *Head,* taken together, had begun to feel like a story, a book, still in need of an ending.

I hadn't put out an issue of the 'zine for more than a year and a half. In that time, I'd written a nonfiction book, lost an ovary, become depressed, moved into an apartment with Bill, recovered from depression, and become a published author. Somewhere amid all that tumult, I'd forgotten about Pagan[1]. When I sat down to produce *Pagan's Head,* I could no longer summon her. Her voice was silent inside me. To finish the 'zine, I had to imitate her voice—as if I were mimicking the work of another author. Despite my efforts to bring Pagan[1] back to life, I never quite could, and I think some of the writing in Issue Eight sounds forced and false.

When did I lose Pagan[1]? Maybe the summer before, when the doctor extracted my mutated ovary—two pounds of tissue, mucus, and precancerous growths. The operation I had was strangely like a birth. When I left the hospital, I was handed a set of instructions written for women recovering from a C-section. Suddenly I'd realized that I'd just had a cesarean—the scar was the same, everything was the same, except no baby. My tumor may have tormented me, but I felt an odd emptiness when it was gone. I didn't want a child—not yet, maybe never. Still, after having borne this growth for at least six months, I felt cheated, barren. Hadn't I made something more than a sack of fluid, something more than flesh to be cut up by a pathologist?

I've heard some women go through a postpartum depression after they have ovarian cysts or tumors removed; other books say that losing even one ovary can throw you into a mini-menopause, a dip in hormones that can cause depression. Whatever the reason, something in my brain went haywire after that operation. During the summer of '93, I had days when I couldn't get out of bed, couldn't even move. Of course I'd suffered through bad moods in the past. But no matter how terrible I'd felt before, I'd always been buoyantly sane. By that I mean that even in my darkest periods, I'd always have this chirping, optimistic voice in my head. "Pagan, get up and take a walk," it would say. "Or call a friend. You've got to do something to make yourself feel better." Now that voice was gone.

By September I was better, but still so unsure of my moods that I began rating each day in my calendar. *Bad,* I scrawled in one square, and then *bad, horrible, OK, bad, good, really horrible, bad, bad, bad.*

Part of what made me feel so down was that I had to spend an inordinate amount of time dealing with the medical establishment. I wrote angry notes to my HMO so they'd pay for my visits to an outside doctor; I read through medical journals; I got myself switched to a new gynecologist; and I tried to get a second opinion. These minor tasks took months of effort, since doctors often failed to return my calls, answer my letters, send slides, or answer questions.

Eventually I had to accept the fact that I'd done all I could. I fought for good care, and I got the best care available—but if you have the wrong disease, the medical establishment doesn't have much to offer you. And ovarian cancer is definitely the wrong disease. Poorly researched and ill understood, the cancer is difficult to detect in its early stages and kills 90 percent of its late-stage sufferers.

I learned to accept my precarious existence and decided to keep my remaining ovary. I've read all different opinions on this matter: Many voices say that a woman at risk of ovarian cancer should "complete her family" and then get a hysterectomy. Well, what if you don't know whether you want a family—not to mention a complete one, which I assume includes a house in Newton, a husband in a Burberry raincoat, and a golden retriever? I'm still trying to figure it all out.

A friend of mine calls Issue Eight the "dark issue." For the first time, I showed my whole self in *Pagan's Head*—not just the happy part of me, but also the despairing and angry part. I'd been able to divide myself during my father's death, writing about my nutty search for a car even as I kept my grief private; but now I no longer seemed able to do that, or wanted to do it. Once, Pagan^1 had helped me through hard times, but now I felt that particular coping mechanism didn't work anymore. Instead of dividing myself into parts, I wanted to pull myself back into one.

I decided to keep my ovary, even if that meant nurturing risk inside me like a baby. But there's no room for Pagan^1 in here anymore. I no longer wanted to live divided into two personas, or three, or four. My body began to divide against itself; the tumor grew with a will of its own. To me, getting healthy involves pulling all the parts of me together, pooling all my resources.

Without knowing quite what I was doing, I think I created a new personality for myself while I was sick. This new person, let's call her Pagan^3, is made out of bits and pieces of all my old selves. Of course, I lost parts of myself, too—like my youthful feelings of invulnerability. And much of Pagan^1 is gone: the woman who masked herself in costumes, the woman who whisked into parties and blew air kisses, the woman who turned dating into performance art. I feel too rubbed raw these days to be anything other than authentic. I pick up other people's feelings almost too easily and can't seem to hide anything about myself—and I've grown to like being this way.

But another part of Pagan^1 is still inside me. She taught me how to become a writer in a way I never learned at Johns Hopkins. Just recently, I finished my novel. This time when I re-re-rewrote the book, I went back to it with a different attitude, a *Pagan's Head* attitude. Before, I'd always tried to make it everything a publishable novel should be: 250 pages long, well plotted, full of beautiful language, etc. But now I stopped worrying about all that. Instead of figuring out what should happen in the book, I simply let the narrator, Frannie, tell her story. And her story turned out to be far more eccentric than anything I could have planned.

I'm not going to publish *Pagan's Head* anymore. Instead, I'm waiting for a new entity to take shape inside me. Let's call her Pagan[3]. She'll have some kind of impracticable, unprofitable, and otherwise kooky scheme she'll want me to carry out. Move to Prague? Have a baby and raise it in an alternative-family, co-op arrangement? Compete in backwards-running races? Turn my yard into a recycling center? And whatever it is, I'll do it.

issue#
8
STRIPPING
Pagan's Head
Books, boyfriends, oophorectomy

UPDATE ON MY LIFE

Oh geez, it's been more than a year since the last Pagan's Head--and what a year. I don't quite know where to begin.

But of course there's only place to begin: My hair. I must apologize to those Pagan watchers who have been hoping I would adopt some outré hair style for the mid-nineties. My look is blander than ever. Since I knew I was going to become a public figure (sort of) after my two books came out, I decided I needed a media-savvy image--a slick look that would make me instantly accessible to a nation not yet ready for the real Pagan. Now my hair is straight and long, its natural red tones enhanced through the magic

NEW PAGAN® with magic-growing hair!

of henna. AND THE GLASSES ARE GONE! I got contacts. Am I a traitor to my nerd roots? Am I intellectual oreo, an egghead masquerading as a normal person? Well, too bad. I feel like I've paid my dues after all those years in chunky, high-profile glasses.

LOVE, EXCITING AND NEW

If you read the last issue of *Pagan's Head*, the infamous Men issue, you probably guessed that I went on a bender. I became a dating Dervish, whirling through clubs with men on my arm. I seemed to be exuding some kind of hormone, because suddenly guys were pursuing me like never before. I wish I could reveal some of the juicier details of this period in my life, but I don't want anyone suing me for defamation.

Dallying with every man in Boston wasn't enough for Pagan. She began a long-distance crypto-courtship with Scot, who lived in California and who originally got sucked into the Pagan vortex because he was friends with her roommate Willie. You may remember Scot as the *Pagan's Head* reader whose letter ran in the last issue. (It was the best fan letter I've ever gotten and included the sentence, "You have become in my eyes like an aromatic, succulent steak, dangled by monofiliment just inches before my quivering snoot.")

After that letter, Scot and I began a correspondence. I'd never met Scot, but long distance made me brazen. One minute I was calling him my "California boyfriend," and the next minute I was demanding that he move to Boston and become my boyfriend for real. Well, little did I know that groovemaster Scot can never resist a challenge like that. I try to live my life like it's performance art; Scot lives his life like it's an Evel Kneivel stunt.

He threw his Tarot, the signs pointed East, so he called me up one day and said "Mama, I'm comin' home!" He then proceeded to send me all his earthly possession, about twenty-two boxes, including his entire collection of K-Tel albums. And soon that crazy Californian jumped on his motorcycle and rode across the country during one of the worst frosts of the year.

I had no idea when exactly he was going to show up. So one night, I was sitting curled up

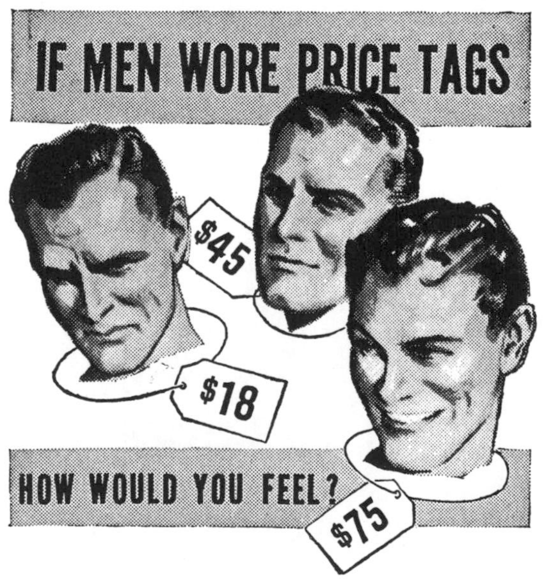

1

in a chair yakking on the cordless, when suddenly there's a banging at the window. I look up, terrified (it's a second-story window, after all) and see a blond guy--as cute as David Soul, I swear--hanging off the fire escape. So I run to the window and point down, indicating that he should enter the house through a more-traditional egress.

Thus began an open-ended romance. Scot found a place to live and began looking for a job. (To be honest, I wasn't the only reason he'd come to Boston. Scot dreamed of getting on the East Coast copy editing fast track.) We spent lots of time together, trying to see if this would really work.

But meanwhile, sensing that a relationship that started as performance art might not last, I continued to go out with other guys--i.e, Bill, this painter who I'd met just before Scot arrived. Since Bill lived on the Cape, we'd only seen each other sporadically, and it wasn't even clear we were dating. (Oooh, I hate that.) And then one day Bill `fessed his love.

It was the classic Victorian gal's dilemma. Do you chose the fair-haired guy (Scot) whose temperament is all sweetness and light? Or do you go for the dark-haired lad (Bill) who storms across the moors, a man with a Russian soul and an ambitious art career? Being a glutton for punishment, I chose the latter.

Actually, it wasn't like I had a choice. Almost immediately, Bill and I fell in hit-by-a-Mack-truck, no-looking-back love. Soon I was trekking out to the Cape all the time to stay at his house (actually his mom's vacation house). Bill had decided to live there because the rent was free, and because he thought the isolation of the Cape (which was nearly deserted during the off-season) would spur him to new heights of creativity. He worked part-time at Head Start, which left his afternoons and evenings free for all his important projects: painting masterpieces, learning to play the accordion, and writing a seminal philosophical tome about consciousness. Actually, by the time I started going out with him (last December), he'd given up on the accordian and the philosophical treatise; instead, he was spending his time painting, drinking beer and listening to talk radio. In the absence of living people, Bill had become "best friends" with Bruce Williams, a financial guru with a nightly call-in show.

As I got to know Bill, I learned to understand why he is so tortured: He is always on the verge of thinking great thoughts but is continually distracted by Jr. Whoppers, *Star Trek: The Next Generation*, the need to dye all his clothes Kelly green, Kraft macaroni and cheese, *Juggs* magazine, media pundits, half-price sales at the supermarket, and naked women on TV (or rather, the hope that if he surfs through the channels long enough, he might see a naked woman). Poor Bill. The modern world torments him with its unwholesome pleasures. In this way, we are opposites. I have made peace with pop culture; once and a while, I sample some bad TV or chemical-laced junk food, get my fill, and then am happy to avoid it for another month or two.

Detail from a self-portrait by Bill

Anyway, after Bill's job ended, he moved to Boston and in September we got our own apartment! Bill sold a lot of paintings, made a bunch of money, and now he doesn't have to "work" for a living either! Every day he goes to his studio and paints while I sit in my office and write. We're back in the high life again!

MY CAREER

Yes, that's right, I don't "work" for a living anymore--I mean I don't go to an office or anything. I use quote marks to describe white-collar drudge work because I actually find that much easier than staying home and writing for a living--which has been my tenuous form of

employment for the last year and a half.

I spent all last year working on my seventies book (*Platforms: A Microwaved Cultural Chronicle of the 1970s*--I didn't come up with that title so don't ask me what it means). That was a very strange interlude in my life, let me tell you. I was so immersed in the seventies that I expected to walk out my door and see Pacers and Gremlins driving down the street, or people clad in Indian wrap skirts and painter's pants walking by. I spent my nights watching blaxploitation movies and old episodes of "Charlie's Angels." The only time I really felt rooted in the nineties was when I went to my health club--those fruity colors (mango, cantaloupe, berry) and the Santa Fe

furniture helped to remind me that, yes, the eighties had come and gone.

Writing a book about an entire decade in nine months was one of the hardest things I've ever done. To complicate matters I had to have major surgery on the *very day* the book was due (see the cartoon in this issue for a full explication of my health problems).

But now the book is out--as is my short story collection from Serpent's Tail press. Right now, I'm caught up in the book-tour whirl (for *Platforms*). Actually, "book tour" isn't really the appropriate term, since I don't go anywhere. I just pick up my phone and get interviewed by deejays at radio stations all over the country.

Typical show: "Hey, today we're remembering the seventies, and we're going to talk to author Pagan Kennedy who will tell us *where they are now.* So if you've been wondering what happened to your favorite superstar, call in and ask Pagan," says the deejay. And I sputter, "Well, actually, I don't know where anyone is now except possibly Freddie Prinze. My book is more about *ideas.*" Or that's what I would say if I had guts. Usually I just play along. And I have to add that many of the deejays who interviewed me have asked me thoughtful questions--*and some have even read my book.*

I may be stuck in radio-promotion hell here in the states, but not in Canada. I've been on three TV shows there, including Much Music, their MTV equivalent. I'm a star in Toronto! (You know you're really cool when you're obscure in your own country but revered in Europe or Japan. But Canada?)

THE MOST DEMEANING MOMENT OF MY BOOK TOUR

It's 9:00 in the morning. I haven't had my coffee yet. And due to some miscommunication between my publicist and me, I have no idea that I am scheduled for a radio interview today. The phone rings. A woman's voice says, "Hi Pagan, this is Brainless Bitch at WXXX in Bumfuck, Connecticut. Are you ready to do the show?"

"Sure," I say, eyeing a pot on the stove, wherein the water for my coffee is about to boil.

"OK, let me put you on hold," she says, and suddenly I hear what's playing on WXXX. It's stupid-guy banter, loud guffawing, mean wisecracks. My heart sinks as I suddenly understand: This is some kind of Howard Stern copy-cat show. The woman I have just spoken to is the host's pathetic sidekick. Her job is to act like an idiot and laugh as he humiliates his guests.

Suddenly the host comes on: "Pagan, Pagan, Pagan, first a little criticism. Your book jacket. Why aren't you wearing any makeup babe? You know, before I started dating her, my girlfriend went through a geeky stage--she looks great now. But you look like your stuck in that stage. I mean, the hair. It's just hanging straight down. You look like you should be on the corner of Haight and Ashbury trying to overthrow the government."

"Well, actually, I would like to overthrow the government," I say.

He ignores me. "And why no makeup? What's wrong with you?"

"You're absolutely right," I say. "I think I should spend several hours a day applying makeup. That would be a very good use of my time."

As he insults me, I continue to agree with everything he says. This is a tactic I learned when I was tormented in junior high.

But then finally he goes too far. "Look, Pagan, I'm just trying to help you. Because if you don't wear makeup and stuff, no one's going to go out with you."

"Ooooh," I coo. "You are just soooo funny." And then, in my most innocent voice: "Are you trying to be like Howard Stern?"

"Never heard of him," the host snaps, and goes directly to the commercial break. During the break, I contemplate all kinds of attacks--I really want to address myself to his female sidekick, say to her "You are a such a slug for laughing along with this creep. I have never seen such a pathetic example of slave mentality in my entire life."

But when the host comes back, he is all lovey-dovey. He talks about my book and pitches me easy questions about the seventies. I play along, eager to be done.

After that experience, I feel I have seen the real America. It is nothing but a big junior high school.

3

WE BUILT THIS CITY ON ROCK AND ROLL

ALLSTON, MA

In the mid-eighties I lived in the far reaches of the Lower East Side in a jack-legged loft; my neighborhood consisted of abandoned buildings, a needle-strewn park, crack factories, Hassidic businessmen, poor people and the occasional artiste.

I thought I would be there forever. Then some friends visited from up north, bringing back tales of an enchanted neighborhood just outside of Boston where punkers lived in harmony with old Irish people, where rent was cheap and the streets were safe. ... A place called Allston.

It sounded intriguing, but I had been so brainwashed by New York that I thought I couldn't leave--after all, nothing artistically important could ever happen outside of Manhattan, right? How would I ever make it as a fiction writer if I left this urban hell of hipness?

One day my Boston pal Max called and told me about some new people he'd met. They lived in this falling-apart, Addams-Family-style house that backed up on an electric plant. The house, called "The E Ranch" (and listed in the phonebook under "Ranch, E"), had been decorated in thrift-shop Western style, with a jackalope head mounted on the wall and cowboy souvenirs plastered all over the kitchen. Oh, yes, and someone had built a gazebo in the backyard so you could sit in Victorian splendor only a few feet away from the "Danger: High Voltage" signs.

I think it was hearing about the E Ranch that made me realize there was life outside of New York. I knew I belonged in that house. What can I say? Sometimes it seems my life is a series of nutty hunches that I follow like signs pointing into some alternate Pagan universe. I moved to Boston and soon shmoozed my way into a room at the E Ranch, acres of transformers right outside my window and a crazy roommate with a gun. My dream house!

Now, looking back, I understand my move from New York to Allston was also a spiritual one. If you're artist in New York you can't help being career-minded--every time you show off your latest poems in some Lower East Side "performance space," you feel like maybe it will be your first big break. Maybe some editor in the audience will make you a star. (Am I being unfair to New York? I just mean that there's no room for amateurism.) In Boston the emphasis is on having fun. It's easy to get gigs; often, everyone in the audience knows each other. It was after moving to Boston/Allston that I became less interested in serious fiction and more interested in just-for-fun stuff like making this zine and starring in a talk show on Somerville cable.

Well, enough of that. Enough over-intellectualized explanations for why I've settled down in Allston without moving my butt (except to go to grad school) for seven years. Enough talk. I want to show what it's like here in Allston. So come, come with me as I escort you around the sleazy little punk-rock suburb I call home.

A beautiful turnpike runs through the neighborhood!

Let's picture ourselves walking down the quiet streets of dear Allstonia on a summer day. The annoying B.U. students have gone home, so all we hear is the twittering of birdies and the roar of the turnpike. A punkette sits in her lush lawn, amidst the morning-glories and posies, carefully brushing glitter on her toenails. A nice Vietnamese man wheels a shopping cart full of cans, stopping at each house to look in the yard. A self-proclaimed witch tends her herb garden. An old Irish woman adds one more plastic gnome to her lawn menagerie. A rasta guy watches the scene from his porch. A crazy old man with a heart condition mutters about property values while he mows the only normal-looking yard on the street. What is Allston? It's a little bit country and a little bit rock 'n' roll.

Come, my friend, let's leave the garden district of Allston and stroll down bustling Harvard Street. Here's an auto parts store. And here's another auto parts store. And, yes, here's another auto parts store. And here's my favorite place in the whole wide world...AMVETS, the caviar of thrift stores. Whenever I try to tell someone about Amvets, I become so emotional that all I can do is stammer and drool. Let me just say this: for under forty dollars, you could fill your living room with furniture--if you weren't too picky. And let me say this: If you want to buy some knick-knack that's smaller than a bread box and it isn't marked down to $1.29 yet, then hold out for the green-tag sale.

Shop daily for best selection? Believe me, I try to.

Now come with me across the street to the Allston Mall. We enter an inauspicious doorway and walk up a narrow flight of stairs. The walls are plastered with flyers ("band seeks singer," "woman wanted for lesbian household") that flutter as we pass. At the top of the stairs we find ourselves in a wide hallway with wildly painted walls and rooms on each side; each room houses a tiny, doomed business--a piercing parlor, an art gallery filled with "installations," a store that sells 'zines and Betty Page porno, a comic book store with the windows painted black. Years ago people started calling this place "The Allston Mall" as a joke, but the name stuck, and now the words are hand-painted near the entrance to the stairs.

There used to be a dental lab up there, owned and operated by a shabby Eastern European gentleman who scuttled past the punk rockers to get into his teeny room. The dental lab was the most pitiful example of market capitalism I've ever seen. You would catch glimpses of the guy in his slime-green room, valiantly wearing his lab coat and whittling away at plastic teeth. Dust hung in gray strings from the ceiling; crud clung to every surface.

The guy finally went belly up--it's really sad because he had to close the business after his eyes started going. My boyfriend Bill took over the room, repainted it, and turned it into his studio. He inherited a lot of dental paraphernalia, and now we have a huge collection of plastic teeth.

Look, here's Bill's beautiful studio and here's Bill hard at work on one of his masterpieces. But hush!, we must not disturb him because he has a show in New York in June and he has to finish five more paintings.

So enough, enough of the Mall. Let's away! It's off to Herrell's! Down the block we go, past the Laundromat that's become an impromptu homeless shelter, past the hardware store run by babbling alcoholics, past the Thai porno video store. And here we are at Herrell's ice cream parlor--oh, what a cute place with stuffed teddy bears everywhere! But as we walk through the door, we are assaulted by a grinding sound so loud we have to clench our teeth. It's some band like Ween or Metallica or Psychic TV or Gwar being cranked on the Herrel's sound system. Behind the counter lurk young men and women in various stages of baldness. The staff of Herrell's--lounging underneath stuffed bears and paper rainbows--looks like a bunch of acid ravers who inadvertently ended up at a kid's birthday party.

Many times I've stood before the picture of Steve Herrell (it hangs in the back of the store) and looked into the eyes of this shaggy prepster who became an ice cream mogul in the '70s (?). "Steve, Steve," I've appealed to him in my thoughts, "how could let your Allston store turn into Lollapalooza? You entered the ice cream market with a rainbow as your sword and a teddy bear as your shield. You had a vision--you would create an atmosphere of cuteness and sugary sweetness where everyone could feel cuddly and warm. But now look at it! Steve, why don't you swoop down from Martha's Vineyard or wherever you are and discipline these slackers?"

Shaking our heads, we leave Herrell's and follow Harvard St. (past Farrington Street with its former Pagan abode) to Cambridge Street and thence to the Harvest Food Coop. As we enter the Coop, pass through the juice aisle and make our way into the produce section, we notice that every example of

When you're in downtown Allston, liquor is never more than a few steps away.

"alternative" humanity mingles here. This is also the most happening pick-up spot in Allston. If you stand near the kale too long, some bearded guy is likely to sidle up to you and ask, "How do you cook that stuff?"--in Coop lingo that phrase means "Your place or mine?"

But away, away, we must leave this New Age Peyton Place and travel on. We rush out of the glass doors and down Cambridge street, speaking in awed whispers, for we are approaching the very soul of Allston, its ground zero, its Taj Mahal. Yes, there it is in the distance, a low, brownstone building that sits beside the train tracks.

Once upon a time in the 1800s, this was a train station called Cambridge Crossing (it was built by the famous architect who also designed the church in Copley Square, but I can't remember his name). The train station served a sleepy hamlet on the outskirts of Boston, a place that became also became known as Cambridge Crossing. The trouble was, people kept getting this Cambridge confused with the tonier one that lay across the river. And so, the city fathers, in their wisdom, decided to rename the train station--they called it Allston station, after the then-famous painter Washington Allston.

These days, the building still stands, a reminder of our neighborhood's proud legacy as a train depot that people got off at only because they thought they were in the other Cambridge. But the building is more than a mere monument; it operates as a bustling ... sports bar. Yes, the historic Allston Depot was once again renamed. A few years ago, it became the Sports Depot. Does that mean we're going have to start calling our neighborhood "Sports"?

"I avoid doctors like the serpent."
--Pagan's grandma

"Why can't you use PageMaker on a Mac? Because PageMaker is for pussies."
--Jennifer

"But I need to watch this women-in-prison movie as part of my research project on the decline of American culture."
--Bill, after I tried to get him to watch a Shakespeare play instead of *Bad Girls in Chains.*

"We were thinking of using the lyrics from a Carpenters song as our wedding vow, but we decided against it."
--Terry

"When I saw the top floor of the Salvation Army in Woonsocket, I nearly got down on my knees and kissed the floor."
--Diane

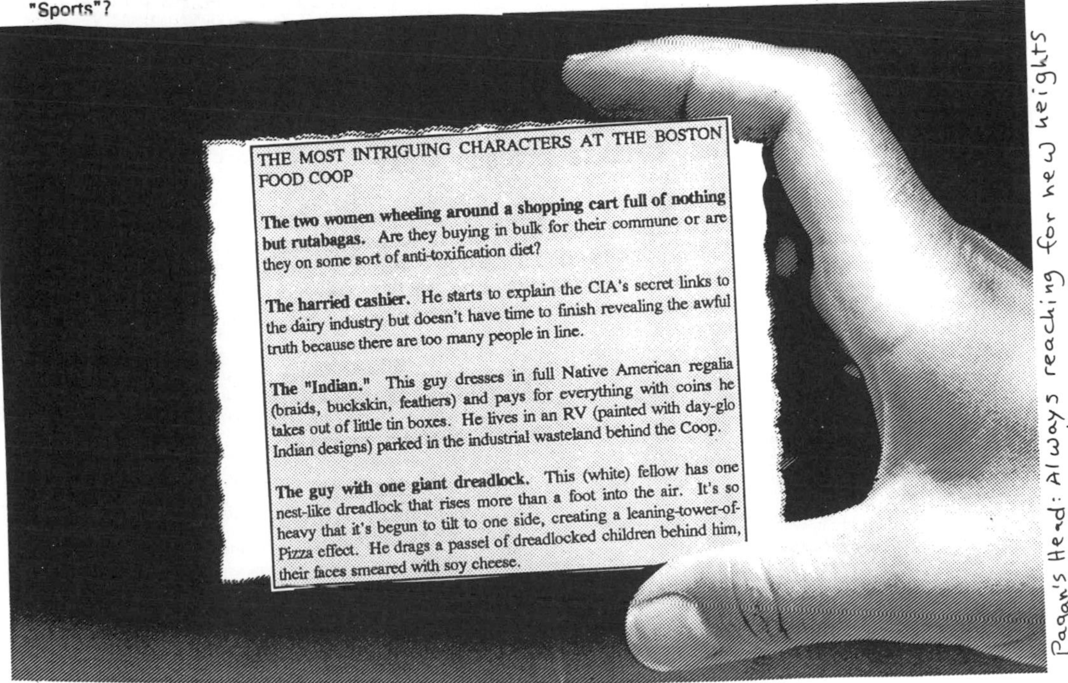

THE MOST INTRIGUING CHARACTERS AT THE BOSTON FOOD COOP

The two women wheeling around a shopping cart full of nothing but rutabagas. Are they buying in bulk for their commune or are they on some sort of anti-toxification diet?

The harried cashier. He starts to explain the CIA's secret links to the dairy industry but doesn't have time to finish revealing the awful truth because there are too many people in line.

The "Indian." This guy dresses in full Native American regalia (braids, buckskin, feathers) and pays for everything with coins he takes out of little tin boxes. He lives in an RV (painted with day-glo Indian designs) parked in the industrial wasteland behind the Coop.

The guy with one giant dreadlock. This (white) fellow has one nest-like dreadlock that rises more than a foot into the air. It's so heavy that it's begun to tilt to one side, creating a leaning-tower-of-Pizza effect. He drags a passel of dreadlocked children behind him, their faces smeared with soy cheese.

Pagan's Head: Always reaching for new heights of clip art abuse.

PAGAN'S HEAD: SOME CRITICAL REFLECTIONS

BY BILL

I don't like "Pagan's Head"--in fact, I hate it. Oh, its funny all right, and entertaining enough, but compared to Pagan's other work it's superficial and sloppy. It burns me up when her friends say they prefer it to her fiction, and I'm endlessly annoyed by Pagan's own suggestion that these silly scrapbooks tread some new literary frontier between the worlds of fiction and autobiography. What makes me an authority on such matters? Why, I'm Pagan's boyfriend.

Just over a year and a half ago, Pagan was a name from my past, a college classmate who I'd noticed but never known, and whose stories I'd seen once or twice in the VLS. I had foolishly decided to spend the winter in my Mom's summer house on the Cape and knew no one in Boston but my brother; he, it turned out, knew Pagan. I called her out of the blue, we talked, and a day later I found a thick bundle of "Pagan's Heads" in my PO box. Since I'd hidden the TV away in an upstairs closet, this unasked-for series of "zines" proved the best available distraction from painting. I read them all.

I'll admit that reading PH made me want to meet Pagan. Aside from the fact that I was desperate to meet ANYONE in the Greater Boston Area, the 'zine gave me the impression that she was very funny and very smart--and on the fast-track to a successful publishing career. In fact, it gave me <u>such</u> a good impression of her that I started wondering whether her claim of "self-parody" was really justified.

I mean a parodist, by definition, is supposed to <u>undermine</u> some one's serious purpose--the way Dana Carvey's incisive imitations deflated the effect of Bush's posturing during the last election. Good parodists reveal the true natures of the two-faced people and institutions that make their best targets, and so earn our respect as *de facto* advocates for virtues like common sense and sincerity.

So what happens when a person tries to parody herself? Pagan's serious purpose in these pages is self-promotion and self-aggrandizement: among the fans of PH are editors around the country who give Pagan lucrative freelance assignments and book contracts on the basis of what they read here *[Hey! Now who's guilty of aggrandizing Pagan's life? -ed.]*, and subscribers know that I wasn't the first man to receive issues in the mail as a prelude to a date *[Hey! My motives were pure. -ed.]*. Pagan the parodist, however, ridicules her own tendencies toward myopic egotism and shameless self-promotion by exaggerating them to a laughable degree--of course it's preposterous that readers throughout the land might care about the hair troubles of a little-known writer and copy-editor living in a group house in Allston. The question then is, does this "parody," hilarious as it may be, at all undermine Pagan's serious purpose, that of self-promotion and self-aggrandizement?

And the answer, of course, is no. Pagan's long-winded boasting would be unbearable, and ineffective, if it were seriously intended--by making light of her boasts she paradoxically slips them right by us. She achieves her serious goals and also deflects anyone else's efforts to criticize or parody her--hey, she already knows she's ridiculous. What looks like self-criticism, assuming the moral high ground of the parodist, is actually the perfect armor against criticism of any kind. Pagan has created a version of herself that is weirdly invulnerable.

This bothers me because I see it everywhere, not just as entertainment, but as a complete substitute for honest discourse. Other commentators have pointed out the narcissism of late 20th C. America, and that the narcissist's fantasy of an invulnerable self is [illegible] only protection for a real self that is so vulnerable and insecure that the slightest blow might wound it. Cloak everything you say in irony, leave people guessing about your serious intentions, express your deepest feelings in jokes, all so you can cover yourself later by saying, "I was sort of kidding,"--these are the annoying narcissistic stunts I find, not only in PH, but in everyday conversations with many of my peers.

Fortunately, though, the real Pagan is capable of leaving these defenses behind around people she trusts--and in her fiction. Her stories concern people with real problems, weaknesses, and fears, and so reflect Pagan's own vulnerabilities. They're funny sometimes, but not all the time, and you know when you're reading the serious parts. Pagan

NOTE: Bill isn't cranky like this in real life

tells me that most people find PH more entertaining, but what's more entertaining than the adventures of a super-hero? Our scared, narcissistic selves love to identify with the well-armored, and are always looking to pick up some of their tricks, but good art goes deeper than that and feeds the rest of our souls as well.

Which brings me to my final point--contrary to what Pagan and some of her fans would have you believe, there's nothing much original about PH. Pagan calls it fiction--a new kind of autobiographical, illustrated fiction that doesn't "constrain" her the way "traditional" fiction does. When pressed she'll tell you that she hasn't made any of it up, though, only embellished things a little. So doesn't PJ O'Rourke embellish his narratives--don't we expect him to? These are mostly humorous, autobiographical essays combined with Pagan's ham-handed cartoons and out-of-focus Polaroids. A new form? I don't think so.

Well, I've done it. At Pagan's request I've committed my criticisms of her harmless 'zine to print. I don't really hate PH, but since Pagan thinks it's her "best work" my luke-warm reaction to it has actually caused her a great deal of distress. I think she's trying to neutralize my critique by brashly airing it in this fantastic realm of hers, a realm where the invincible "Pagan" reigns supreme. She figures her loyal fans will laugh at humorless old stick-in-the-mud Bill, who just doesn't get it. Go ahead and laugh your ironic laughs, you scared, narcissistic sycophants. There are others like me--others who are willing to fight for sincerity and straight talk, and my message will not go unheeded, even as you so easily write it off as the raving of a humorless old grouch. Maybe I'll never get as popular as Pagan by telling the truth, but I don't need friends like you anyway!

Boston rules, but sometimes the great city alone isn't enough to wipe away the ennui we all feel from time to time. Sometimes you need therapy. But with all the different psychologists, psychiatrists, and social workers around, what's a depressed person to do? Well, after some extensive research, I've compiled this guide to Boston-area mental health.

If you belong to an HMO, you are allowed (+ or -) 4 sessions with a psychiatrist at full coverage. This nascent model of mental health care has given rise to an elegant, short-term therapy, one ~~who~~ that can cure in just a few sessions. Janice Clark practices such a therapy.

Janice Clark, HMO Whore. Actually, Dr. Clark, a psychiatrist, is more call girl than whore. Her plush Cambridge office has a view of the river, and it's no coincidence that a video parlor called The Games People Play occupies a ground floor space in the same building.

Janice looked lovely that first visit. She wore a loose, flower print dress and her lips were painted up to a ripe glossy plum. I avoided the couch and sat in a supple leather chair opposite her, anticipating a Margaret Bean-Bayog-type treatment.

She crossed her legs non-aggressively and the flowers settled over health club toned thighs. "So, what brings you to my office?"

"I'm depressed."

Janice asked me briefly about my history, inquired if I was allergic to any drugs, and wrote me a Prozac prescription on the spot.

This seemed reckless and irresponsible, but she explained the risks of the medication: "If you suddenly feel like hurting yourself or hurting other people, just stop for a minute and tell yourself 'It's just the drug'. Then call me." The plums gave way to perfect white teeth.

Because the treatment involved medication, she told me, we would need to involve a psychopharmacologist. Dr. Clark gave me the Prozac prescription, a cool handshake, and sent me to the Psycho Pharm.

Dr. Dan Krausshoffler, Psychopharmacologist/Pusher. Not all Nazi war criminals fled to Paraguay. Dr. Krausshoffler, my new psychopharmacologist, made it all the way to Watertown and managed to start a practice where he gets paid to continue his experiments of terror. After asking me to interpret a couple of proverbs, he decided Prozac might not be the answer, probably because it takes up to six weeks to work and that would exceed the 5-session cure I had been allotted. Also, Prozac is relatively new and perhaps not evil enough. He recommend a monoamine oxidase (M.A.O.) inhibitor.

"The M.A.O. inhibitor can be quite effective," he told me.

"I thought they only used them in China, you know, to stop the spread of communism."

This comment caused Herr Doktor to write furiously on his pad. The only time he smiled was when we scheduled the next appointment, the damn enabler.

A Clinic Somewhere in Allston. With no more insurance and a dolorous outlook, I tracked down this sliding-scale clinic. The place seemed stolid and reputable from the outside, however, I soon discovered it was run like a sales operation, with incentives and prizes going to the clinician who collects the most clients with DSM IIIR disorders. Here's how my session went:

WENDY (after taking a bit of history): You know, sometimes I put something down, and it disappears. Does that ever happen to you? You ever put something down and have it vanish?

ME: No.

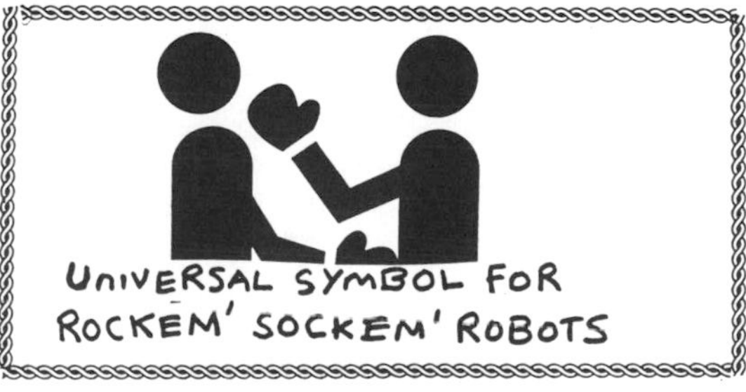

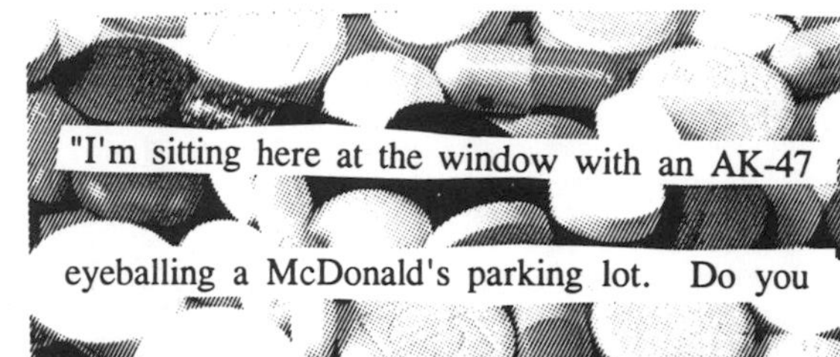

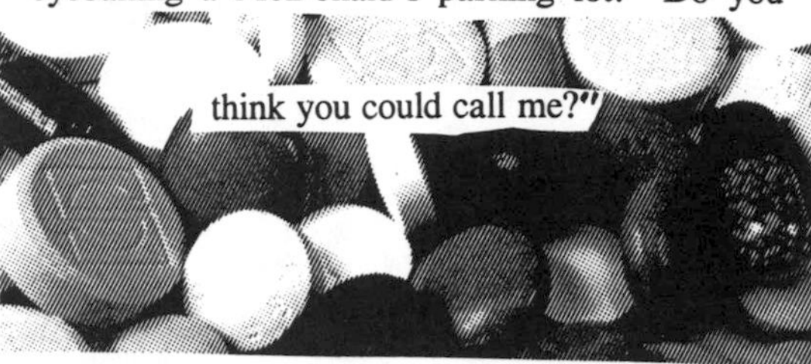

WENDY (disappointed): Oh. Your keys never vanish? Sometimes I loose my keys...
ME: Yeah, I've misplaced keys, but I haven't seen any vanish.
WENDY: Are there any behaviors that you have to do every day?
ME: Well, I floss every day.
WENDY (suddenly excited but trying to hide it): Ummhmmm. Could you go a day without flossing?
ME: I could...
WENDY: How about two days?
ME: Well, I suppose I--
WENDY: What about a week? Could you go a week without flossing?
ME: I could, but I wouldn't want to. Flossing is the key to preventive dental care.
WENDY: So you have to floss every day...
ME: You brush your teeth everyday, right? Could you go a day without brushing? Two days? A week? Would you want to?

I wasn't about to help her win the set of steak knives, so I did what I should have done in the first place: I networked. My friend Danny gave me the name of shrink who referred people to therapists. At first the shrink wouldn't return my calls. So I finally left a serious message: "Dave, this is Willie. I'm sitting here at the window with an AK-47 eyeballing a McDonald's parking lot. Do you think you could call me; it's important."
He called, and I got Dr. Elizabeth Smith

Dr. Elizabeth Smith, Brookline Location, Sliding Scale, Oh So Clean. Brookline location, sliding scale, and oh so clean.

Dr. Smith lets you call her Beth right away. Two chairs, low lights, a dab of Channel #5 and Beth is ready to help.

She started each session by tipping her head slightly to one side, flipping her hand, and asking, "I'm wondering how it is for you to come in here this week." She closed each session with a gentle "it's time to finish now."

Beth focused on "the relationship" and actually thought I wanted to date her! It's important to remember that not even the trained therapist is immune to projecting and it is ok for you, the client, to call him/her on it. Beth vehemently denied wanting to date, but we all know what that means!

Down the street from her office is a cafe. After therapy I'd get a latte and something chocolate. This was the only time I genuinely felt better. With a near-by espresso machine, therapy works!

Hey Bill and Hillary, how about lattes and cookies for a small co-payment?

THIS CAME TO ME IN A REVELATION ONE DAY WHILE I WAS OUT JOGGING.

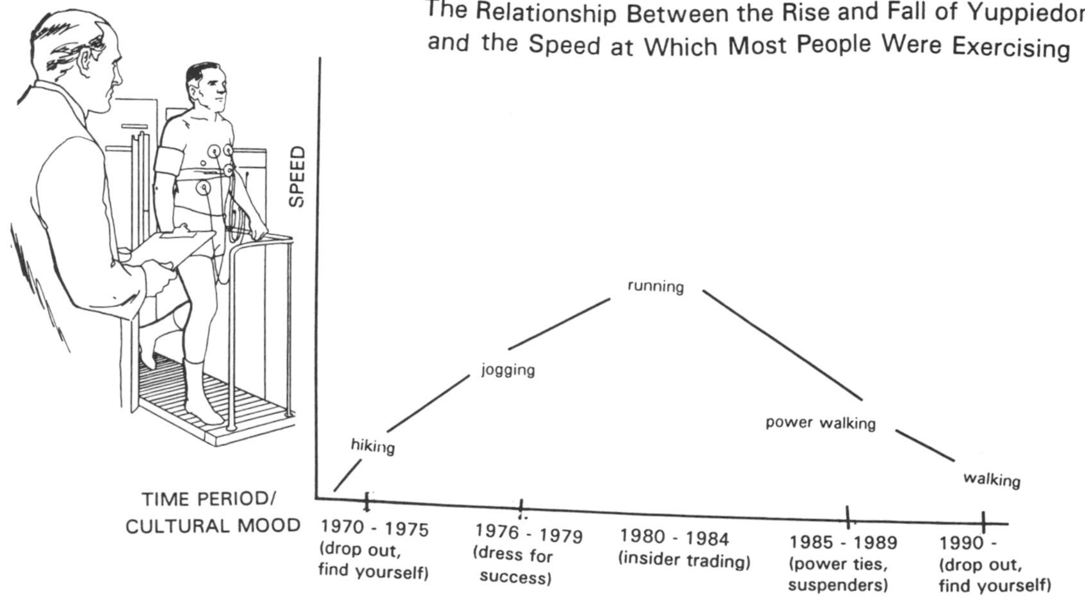

A TRUE MEDICAL HORROR STORY ABOUT SOMETHING THAT HAPPENS TO LOTS AND LOTS OF WOMEN...
THEY WANTED TO CASTRATE ME
BY PATIENT PAGAN KENNEDY
WRITTEN, DRAWN AND INKED BY THE AUTHOR, WHO SAW IN A VISION THAT HER OVARIAN ADVENTURES HAD TO BE TURNED INTO A COMIC BOOK

I always thought of myself as stunningly healthy.
I ate sea vegetables.
I belonged to a gym.

Then one night...
Owww... my stomach

It hurt so much. All night I threw up...
Bill

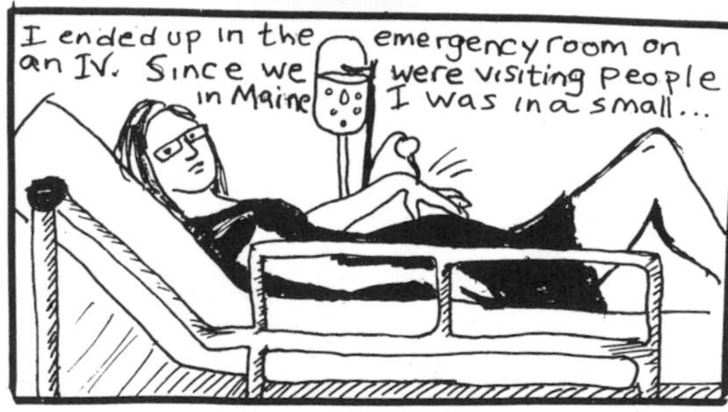
I ended up in the emergency room on an IV. Since we were visiting people in Maine I was in a small...

... hospital where they gave me every test.
C'mon, honey, we're going for an X-ray.

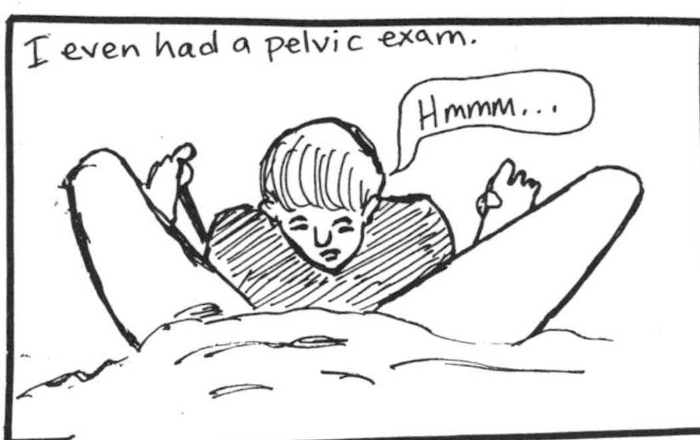
I even had a pelvic exam.
Hmmm...

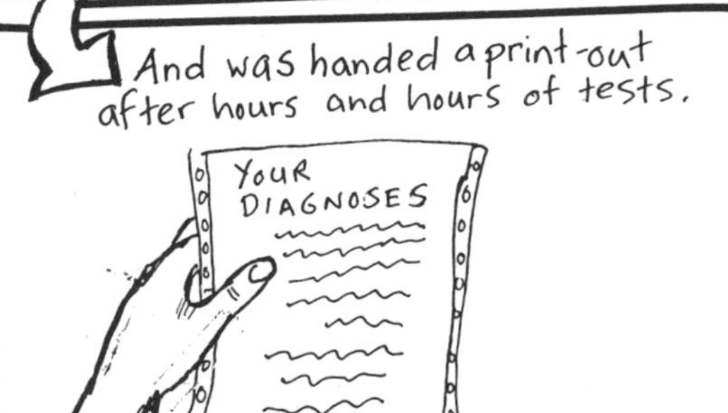
And was handed a print-out after hours and hours of tests.
YOUR DIAGNOSES

They say it's basically just gas. But I still say it felt like food poisoning.

I was puking all the way to the hospital — even in the emergency room. I thought I would pass out from the pain. After several hours I saw a doctor who gave me a pelvic exam...

That night, I went back to Boston. The doctor told me I was supposed to get a sonagram first thing next morning. But when I called my HMO, they wouldn't let me have a sonagram for several days ... And I couldn't see a doctor for two weeks.

But after landing in another emergency room I became a "priority" case and my appointment was moved up.

And then the doctor went on...

"It may be necessary to take out the entire ovary. From what we can see on the sonagram the cyst is made up of pockets of mucous. The whole thing has become swollen and the tissue on the outside of the ovary is stretched thin. We have to be careful of the fluid—keep it from leaking out—on the off chance it's cancerous.

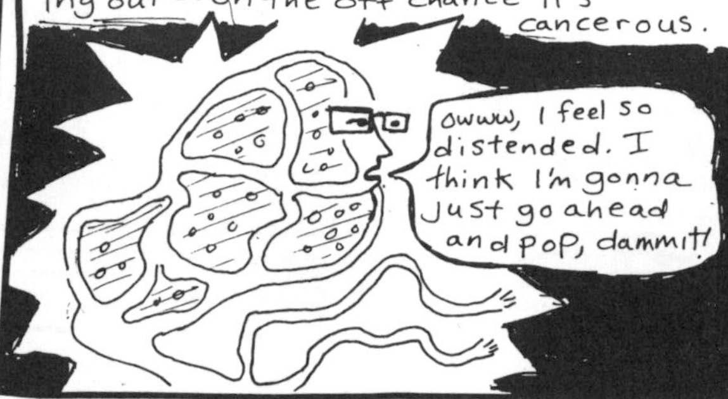

Right before I went in for surgery my mom came up to Boston. I was really glad she was there—although she was rather overenthusiastic.

On the big day, I was terrified. My anesthesiologist tried to ease the tension by making Monty Python jokes.

Bring me the machine that goes PEEP... Nurse, I need the machine that goes PEEP. Hey don't scowl at me like that. I'm trying to cheer you up.

That night, I thought of my father who had died of lung cancer the year before. My mother, my sister and I took care of him at home for the last two weeks. The oral medication we were supposed to give him hadn't worked and he had become pitifully terrified of the pain. We fought with the doctors and finally got him the same intravenous morphine pump I used now. Why had it been given so readily to me and kept from him, a dying man?

Mom on the warpath... Woe to anyone who stands in her way. Within hours she found that I didn't have to have chemo. No harmful cells were left in my body.

Luckily, the rest of my body was so healthy that I was out of the hospital in 2½ days instead of 5. My stomach looked like this:

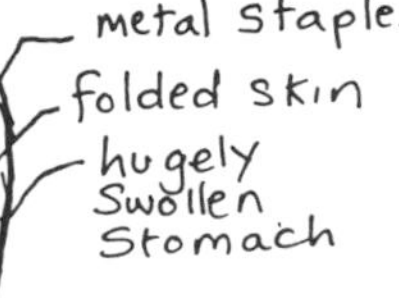

So I went home to my group house.

Could somebody get me another glass of water?

A few weeks later I went in for my follow-up appointment. I still wasn't allowed to lift anything heavier than a phone book, but I was basically OK, or so I thought...

I made an appointment with one of the top doctors in Boston and a few weeks later walked into his office and told him my story

Congratulations, Miss Kennedy. You don't need a hysterectomy. In fact, I think that advice borders on malpractice. I can't tell you how many women come in here thinking they need everything taken out. It's shameful!

Such a good doctor that he's drawn better.

And you're right — It's very important that you go on the Pill. I'll give you some free samples.

As soon as I got out of the office
I'm so happy!

But then one day my HMO doctor called.
Miss Kennedy? That pap smear you had in your follow-up appointment? It turned out to be abnormal. You need to come in for a colposcopy

Oh Jesus. A colposcopy involves some sort of biopsy. No way am I going to let that quack cut a piece out of my cervix. I'll make an appointment with the expert and pay for this myself.
Doctors Suck
The AMA Bites

I made a long list of questions to ask Dr. Expert. Finally the big day arrived.
Well, I'm glad you came to me. You're going to need a LEEP extraction. It's a new technique and the doctors at your HMO won't know how to do it right. I, however, have performed it hundreds of times.
All right, Dr. But I'm still really confused. I brought a list of questions...

But before I could say anything else...
Yes, yes. Make an appointment for the procedure with my secretary
no longer looks so perfect

I ran out after him.
Doctor? Where are you?

Then I spotted the nurse who'd been in the room when he examined me.
Excuse me. What's the name of the procedure I have to have?
Ask your doctor!

THAT WAS THE MOMENT I realized I was in This alone. From NOW ON I would have to FIGURE everything out myself, MAKE MY OWN Decisions. I WAS SCARED AND I DIDN'T EVEN KNOW WHAT THEY WERE GOING TO DO TO MY CERVIX.

FOLLOW-UP TREATMENT

I met one last time with the HMO surgeon who had cut out my ovary. "Well," he said, "the tumor board at the hospital has reviewed your case and, just as I thought, they suggest that you be monitored. No further treatment is necessary."

"But last time I saw you, you told me that I should get a hysterectomy. You said I should have one in a year or so!"

"Oh no, you must have misunderstood me."

How could I have misunderstood him? He told me to think of myself as a woman of 40, a woman who had to make an immediate decision about whether or not to have children. I remember, after he mentioned the hysterectomy, that I had asked incredulously, "But why would you have to take out my uterus too?" I did not misunderstand anything.

So anyway, I switched to a woman gynecologist at the HMO. I had my first appointment with her the day before Dr. Expert planned to perform the LEEP operation on my cervix. (After reading several medical articles I'd learned that in a LEEP procedure the doctor uses a hot wire to cut out a chunk of your cervix. I wasn't sure what the long-term implications of the LEEP could be--since it's a new procedure.) My HMO doctor, Dr. Woman, was shocked to hear that I would be having the procedure. "That's an awfully aggressive treatment. You haven't even had a biopsy yet." Well, the treatment sounded awfully aggressive to me too, but at that point I was so beaten down that I just went ahead and had it done.

A few months later, I volunteered to be part of an ovarian cancer study. They tested my ability to turn milk sugar (galactose) into normal sugar (glucose). I rated a 9 in the galactose test; the average person is a 23. Being a vegetarian, I also happened to eat a lot of dairy. That meant I had a lot of galactose hanging out in my body, screwing up my hormones and generally causing havoc. A previous medical study had indicated that women with a low ability to break down galactose--or who eat more dairy than their body can handle--are twice as likely to get ovarian cancer. Galactosemia has also been linked to cataracts and retardation in babies (and it has nothing to do with being lactose-intolerant). So I've quit dairy. Yikes! What's left to eat?

When I tell people about my medical odyssey, they always say, "So, but your fine now, right?" Some days I do feel fine. Other days, I wonder if I *should* have a hysterectomy. Because if I do get ovarian cancer, it will be *my fault* for not having taken the right precautions. I know that's not terribly rational, but that's what goes through my head.

I used to spend a lot of time reading medical articles, but I've since given up. I'm beginning to think *there just isn't very much information out there.* I am hoping that, in the next few years, someone will develop a more-effective screening method for ovarian cancer. Until then, I'm learning to live with uncertainty.

HYSTERECTOMY FUN FACTS

- The hysterectomy is the most commonly performed operation in the U.S. Almost 90 percent of the operations are used in the absence of cancer.
- One Swiss study showed that women doctors are half as likely as their male colleagues to perform hysterectomies.
- In the 19th century, women had their ovaries removed to cure such perceived pathologies as bad temper, large appetite, masturbation and depression.

--Information derived from *No More Hysterectomies* by Vicki Hafnagel

Since my operation, I've been given tests every three months--the CU-125 (a blood test that is used to monitor tumors) and a sonogram. Both tests are wildly inaccurate and were not designed to be screening tools. For instance, in a sonogram, my remaining ovary appears as a shadow on the computer screen. The technician can see whether the ovary is abnormally large, but cannot detect cancer cells--and by the time a ovary appears abnormally large in a sonogram, the cancer may have progressed to a life-threatening stage. Then there is an added problem with the sonogram: What do ovaries do, as a matter of course? They swell and shrink every month. It is often difficult to tell, when you look at a sonogram, whether an ovary is enlarged because of a "functional cyst" or because of something else.

Right now, there is no effective screening device for ovarian cancer. And as it happens, the type of borderline malignancy I had may spread to the other ovary --even years after the original ovary was removed. But only one study was ever published about the type of tumor I had, so I don't know whether to trust that data. Welcome to the wonderful world of women's health!

KARMIC KOMIX PROUDLY PRESENTS
CHAPTER III "THIS TIME I SWEAR IT'LL BE DIFFERENT"
FATAL FUNNIES
PART IV ROMANCE
APPROPRIATE RESPONSIBILITY GOES TO JIM KENDALL ©1993
WHEN LOVE GOES WRONG SOME PEOPLE TRY BLAMING THEIR PARENTS.
AH, THE REPETITION SYNDROME- IT'S THE SUBCONSCIOUS'S TWISTED VERSION OF THE GOLDEN RULE.
"DO UNTO OTHERS AS OTHERS HAVE DONE UNTO YOU."
THAT APPLE DOES NOT FALL FAR FROM THE TREE.
BUT
I LIVE ON A HILL
IT'S EASIER AND SAFER THAN BLAMING YOURSELF- TOO PERSONAL
RINSE
REPEAT
I AM NOT BE-COMING MY PARENTS.
IT'S MOST FUN TO BLAME THAT MOST DEVIOUS OPPOSITE SEX.
LOVE IS THE STORY OF THE TROJAN HORSE. WE ARE THE HAPPY FORTRESSED CITY.
THE ENEMY HAS FLED. SAFE AT LAST.
THIS HORSE CAN'T FIT THROUGH OUR GATES. LET'S TEAR DOWN THE WALLS AND CELEBRATE.
LATER THAT NIGHT, THE SOLDIERS WILL COME TO SLAY US IN OUR SLEEP AND THE ENEMY ARMIES WILL AGAIN RETURN TO CONQUER OUR UNPROTECTED CITY.
SAFETY & SEDUCTION
LIMITLESS JOY!
TREACHERY & DEATH
BUT IT'S WRONG TO THINK IN SUCH ADVERSARIAL TERMS. BLAME IS ALWAYS A DEAD END. LIVE AND LEARN IF LUCKY.
KINDA ANNOYINGLY CYCLICAL
I LIKE THE IDEA OF THAT YIN-YANG THING- TO LET GO OF ALL CONCEPTS OF OPPOSITION. Y'KNOW, BALANCE AND HARMONY AS THE KEY- EACH THING IS DEFINED BY THE OTHER- A DANCE OF BEING & BECOMING EACH OTHER.
TOO DEEP...
CAN I WATCH T.V. NOW?
I'M ALL IN A LATHER
I AM NOT BECOMING MY PARENTS.
RINSE
MAYBE JUST A LITTLE BIT- JUST A LITTLE
REPEAT
HEY, DIDN'T I HAVE THIS SAME FIGHT WITH SOMEONE LIKE YOU LAST YEAR?
OKAY, MAYBE HISTORY DOESN'T REPEAT ITSELF, BUT IT SURE AS HELL RHYMES.

"What Would Freud Say?"

©FITZ '89

I HAD BEEN READING A HUGE BIOGRAPHY OF ADOLF HITLER BY JOHN TOLAND ...RIGHT BEFORE HITTING THE SACK...

WHEN I WENT TO SLEEP, I HAD THIS DREAM......

IN THE DREAM, I WAS A SMALL CHILD. I WAS SITTING ON SOMEONE'S FRONT PORCH WITH THIS CHUBBY RED-HAIRED KID. THERE WAS A LARGE POPULATION OF **DADDY LONGLEGS** THERE. WE WERE CATCHING THEM AND PULLING THEIR LEGS OFF....

THIS IS STRANGE BECAUSE, EVEN AS A CHILD, I NEVER FELT COMPELLED TO TORTURE INSECTS OR SMALL ANIMALS. I DIDN'T EVEN KNOW THE NAME OF THE RED-HAIRED KID, BUT I HAD THE VAGUE FEELING THAT HE HAD BULLIED OR COERCED ME INTO DISMEMBERING THE DADDY LONGLEGS...

WE HAD A BIG PILE OF THEIR LEGLESS BODIES

I BECAME AWARE THAT WE WERE BEING WATCHED... BY ADOLF HITLER!

HITLER ACCUSED US OF MONSTEROUS EVIL!

I WAS TERRIFIED AND UNABLE TO SPEAK ... WORDS SEEMED TO STICK IN MY THROAT... FINALLY, I MANAGED TO STAMMER...

THE CLOUDS IN THE SKY BEGAN WHIRLING. HITLER'S VOICE THUNDERED IN THE MAELSTROM...

SUDDENLY, THE DISMEMBERED BODIES EMITTED A HORRIBLE SCREAM THAT SOUNDED LIKE MUTILATED CHILDREN...

I LITERALLY AWOKE IN A COLD SWEAT!

THE ENTIRE NEXT DAY, I FELT CREEPY AND UNEASY...

SORRY, KIDS... NO PUNCH LINE...

EPILOGUE

THIS PAST WINTER, I began to hope *Pagan's Head* could become more than just a sheaf of Xeroxed papers that I handed out to friends. I wanted to republish the 'zine as a book. So I sent a bunch of issues off to my editor at St. Martin's, and a few months later—right after I'd printed up Issue Eight—the amazing happened. He said he wanted to buy *Pagan's Head.*

I still find it very strange that my 'zine, which I put together and copied myself, will someday be wedged into the shelves of bookstores. The idea elates and terrifies me. I can't wait for strangers to read all the bits I'm most proud of—like "Wild in the Streets" or "I Pulled the Legs Off." But, still, it's frightening to think that soon so much juicy gossip about me will be on sale at Barnes & Noble. Worse still, what I'm showing to the world isn't just the cleaned-up, mature, thirtysomething Pagan my friends know today; it's also the fame-obsessed Pagan of yore. When I read through the back issues of the 'zine, I'm confronted with what a superficial and self-promoting fool I often was; still, I did some of my best work because I was a fool and wasn't afraid to admit it.

All in all, the *Pagan's Head* book seems inevitable and right. For six years, I lived as a literary character. I struggled to merge life and art; to turn every trip to the supermarket into an epic adventure; to transform myself from a short, whiny, bespeckled woman into a superstar. These days, I have no desire to do that anymore, but I'm glad I documented my Pagan[1] years in such detail. Now other people can see what it's like to turn reality into something that approaches your inner landscape—the murky, psychedelic place where you have your own theme song and Saturday morning cartoon show, where you can nurture several personalities at once (without going crazy) and can parade around, unembarrassed, in white go-go boots.

So anyway, this summer I started work on *Pagan's Head,* the book. My editor wanted it to be more than just a compilation of 'zines. I guess he was worried that readers wouldn't understand *Pagan's Head.* My editor wanted me to turn all the issues of the *Head* into one big story, a narrative of my not-necessarily-true adventures as the 'zine queen of Boston. To that end, he told me to write a series of essays, one to go with each issue of the 'zine. The essays would explain what was going on in my life while I produced the *Head* and how each issue came into being.

At first I wasn't too psyched about writing these essays. I thought *Pagan's Head* stood on its own. I'd handed out a lot of issues over the years, and no one had ever seemed confused by it; on the contrary, people flipped through the pages eagerly, sometimes laughing out loud. So why should I have to explain the 'zine to readers now?

But then, as I began work on the essays, the idea grew on me. Instead of speaking as Pagan^1 in these pieces, I would use another voice. After a few false starts, I stumbled on just the right persona: The woman who explained *Pagan's Head* to her readers would be scholarly, thoughtful, a little weary and Weltschmerz-y. Let's call her Pagan^2.

As I worked on the essays, I found out more and more about Pagan^2, for she was not so much a voice I made up as a person who had always been there inside me. She's the no-nonsense one who watches, who takes stock. If Pagan^1 is Mork, then Pagan^2 is Mindy.

In the essays, I knew Pagan^2 could tell a story, but it wouldn't be the story my editor had envisioned. Instead, Pagan^2 would narrate the tale of a woman who creates a literary character with her own name and face. At first, this woman's character lives only on paper; and then one day the woman realizes that she herself has turned into her own literary invention. For a while, the woman finds happiness this way: Her own life seems to unfurl with all the drama and meaning of a novel. People enter her sphere like characters in a movie. Life seems larger than life.

But then, some hard things happen, things she did not write into the script. The woman's father dies. She herself battles with illness. She falls in love, but after two years, what seemed like a long-term relationship suddenly dissolves.

And so the woman is no longer able to imagine herself as a literary character. Because when she believed herself to be a character, she also believed herself to be the author—she thought she could twist her own plot, map out the story of her own life.

The woman, chastened by circumstance, learns that she is not the author of her own experience. Nor is she the one who creates her own personality; rather, it is tragedy and chance that do that. And so she begins to search for a new way to move through the world, a humbler attitude that will allow her to make peace with all she cannot control.

Why did I want fame so passionately during my Pagan[1] years? I guess the reason is obvious: I wanted to be loved by lots of people. But eventually I realized that fans are not the same as friends, and instead of fame I began to hunger for community—a swirl of supportive people around me, a sense of belonging to something larger than myself, a family made of friends.

So the 'zine started as an advertisement for myself, but became much more. It documented the personalities of my friends, the legends of my family, the goings-on in my group house, the aimless-hipster culture of Allston. As time went on, *Pagan's Head* became less *mine* than *ours;* other people began writing and cartooning for the *Head,* and often my best ideas came from friends. "You should do an issue about dating, Pagan dating," Diane suggested, and out of that came the *Men* issue. "You always have a different image—first you dressed messy, then you dressed neatly. I don't know how to keep up," Max said, so I began naming and photographing my various images, from Classic Pagan to the L.A. Pagan. And so the 'zine turned into a group project, an imaginary world I could live in with my friends.

When my father was dying, that world became a retreat; and when I lost my ovary, *Pagan's Head* became a forum in which I could vent my anger—through both tragedies, the 'zine helped me survive.

My most recent ordeal happened a month ago: Bill and I broke up. Of course I had a major panic attack when he moved out of my apartment—

and for more than just the obvious reasons. You see, during the past two years, I had been working at home full time; I'd been a prolific writer during those years, but the price had been high. I often felt isolated and depressed as I struggled in front of the computer screen. Sometimes Bill was the only person I saw during the day. So I was terrified that without him I'd become even more cut off. I'd turn into a hermit, lose my mind—*Yikes!*

I panicked about this for a day or two. And then the phone began to ring. And ring. And ring. It was Meg: She wanted me to come stay with her in Iowa so she could heal my broken heart with her homemade breads, her carrot sauces. It was Lauren: She said that she'd heard I needed a car, and I could have her Dodge Colt for free. It was Max, Willie, Maggie, Diane, Marcus, Mary, Jan, Karen, Scot, Amy, Terry, Peter, Carl, Ingrid, Gregg Z., Orin, Jimmy, Jim, both Leslies, Paul, John, Elizabeth, Simon (formerly Mina), Dana, Anna.

My dear friends hold me close. I hug them, not wanting to let go. Our arms weave together into a net; the net hangs beneath us; it cushions us when we fall; it saves us.

Where did I find all these friends and how did I build this community? I'm not quite sure, but I know that *Pagan's Head* helped. Over the years, so many of my close friends contributed to the 'zine, or appeared in it as "celebrities," or read it faithfully and gave me suggestions, or wrote in letters. *Pagan's Head* became like an imaginary group house where we could all live together, talking aimlessly into the night and laughing at our own stupid jokes. The world outside this house of ours is lonely—a place of Personal ads, identical Burger Kings, strip malls, TV laugh tracks, lite rock. But luckily we don't need mass culture, because we can stay home and make our own fun.

I'm a very different woman from the one who started *Pagan's Head* so many years ago; I think I've changed too much to keep on producing the 'zine. Now I want to move on and find new projects—projects more appropriate for a woman with one ovary and a few wrinkles starting around her eyes. But even so, even if I give up the *Head,* I know I'll never move out of this house made of art, this secret garden that sits in the midst of an anonymous city.